AMERICAN RACING MOTORCYCLES

Jerry Hatfield

Motorbooks International
Publishers & Wholesalers Inc
Osceola, Wisconsin 54020, USA ®

This edition first published in 1989 by Motorbooks International Publishers & Wholesalers Inc, P O Box 2, 729 Prospect Avenue, Osceola, WI 54020 USA

Previously published by Haynes Publishing Group, England, 1982

© Jerry Hatfield, 1989

Motorbooks International is a certified trademark, registered with the United States Patent Office

Printed and bound in England

The information in this book is true and complete to the best of our knowledge. All recommendations are made without any guarantee on the part of the author or publisher, who also disclaim any liability incurred in connection with the use of this data or specific details

We recognize that some words, model names and designations, for example, mentioned herein are the property of the trademark holder. We use them for identification purposes only. This is not an official publication.

Library of Congress Cataloging-in-Publication Data
ISBN 0-87938-355-0

On the front cover: Cyclone racer. *Stephen Wright*

On the back cover: Jay Springsteen aboard a Harley-Davidson XR road racer. *Harley-Davidson Motor Company*

DEDICATION

Dedicated to all the motorcycle racers who never won a championship – their presence forced champions to greatness and made motorcycle sport possible.

FOREWORD

It was sixty-one years ago when I was working in a motorcycle shop in Denver, Colorado. The company I worked for was named 'The Western Supplies Co.,' whose business was about twenty-five percent retailing motorcycles and the rest a large mail order motorcycle business. The company carried about four hundred used motorcycles of all makes and shipped them all over the country.

One day the foreman told me to go to the basement and bring up a Cyclone motorcycle for which they had just received an order. When he said Cyclone, I thought he was kidding, as I had never heard of such a motorcycle. He then told me it was a yellow motorcycle and was the only yellow one down there. Sure enough, there was a yellow Cyclone down there. Little did I know at the time that I had the chance to work on one of the best engineered motorcycles that was ever built.

After sixty-one years, I had the opportunity through the pages of *American Racing Motorcycles,* to learn the details of how this motorcycle was engineered. It now makes it more clear that the engineers at Excelsior and Reading Standard must have cut corners when they tried to copy the Cyclone engine, and without success.

The above story is one of the many, many details that are laid out in the pages of *American Racing Motorcycles*. I am quite sure that people in all walks of life in the motorcycle world will learn as I did by reading the pages of this wonderful book by Jerry Hatfield.

Charles 'Red' Wolverton
Feb. 28, 1981

AUTHOR'S PREFACE

In the annals of American sport, the forgotten players have long been the professional motorcycle racers. There are perhaps more motorcyclists than golfers in the USA, yet more press coverage is given a chance interview with a golf star practicing his putting, than to national championship motorcycle racing. The perennial exceptions are flashy photos of motorcyclists spilling, and sensationalized written accounts of racing accidents. Why this is so, is a curious matter. The cause cannot be the danger alone, for automobile racing generally does not suffer a bad press with each fatal accident. The cause cannot be relative popularity because for years tennis has enjoyed the coverage it only recently has merited by the standard of participation.

I submit that the reasons for American motorcycling's lack of public recognition lie deep in the distinctive psychological/sociological evolution of the American public. The motorcycle should have replaced, image-wise, the horse; and the car should have replaced the buggy as a more genteel mode of locomotion. Alas, affluence undid this natural progression. The automobile at last stood for maturity and success; the motorcycle spelled the lack thereof.

Thus, winning in a Ferrari is more important than winning on a Harley-Davidson. The same press that periodically rises with moral indignation against the evils in the 'blue collar' sports of boxing and motorcycle racing, almost never finds immorality in the Indianapolis 500. Another contrast is bullfighting, in which the toreador receives lavish outpourings of glory and sentiment, aided both by Hemingway and Hollywood. Is the toreador game more socially worthwhile, when judged by the standards applied to motorcycle racing? Hardly.

Superimposed over it all is a reminder of the potency of the press. In England, Hailwood flashed his smile for a toothpaste ad. In El Paso, Daytona-winner Buddy Elmore's hometown obituary is the kind of stuff written about us ordinary mortals. We 'ordinaries' deserve our obscurity. But the elite riders of motorcycle racing deserve a better break, and with them, the engineers, official and unofficial, who make the best run better.

In the USA, there is a growing interest in motorcycle history. This trend is exemplified by a surge in the collection of old motorcycles, and by the acceptance of a succession of historical motorcycle books. To date, the USA trails well behind Britain and Europe in its attempt to discover its motorcycle history. Hopefully, *American Racing Motorcycles* will in some small way help to close the gap. For we can never expect American motorcycling to receive its fair shake when we, as American motorcyclists, don't pay homage to our own heroes.

I've been preaching to my fellow countrymen, but this book has been written with the secondary intent of dramatizing the impact of the British and Japanese on American motorcycle racing. Happy reading to one and all, wherever you live, whatever you ride.

Jerry H. Hatfield

ACKNOWLEDGEMENTS

I greatly appreciate the time and effort of many knowledgeable people who helped in the preparation of this book. Maldwyn Jones loaned his photograph collection and letters file, and granted an interview. Maldwyn's efforts provided a rare personal view into the pre-World War I days of racing, an insight which becomes increasingly difficult to obtain with each passing year.

Sam Arena copied photographs, granted an interview, and introduced me to Tom Sifton. Tom devoted several hours to the interview process, and provided technical information which was critically important to Class C history, and otherwise unobtainable. Hap Jones' interview defined the scene for 1930s and 1940s club-promoted amateur competition.

Ed Kretz discussed his riding career and assisted with photographs. Mike Partee introduced me to Roland 'Rollie' Free, now deceased. Rollie disclosed his tuning techniques annd reminisced concerning his several successful speed records, his experiences as an Indian dealer, and his employment by the Indian factory. Charles L. 'Red' Wolverton loaned photographs and devoted several hours to the preparation of recorded messages which detailed his long career as a rider, tuner, and dealer. Jim Davis and Woodsie Castonguay discussed their racing careers.

Dick O'Brien conducted a tour of the Harley-Davidson Racing Department and granted an interview which provided information gleaned from his long tenure as Chief of Harley-Davidson racing. Carroll Resweber discussed his brilliant racing career.

Bob Klein of AMF Harley-Davidson arranged for provision of photographs and information from the factory archives. Midge Kimball enthusiastically assisted in locating Harley-Davidson photographs and information, and arranged for my meetings with Dick O'Brien and Carroll Resweber.

Gene Rhyne discussed his hillclimbing career with Excelsior/Super X. He also related Crocker speedway motorcycle information.

Emmett Moore, former publicity director for Indian, made copies of original photographs from the Indian archives. Ted Hodgdon, a co-founder of the Antique Motorcycle Club of America, made available original Excelsior photographs. Bob Smith and Dan Myers loaned rare photographs.

Ernie Beckman, Dick Gross, Art Hafer, and Bobby Hill provided information on the last racing Indians. Max Bubeck discussed his desert riding and speed runs on Indians, and provided photographs and editorial assistance. Sam Pierce provided photographs and information. Dick Barth researched the development of the Indian model 648 Scout. Bob Stark loaned many old magazines. Dick Klamfoth provided insights as a champion rider of British motorcycles.

The last two surviving companies formerly manufacturing American motorcycles helped with information. These were: The Schwinn Bicycle Company (Excelsior, Super X, Henderson) and Stewart Warner (Thor). Otis

Spiker (and Red Wolverton) put me in touch with Maldwyn Jones.

Geoff Hockley informed me about American motorcycle racing in New Zealand, and loaned valuable photographs. Stephen Wright, author of *American Racer*, loaned many rare photographs, helped with information, and made his restored motorcycles available for photography. The staff of the Cincinnati Public Library rendered competent and cordial assistance.

Sam Hotton shot and processed many of the better photos, including the dust jacket subject, proving himself both an artist and technician. Bob Mosely and Marvin Fredericks of Pohlman Studio in Milwaukee provided outstanding photographic services. Likewise, the Dark Room Plus studio of Lancaster, California provided outstanding service.

Many enthusiasts responded to my requests for assistance. Several arranged for the photographing of their restored machines, or loaned historic photos, and are appropriately credited elsewhere. Others provided information. A few influenced me in general, prior to the formalization of this project. All provided some help and encouragement. These were: Dewey Bonkrud, Ted Buhl, Ira Bullock, John Cameron, Corine Capuda, Woody Carson, Charlie Carter, Earl Chalfant, Jimmy Chann, Peter Chann, Stephen Chann, Lee Cowie, Charles Darling, Bud Ekins, Del DuChene, Don Frauendienst, Allan Girdler, Ernie Hartman Jr, Charles H. Hostetter, Gene Hunt, O.H. Klausmeyer, G.W. Knudsen, Leon Landry, Stark Leighty, Charles Lipsky, Jim Lucas, Marc Madow, Fred Markwick, Col. Edwin L. Marsh, Harold Mathewson, John McCabe, Carolyn Mijokovic, F.R. Miller, Char Orcutt, Herb Ottaway, Carleton Palmer, John Parker, Jo Ann Plezek, Layne Plotner, Gary Porter, Bill Potter, Sandi Pyle, Ted Pratt, Will Quombly, Tim Ragan, Dick Renstrom, Chuck Rouse, Dick and Rita Sanchez, Connie Schlemmer, Col. Charles B. Stratton, Art Sigal, Ernie Skelton, Lee Standley, Herbert Stuart, George Thoma, Chuck Vernon, Buzz Walneck, W.R. 'Sarge' Watkins, the late George A. Williams, Dee Winegardner, David Work, and Pete Zylstra.

Marty Lang, Mses. Sharon Buckley, Bonnie McCabe, Jan Minniear, Judy Ross, and Linda Row deciphered my handwriting, corrected my spelling, and did the typing. My wife, Ella, made editorial contributions and offered encouragement.

Finally, I owe a special debt to George Hays and Harry Sucher for recommending me, and to Jeff Clew for selecting me to write the book. I hope that I've not omitted anyone. To one and all, thanks for helping me along in the adventure of a lifetime.

Jerry H. Hatfield

Jerry H. Hatfield
Lancaster, Ca.
January 1982

Contents

How to Use this Book

American Racing Motorcycles is organized alphabetically to facilitate its use as a reference work. However, the first reading should be done in the manner of a novel, especially the Excelsior, Harley-Davidson, and Indian sections. These three makes account for about 80 percent of the American racing story, and within the sections treating these three makes can be found the events, personalities, and trends which determined the evolution of American motorcycle sport. Repetition has been minimized, and it is therefore highly recommended that the Excelsior, Harley-Davidson, and Indian sections be read in that order to enhance understanding.

Awareness of fundamental trends will make your reading more informative and enjoyable. Considerable attention has been devoted to the evolution of Class C racing in the USA, and this subject is treated within the Harley-Davidson section. The author has mixed facts and interpretation on Class C, so you are forewarned and encouraged to develop your own attitude concerning this controversial subject. In turn, your viewpoint on Class C will largely influence your interpretation of Harley-Davidson racing.

British and Japanese motorcycles have had a dramatic impact on American motorcycling history. The role of the Union Jack marques in the USA is highlighted in both the Harley-Davidson and Indian sections. The influence of Japanese machines is depicted within the Harley-Davidson story.

Unless otherwise qualified, riders' accomplishments were earned on the same make of machine as the section in which mentioned. The USA's technical terminology has changed over the years, so the author has generally used the wording favored for each applicable period. On the other hand, there have always been differences between American and British usage. Therefore, both American and British readers should review the table of definitions, synonyms, and abbreviations.

British readers may find it worthwhile to review a map of the USA, keying on the location of the 48 contiguous states. State titles have generally been included with city titles, for example, 'Sacramento, California'. While the applicable states are usually obvious to Americans, it is hoped that these little 'redundancies' may be helpful to British readers. A continual realization of the USA's far-flung distances will make for more knowledgeable and enjoyable reading.

Constructive criticism is welcomed. Corrections and suggestions should be brought to the attention of the publisher. For corrections, please provide references.

Many American motorcycles have not been discussed. The basis for inclusion of any marque was any one or more of the following: an historic first-time event; the setting of a major speed or distance record; and the fielding of a factory team for a National Championship event. Two exceptions were made: the Crocker was included because the Crocker speedway machine   11 did not fit into the traditional road racing and long track Championships. The Dayton was omitted because a team was fielded for only one Championship the performance at the race was insignificant, and the Dayton had no particularly distinctive features.

TABLE OF ABBREVIATIONS, DEFINITIONS, AND SYNONYMS

Aluminum : aluminium
Board Track: any wooden track

Cubic Displacement:			
	15	cubic inches	250 cc
	21.35	cubic inches	350 cc
	30.50	cubic inches	500 cc
	45	cubic inches	750 cc
	61	cubic inches	1000 cc
	74	cubic inches	1200 cc
	80	cubic inches	1300 cc

Dry Sump Lubrication: recirculating engine oil supplied from a remote tank
Fender: mudguard
Gasoline: gas, petrol
Gear Shift: gear change
Intake Over Exhaust: ioe, F-head, pocket valve
Motordrome: 1/6 – 1/3 mile board track
Muffler: silencer
Pocket Valve: term applied to both inlet-over-exhaust and sidevalve engines
Short Track: 1/4 mile dirt track
Sidevalve: pocket valve, L-head, flathead, sv
Speedway: in the USA during the thirties, forties, and fifties, a paved board, or steeply banked dirt track one mile or more in circumference; otherwise, a term meaning short dirt track 500cc racing.
Tire Sizes: in the early days, provided on the basis of the outside diameter of the tire and its cross section; in later and current usage, provided on the basis of wheel diameter and tire cross section.
Total Loss Lubrication: metered, non-recirculating engine oil supplied from a remote tank
Transmission: gearbox
TT: tourist trophy; in Britain, the Isle of Man professional road race; in the USA, a miniaturized dirt road course, analogous to motocross but faster and with less extreme jumps and dips.
Wet Sump Lubrication: engine oil supply carried within the crankcase

INTRODUCTION

The term 'American racing motorcycles' within the context of this book, refers to all made-in-the-USA motorcycles used in competitive events or for the establishment of speed or distance records.

As for modes of competition, there have been principally six in the United States. From the earliest days until about 1910, intercity enduros prevailed, only to eventually run foul of speed and traffic laws. That unique American idiom, the board tracks, began in 1908, reached a popularity peak about 1912, and continued as a significant factor until the early thirties. Transcontinental and other distance runs were around from 1903, but were most popular from 1915 to 1925. Hillclimbing, likewise, was prevalent at the outset, but enjoyed its greatest success from 1920 to 1935.

Flat (dirt) track racing has continually gained in popularity since the early thirties, and today represents the dominant American theme. Flat tracking is also the senior form of American racing, as the abundance of horse tracks resulted in their use for secondary status events in the first decade of this century. And finally, there is genuine road racing on pavement, never a highly emphasized form in American factory circles except during the sixties, and apparently abandoned indefinitely due to the all-conquering Japanese.

Although it has been over a generation since American racing motorcycles figured significantly on the world scene, the exploits of riders in Britain, New Zealand, and elsewhere are nevertheless worthy of discussion. Harley-Davidson and Indian accomplishments at Brooklands and the Isle of Man were particularly historic.

The lack of a continuing American venue such as the Isle of Man is, on first thought, a handicap to the historian. However, the continually changing format of American racing is not without its benefit. The wide variety of racing types and ever-changing locales forces one to the realization of a basic truth: the accomplishments of riders from different eras cannot be accurately weighed, one against the other. British riders Mike Hailwood and Charlie Collier were equally great within their environments; so, too, were Americans Carroll Resweber and Jake DeRosier.

The vastness of the United States and the availability of inexpensive automobiles determined the evolution of American motorcycling. In the earliest days, incredibly rough and monotonously straight roads made the big V-twin dominant, while promoting modes of competition which maximized speed and minimized handling requirements. Later, as American motorcycling almost succumbed to the Model T Ford, the American motorcycle press dwindled to impotence. The harsh economic times, journalistic vacuum, and geographical separation, moved motorcycle sport in the United States increasingly toward a sort of county fair operation by the early 1930s. Even today, despite closer international affiliation and the recent accomplishments of Kenny Roberts and others, American motorcycle racing still goes its own way. 13

Though all this sounds like an apology, it is not. American motorcycle racing has not been inferior to the international main stream, for it is closeness of competition, together with the unique blend of technical and human qualities which gives all motorcycle racing its exciting quality. And in these aspects, the impartial reader will appreciate that American racing motorcycles represent the evolution of a branch of the sport that is at least the equal of any other.

Ace

The Ace motorcycle was publicized in late 1919 as the creation of William G. Henderson, who had earlier originated the famous Henderson four. While the Ace engine was very Henderson in appearance, the designer had attempted to avoid legal problems by insuring that no parts were interchangeable between the two marques. The Ace's four cylinder in-line ioe engine had a bore of 2.7 inches and a stroke of 3 1/4 inches, yielding a displacement of near 75 cubic inches (1229 cc).

The 1 1/2 inch valves had a maximum lift of 1/4 inch. The overhead intake valves were enclosed in 'cages', there being two separately cast cages, each handling two cylinders. A pressed steel bonnet, bolted to the top of each valve cage, completed the enclosure of the valves and rocker arms. As in the earlier Henderson, it was necessary to make the intake pushrods offset (i.e., with two) bends), in order to clear the exhaust plumbing. In the top of each bonnet was a depression running the full length of the bonnet and containing six drilled holes. After lifting a snap cover, a generous application of oil via squirt can was intended to suffice for the intake valve mechanism's lubrication.

The crankshaft was mounted in three plain bearings. The cast aluminum crankcase consisted of upper and lower halves, the lower half being ribbed for heat dissipation. Splash lubrication was employed. A pressed steel false bottom in the crankcase contained four cups, one directly under each connecting rod, through which the rods scooped up their oil. An oil cup was also provided for each of the three main bearings, but these three cups were cast into the lower crankcase section. The gear type oil pump was driven from the timing gears. A wet multiplate steel disk clutch transmitted the power to a three speed hand-shifted transmission, the ratios being 9 1/2:1, 6 1/5:1, and 4:1. The wheelbase was 59 inches, saddle height was 29 inches, and total weight (dry) was 365 pounds.

After two years of production, the Ace factory engaged the services of Erwin G. 'Cannonball' Baker, famous for his numerous long-distance rides on Indian machines. On Sept. 22, 1922, Baker left Los Angeles, California with the goal of breaking the late Alan Bedell's five year old Henderson trans-continental record. Two days later, rival Wells Bennett hopped aboard a Henderson four at Los Angeles with the same goal, and the 'race' was on. Owing to his familiarity with the largely unmarked transcontinental routes. Baker prevailed, setting a new cross-country record of 6 days, 22 hours, 52 minutes, and breaking the former Henderson record by over 17 hours. Bennett finally gave up in Philadelphia, when he realized Cannonball's latest feat was beyond his reach. It was Baker's last transcontinental motorcycle record.

On December 11, 1922, William G. Henderson was fatally injured when struck by a car during testing of a new Ace model. The following March, Arthur O. Lemon of the Excelsior/Henderson firm was hired by Ace as chief engineer. Lemon immediately convinced fellow Henderson employee Charles

15

L. 'Red' Wolverton to abandon the 'Hen' for the Ace, and a chain of events was on the way which would add new glory to the Ace name.

Lemon had been granted the authority to build the fastest motorcycle in the world regardless of cost, and he immediately spent the then large sum of $5,000 for a dynamometer. During April, May, and June of 1923, Art Lemon and his staff produced two very special Ace machines, called XP3 and XP4. XP3 was a modified stocker, weighing in at 320 pounds, but XP4 was essentially a completely different machine. With a magnesium crankcase, thin walled frame tubing and shaved-down lugs, the XP4 was startlingly light for a 1200 cc machine, tipping the scales at 285 pounds. For marketing value as well as simplified construction, the unique XP4 had the outward appearance of any other Ace.

At the big Rochester, New York hillclimb on July 4, 1923, Wolverton's team mate 'TNT' Terpening, formerly a Harley-Davidson star, won the four cylinder class of the National Hillclimb Championship. Ace hillclimbing successes continued during the summer and early autumn, culminating in three outstanding victories in October, with Wolverton thrice beating Indian's best hill buster, Orie Steele. One of Red Wolverton's Ace victories earned him the Eastern States Championship. The Ace was now tops in both the 80 inch open class and the four cylinder class.

On November 19, 1923, near Philadelphia, Red Wolverton piloted XP4 to the unofficial world record of 129.61 mph. Red followed this up with a sidecar record of 106 mph, Everett DeLong as passenger. As Red had come so tantalizingly close to 130 mph on his several solo runs, he suggested to Lemon that the sidecar be unhooked for one more solo shot. However, Lemon vetoed the idea as everyone was by now cold soaked in the chill November air, and he offered the opinion that a faster solo run was unlikely. Later, examination of the motorcycle revealed that its specially fitted lightweight Merkel forks had cracked three quarters of the way through the stem! One more run could have been disastrous.

This ace of Aces produced 45 hp at 5400 rpm, and weighed nearly 100 pounds less than stock road jobs. So extreme were the weight saving measures, that a special aluminum carburetor was cast, while pistons, rods, and timing gears were extensively drilled.

As the Ace was over 1000 cc, any speed records would not be recognized by the FICM. This being the case, and since American rules curiously did not require two-way runs, Lemon decided to run the Ace in one direction only. Wolverton recalls that there was a crosswind. It is worth noting that the official world motorcycle speed record in late 1923 was 108.48 mph by Britain's Claude Temple on a British Anzani. Furthermore, it would be another seven

Right top: A 1923 Ace Sporting Solo, the type on which Will Henderson was killed in late 1922.

(Steve McQueen, author.)

Right bottom, left to right: 'TNT' Terpening, 'Red' Wolverton, and Ace chief engineer Art Lemon. Although Terpening's and Wolverton's machines appear nearly identical, Terpening's is the much lighter XP4 and is equipped with Merkel front forks.   *(Charles L. 'Red' Wolverton.)*

16

17

years before an FICM-sanctioned run would better the ACE's 129.61 mph.

The favorable publicity of the new American speed record, and Ace's numerous hillclimb successes, were not enough to overcome the firm's continual financial crises. Not the least of Ace's mistakes was that, for a time, each underpriced Ace was unknowingly marketed at a $50 loss per machine. When failure occurred in early 1924, so soon after the euphoria of the speed records, the Ace plant manager offered to sell the special experimental models to Red Wolverton and Art Lemon. The plant manager took XP4 for himself, while XP3 was eventually sold with a sidecar for the princely sum of $50!

Subsequently, two different attempts were made to reorganize Ace. During the first of these, in 1924, XP3 found its way back to Red Wolverton's hands, and Red won ten consecutive hillclimbs with it before its power began to fall off. Then, in 1925, Art Lemon once again called on Red Wolverton for help. This time the scene was Detroit, Michigan, new home of the newest Ace builder, Michigan Motors.

Lemon had bought XP4 back from the former Philadelphia factory manager, and turned it over to Red for hillclimb action. XP4 and four other Aces were equipped with pressure-fed oiling and taken to Rochester for the big hillclimb nationals, the scene of earlier Ace triumphs. In the words of Wolverton, 'We took a licking'. Art Lemon realized the competition had caught up in the three years since the Ace hillclimbers were all-conquering, and immediately plunged into the task of finding extra power. Although handicapped by the lack of a dynamometer, Lemon nevertheless achieved significant gains. Red said he could feel the extra power on his first trial run, before winning the Milwaukee, Wisconsin hillclimb. He then won the Sommers, New York climb, setting a new hill record.

By this time, in late 1926, it became apparent that the Ace was once again to die. Red's love for the machine and his respect for Art Lemon were no longer enough, and he left Ace in its last days as an independent marque before being absorbed by Indian. For Charles L. 'Red' Wolverton, there were many exciting racing days ahead, first as a rider, and later as a successful tuner. But for the Ace, its brief competitive era was over.

Crocker

Albert G. 'Al' Crocker was one of the more successful Indian dealers, operating the Los Angeles agency from 1928 until 1934. During this period he began taking on contract work for the Indian factory on such items as crankpins and other small components. Having both a large machine shop operation and a skilled foreman, Paul A. Bigsby, as well as his strong interest in sporting motorcycles, Crocker decided to build his own speedway machines. Interest in European-style speedway had exploded after its introduction by Sprouts Elder during 1931. Several high school athletic fields in the Los Angeles area had been turned into speedway courses during the summer vacation periods. The speedway project, accordingly, appeared promising.

For the 1931 season Crocker built a special frame into which he installed a regular 45 cubic inch (750 cc) sidevalve Indian 101 Scout engine. Satisfied with this frame design, Crocker next turned his attention to a better engine. For the 1932 campaign several Scout engines were converted into 30.50 cubic inch (500 cc) overhead valve units.

Quoting from a 1934 Crocker catalog: *'These machines competed continually at Long Beach, San Diego, Los Angeles, and Santa Ana. In the winter they were sent to Mexico City for a series of eighteen races, where practically every event was won by a Crocker machine.'*

'Competition with the imported equipment forced the decision in favor of a newly designed power plant – a type which would have acceleration, the right power output, low cost of maintenance plus a low first cost. A single cylinder type was decided upon.'

The first of the Crocker-powered overhead valve singles debuted on

The Crocker speedway bike was a consistent performer, but needed more investment of time and money to be competitive with the JAP-powered machines.   *(Bud Ekins, author.)*   19

November 11, 1933 at Emoryville motorcycle speedway in California. Out of his twelve starts, Cordy Milne took nine 'firsts' and one 'second' during the meets of November 11 and 14. During the same stand, his brother Jack won four 'first' places. (Just four years later, on JAPs, Jack and Cordy were destined to place first and third in the World Speedway Championship at England's Wembley Stadium, with fellow American Wilbur "Lammy' Lamoreaux taking second.) Another top rider on the first of these Crocker dirt trackers was Miny Waln. Earl Farrand and Snooky Owens also rode Crockers, so the marque did not suffer for the lack of good jockeys.

Unfortunately for Al Crocker, the JAP-powered British bikes were coming on strong and were rapidly replacing the Rudge machines which had been dominant in the sport for several years. The 40hp Crocker proved itself the equal of the Rudge, and was superior to the Harley-Davidson CAC. However, the JAP machines were good for 42-43 hp, so Crocker's new baby needed further development to be competitive. He therefore had two overhead cam motorcycles built during 1934, one of which was ridden a few times by Miny Waln.

Meanwhile, Crocker's attention was turning to a long cherished dream of building the fastest road-going motorcycle in the nation – perhaps the world. Facing stiff competition from the JAPs, and not being a true factory owner, he abandoned his shop-built speedway bikes at the end of 1934 to launch the far more famous Crocker v-twins which debuted in 1936. During the speedway project, the Crocker machine shop had built between forty and fifty of the pushrod speedway motorcycles.

Key specifications of the 1934 Crocker speedway machines were:

Bore:	3 1/4 in
Stroke:	3 5/8 in
Displacement:	30.06 cubic inches
Compression Ratio:	14 : 1
Crankpin:	1 1/8 in, drilled for oil
Main Shafts:	1 in, with 7 degree taper
Bearings:	roller for mainshafts and crankpin
Valves:	1 3/4 in, set at 'close angle' in 'shallow domed interior'
Valve Springs:	three coil springs per valve
Ignition:	gear driven Lucas magneto
Carburetor:	two bowl Amal
Power Peak:	at 6,000 rpm
Fuel:	alcohol
Frame:	chrome molybdenum tubing
Gear Ratio:	for 1/5 mile track, 8.75 : 1
Weight:	235 pounds
Finish:	blue frame, forks, and fender; polished aluminum tank; rims, bars etc., chromium plated
Cost:	$385, f.o.b. Los Angeles

Curtiss

Glenn H. Curtiss' motorcycles provided the most serious and sustained challenge to Indian supremacy during the 1902-1907 period. First mention of the marque was September 1902 (Labor Day), when a Curtiss motorcycle made the fastest time of all 'regular stock or road machines' in the New York Motorcycle Club's road race. The following May (1903), Glenn Curtiss was the winning rider at the **first American hillclimb,** also sponsored by the New York Motorcycle Club. This first Yankee hillclimb was conducted on a public road in the manner later adopted by Europeans but abandoned in the USA in favor of the dirt-hill bronco-busting variety. Not long afterwards, Curtiss startled observers at a Providence, Rhode Island meet when he piloted his 190 lb, 680 cc single (3 1/2 inches by 5 inches) through a one-mile run in 56.40 seconds (63.8 mph), a record for single cylinder machines.

On January 28, 1904, Glenn Curtiss made the first of his historic speed runs along the Atlantic shores at Ormond Beach, Florida, setting a 10-mile record of 8 minutes, 54 2/5 seconds (67.3 mph). This record remained unbroken over the next four years. In 1905, at Syracuse, New York, Glenn rode a Curtiss twin over a one-mile flat track course at a record pace for the dirt, turning the mile in 1 minute, 1 second (59 mph).

The specifications of the 1904 Curtiss twin were provided by *Scientific American* for February 29, 1904, in the following account. Note that the Curtiss was **the first motorcycle with twist grip controls,** not Indian as popularly believed, for Indian adopted this feature a year after Curtiss.

'One of our cuts shows a motor bicycle with an air-cooled V-shaped motor of 5 horse power, which made the fastest time at the recent Florida Race Meet. The machine is made by the G.H. Curtiss Manufacturing Company, Hammondsport, NY, and it is intended for use as a powerful roadster for use on all kinds of American roads. Its weight complete is but 165 pounds, and it has gasoline and oil tanks of sufficient capacity for traveling 150 miles. The double-cylinder, V-shaped motor is placed in a 23-inch frame, and transmits its power directly to the rear wheel by means of a 2-inch flat belt made of two-ply Russian rawhide. A wooden pulley is used on the rear wheel, and a leather-covered pulley on the motor. The motor itself weighs but 60 pounds, has a 3-inch bore and stroke and develops 5 horse power at 2,000 rpm, thus making the bicycle one of the most powerful motorcycles ever built for use as a regular road machine. The crankshaft runs on roller bearings in hardened and ground steel bushings. The two cylinders add greatly to the flexibility of the motor, and make it possible to obtain a wide variation in speed. With the regular gear of 4 : 1, the machine will climb any hill where the road is of fairly good surface, and will travel at the rate of 45 miles per hour on the level. With the racing gear of 2 1/2 : 1, it made a mile in 59 1/5 seconds and 10 miles in 8 minutes, 45 2/5 seconds on the Ormond-Daytona Beach.'

'The switch and spark advance are controlled by turning the left grip, while the exhaust valves can be raised by a small lever on the frame. The batteries and spark coils are placed across the upper part of the frame, the gasoline tank behind the seat. The carburetor is seen between the two cylinders of the motor. The company also builds a single-cylinder, 120 lb, 2 1/2 hp machine. The two sizes of machines are respectively fitted with 2 1/2 and 2-inch detachable tires, having a 62 and 58-inch wheel base.'

The Curtiss motorcycle peaked early, for 1907 was destined to be the best year for these Hammondsport, New York creations. Ormond Beach, Florida was again the place, and January 28 was the date, when Glenn Curtiss earned the title of 'fastest man in the world.' Riding a special 40 hp V-8 of his own design, Curtiss did the mile in 26.40 seconds, a rate of 137 mph. Unfortunately, the V-8 record was not official, but there seems little doubt that, whatever his exact speed, Curtiss had indeed traveled **faster than any man in the world in any kind of vehicle.** A contemporary account of the V-8 speed trial was provided by *Scientific American* for February 9, 1907, and is worded as follows:

THE FASTEST AND MOST POWERFUL AMERICAN MOTOR BICYCLE

'What is unquestionably the most powerful, as well as the fastest, motor bicycle ever built in this country made its appearance at the races at Ormond Beach recently; but, owing to the breaking of a universal joint and subsequent buckling of the frame, this machine made no official record. It was built by Mr. G.H. Curtiss, a well-known motor-bicycle maker, with the idea of breaking all records. The machine was fitted with an 8-cylinder air-cooled V-motor of 36-40 horse-power. The motor was placed with the crankshaft running lengthwise of the bicycle and connected to the driving shaft through a double universal joint. A large bevel gear on this shaft meshed with a similar one on the rear wheel of the bicycle. The total weight of the complete machine was but 275 pounds, or 6.8 pounds per horse-power. In an official mile test, timed by stop watches from the start by several persons who watched through field glasses a flag waved at the finish, Mr. Curtiss is said to have covered this distance in 26 2/5 seconds, which would be at the rate of 136.3 miles an hour – a faster speed than has ever been made before by a man on any type of vehicle. Unfortunately, before this new mile record could be corroborated by an official test, the universal joint broke while the machine was going 90 miles an hour. Fortunately, it was brought to a stop without injury to its daring rider from the rapidly-revolving driving shaft, which was thrashing about in a dangerous manner. Later on, the frame buckled, throwing the gears out of line, and the official test had to be abandoned. With his 2-cylinder machine, Curtiss rode a mile in 46 2/5 seconds in a race with Wray on a 2-cylinder 14 horse-power Peugeot motor bicycle, only to be beaten 2 seconds by the latter in a subsequent race, wherein a speed of about 80 1/2 miles an hour was obtained. With one of his single-cylinder machines, Curtiss made a mile in 1 minute, 5 3.5 seconds on January 21.'

Right top: **Glenn Curtiss on his V-8 special, which, although not officially recognized, was undoubtedly the fastest motorcycle in the world. The V-8's reported run of over 136 mph in 1907 would not be officially exceeded until 1930.** *(Motorcycle Illustrated.)*

Right bottom: **The Curtiss triple, surely the fastest stock 1909 motorcycle in the world, as claimed.**
(The Antique Motorcycle.)

Further success awaited Curtiss machines in 1907. On July 4, at Manhasset Hill, Long Island, New York, Curtiss machines won the 33.67 inch, 61 inch, and unlimited hillclimb events, defeating Indian stars Stanley T. Kellogg and George Holden. Glenn Curtiss was the jockey in the 61 inch and unlimited classes. In August, at the Providence National Endurance Contest of the Federation of American Motorcyclists (FAM), A. Cook rode a Curtiss to victory in the double-cylinder class. Glenn Curtiss and A. Cook finished first and second in the 30.50 inch 1-mile race and in the 30.50 inch hillclimb.

By 1909, two special racing models were offered, a 61 cubic inch (1000 cc) twin, and a 30 1/2 cubic inch (500 cc) single. Both machines featured roller bearings throughout.

Mention of the Curtiss would scarcely be complete without reference to the 1909 triple cylinder model. No records of competition success have been found, but the Curtiss triple was advertised as *the most powerful regularly built motorcycle in the world,* and had a claimed top speed of 90 mph, quite a claim for 1909. The engine appears to be formed from three 30.5 cubic inch cylinders, yielding a cubic capacity of some 1500 cc or 91.5 cubic inches. Such a motorcycle, weighing but 175 pounds as advertised, and with either the optional 3 : 1 or 2 1/2 : 1 gearing, was no doubt outstandingly fast for its time.

It was during this period of time that Glenn Curtiss was giving increased attention to aviation, and hereafter he would achieve great fame as a pioneer aircraft builder. Meanwhile, the Curtiss motorcycle, and its badge-engineered 'Marvel' brother, would continue in moderate production until the advent of the First World War.

Cyclone

The Cyclone probably aroused more curiosity and excitement than any other American racing motorcycle, a situation made all the more interesting by its brief four-year life. Two factors accounted for the yellow V-twin's special hold on the public's imagination. First, the Cyclone was far and away the most technically advanced motorcycle ever seen in the USA; indeed, in terms of raw horsepower, there was likely no equal anywhere on the planet. The second ingredient of Cyclone excitement was the spectacular riding style of Don Johns, whose name became inseparably linked with the Cyclone, despite the fact that Johns spent ninety percent of his career astride other marques.

A product of the same Minnesota firm which had once made the conservative and obscure Theim, the 61 cubic inch (1000 cc) Cyclone was a force to be reckoned with during the 1915 racing season. Its standout features were its bevel driven single overhead camshaft valve gear, and a similar gear and shaft layout which operated the Bosch magneto, giving the engine its unique appearance. All other features represented the limit of state-of-the-art technology. The forged steel flywheels were of spoked style, final balance adjustments being achieved by hand filing the bobweight in the spoke opposite

With the exception of the connecting rods' little ends, ball and roller bearings were used throughout. *(Bud Ekins, author)* 25

to the crankpin. Big end bearings were 1/4 inch rollers carried in three rows. Amazingly, the dainty looking connecting rods weighed but six ounces for the straight and a little less than eight ounces for the forked rods. Machining of the crankcases was so accurate that no shims were required to achieve the maximum of 0.001 inch end play necessitated by use of bevel gear cam drive. The cylinder walls were very thin, but additional strength was achieved by two ribs cast around the lower part of the barrel. The upper rib was drilled to provide for pressure-fed oiling of the pistons and cylinder walls. The cylinders were deeply recessed into the crankcase.

The valves were sized at 1 3/4 inches and disposed with an included angle of 70 degrees with the near-hemispherical combustion chamber. Valve actuation was through a rocker and stirrup affair which eliminated all side thrust. The compression ratio was 5.5 : 1 and maximum engine speed was 5,000 rpm. Four rows of caged rollers supported the drive side of the crankshaft assembly, while two rows of SKF self-aligning ball bearings handled the timing side. The flat-topped cast steel pistons were of solid skirt design and had only two compression rings. The piston pins ran directly in the unbushed connecting rods' little ends, and these were the only plain bearings in the engine.

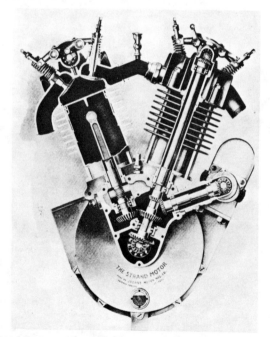

Cutaway of the Cyclone engine. Note the unique stirrup linkage between the rocker arms and valve stems, effectively eliminating side thrust. As this is not a racing engine, it does not have the reinforcing cylinder ribs below the bottom fins. The combustion chamber walls are surprisingly thin and the porting is awkward.

(The Antique Motorcycle.)

In keeping with the era's theories, the cylinders were ported, i.e., vented to the atmosphere through several rectangular cuts or ports, so that the ports began opening when the pistons were 5/16 inch from bottom dead center. At the time, popular theory was that such porting achieved greater power by permitting rapid expulsion of the exhaust gases, but modern technical hindsight explains the resultant power improvement as a crude supercharging effect. Regardless of the explanation, such open-ported machines set the speed standards of their day, while the resultant noise and thick smokescreen from the pressure-oiled cylinder walls inparted a definite Baron von Richthofen atmosphere. At night, the effect was even more spectacular, as blue flames busily surrounded the engine works and the rider's legs.

A by-product of porting was the need to provide a very rich fuel mixture due to the large amounts of air inhaled through the open ports. Furthermore, as the amount of intake air could not be effectively regulated, the proper

J.A. McNeil at the Omaha, Nebraska, board track on a Cyclone. The reinforcing cylinder ribs may be seen below the bottom cooling fins. At this same track on Oct. 1, 1914, McNeil did the mile in 35 2/5 seconds (101 mph), and later in 32 2/5 seconds (111.1 mph), breaking Hummiston's Excelsior record of 100 mph. The official World Record at that time was 93.48 mph by S. George of Britain, on an Indian. *(Bud Ekins, author.)* 27

fuel/air ratio occurred only at peak power and engine speed. Consequently, there was no throttle, speed being governed by the use of an ignition cut-out or 'kill' button on the handlebar. Speed control, therefore, was a jerky on-again-off-again proposition which produced hairy amounts of wheelspin on the dirt tracks. The overall 250 pound package was peculiarly suited to Don Johns' hell-for-leather style.

During 1913, Cyclone's original factory riders J.A. McNeil and Larry 'Cave Man' Fleckenstein were turning 108 mph laps at a Minneapolis motordrome. Moreover, in 1914 at the Omaha, Nebraska board track, McNeil traveled a mile in 32.4 seconds, or 111.1 mph, a speed which was well above both the recognized world record of 93.48 mph by Britain's S. George (Indian) and Lee Humiston's (Excelsior) FAM mark of 100 mph. However, the FAM refused to recognize McNeil's record, doubtless being suspicious of such a high speed margin over other motorcycles of the time.

During the spring of 1915, the reputation of the Cyclone as the ultimate in speed continued to grow out of its reported victories and good showings in several secondary-status dirt track races in Ohio and Illinois. However, as a new model, the Cyclone was predictably experiencing some reliability problems; these included piston, exhaust valve and control linkage failures. At the big Venice, California 300-mile road race, Dave Kinney suffered carburetor failure, and Johns was eliminated with a broken chain. These problems, and the fact that both Don Johns and Bill Goudy had generally faced less than stellar competition in midwestern dirt track events, meant that many racing fans remained unconvinced.

The 1915 Dodge City, Kansas 300-Mile National Championship road race on July 4 was another Cyclone opportunity in all-out head to head battle with the three established marques, Harley-Davidson, Excelsior, and Indian. Kinney had the fastest qualifying lap at 88.5 mph, but during the race Johns turned in a 90 mph lap. Johns led laps two through sixteen on the two-mile dirt oval, before stopping for fuel and oil. Oil consumption, incidentally, was atrocious, being about one quart per five miles.

Johns' performance was termed 'championship caliber' by *Motorcycle Illustrated,* which went on to say *'Johns' work was nothing short of spectacular and it was generally understood that he was gaiting himself for a new 100-mile record.'* John again took the lead on lap 24, *'...setting a terrific pace and looking for all the world like a winner.'* Alas, the Cyclone began to falter, and Johns gave up the lead for good somewhere between the 70th and 80th mile, depending on which of the conflicting lap counts you prefer. One thing is for certain, after 90 miles Johns suffered a broken fuel tank and was forced to retire, joining team mate Dave Kinney on the sidelines. Kinney had earlier experienced a broken frame on his Cyclone.

After Dodge City, the promise of the Cyclone was not fulfilled. Johns journeyed to Sacramento, California, where he managed to win a one-mile National Championship, after 16 miles of pacing with the other riders before getting an acceptable rolling start wave-off from the referee! Most of the Sacramento wins, however, went to Ray Creviston on his Indian. Symbolically,

28

on July 24, 1915, Johns was eliminated from the 15-mile Sacramento feature event by another breakdown, this time the magneto. After Sacramento, Don Johns abandoned his one year of spectacular riding for Cyclone, riding which had produced much excitement but little reward. He returned to the Indian team in 1916 for his last full season of racing, finishing his career after one year with Thor, two with Excelsior, four with Indian, and one with Cyclone; but he will always be remembered best as 'that Cyclone racer.'

Cyclone racing continued after July 1915 in the hands of riders Dave Kinney, Bill Goudy, Carl Eschereich, and a rider known as Fabian. The latter won a 10-mile event against Creviston and Johns on August 8 at Fresno, California. On October 19, announcement was made that the Cyclone firm (Joerns Mfg. Co. of Minneapolis, Minnesota) was ceasing production, but somehow this decision was shortly reversed.

Kinney made the Cyclone's best long distance showing a few weeks later, when on November 25, 1915, he placed second to Bob Perry (Excelsior) at the Phoenix, Arizona 100-mile flat track event. Such was the pace that Perry was forced to a new record for the distance.

Cyclone victories were few and far between in 1916. Kinney managed to win the Stockton, California 10-mile pro event over a good field on June 20, 1916, before following in Don Johns' footsteps and joining the Indian team. After Kinney, there weren't enough racing dollars and good riders to extract the full potential from the Cyclone overhead cam twin. There were aborted attempts to resurrect the company in the early twenties, Joerns Mfg. having finally gone under after the 1916 season. Meanwhile, both Excelsior and Reading-Standard flattered Cyclone designer Andrew Strand by racing their own bevel gear driven overhead cam V-twins. Somehow, though, neither of these ohc motorcycles ever found the magic, and American motorcycle racing eventually started down the long trail of sidevalve racing. How different things might have been!

Emblem

The maker of the Emblem, W.C. Schack, never made a total leap into big-time racing, but he did flirt with the idea for quite some time. First mention of the Emblem's racing career occurred in 1910. In August, W.E. Gale set a New York to Chicago record of 35 hours. At Columbus, Ohio on Sept. 10, L.S. (Lee) Taylor set a 100-mile dirt track record for single cylinder belt-driven machines. His time was 1 hour, 56 minutes, 57 2/5 seconds, an average of 48.7 mph. Taylor's machine was a 38.5 cubic inch (630 cc) model, available with optional 1 3/4 inch flatbelt or 1 1/8 inch v-belt drive. The engine had a 3 1/2 inch bore and a 4 inch stroke, and was a typical ioe (F-head) unit. One year later, and on the same track, George Evans rode a belt drive twin-cylinder Emblem to a new 100-mile dirt track record of 1 hour, 42 minutes, 9 2/5 seconds, an average of 35.2 mph.

Although the general specification of this 1915 twin followed typical ioe practice, the cast-in horizontal motor mounts and corresponding frame lugs were unique. Likewise, the method of securing the timing gear cover with a single nut was distinctive. *(Earl Chalfant.)*

As close as Emblem ever came to real glory was the 1915 Dodge City, Kansas 300-mile National Championship, in which a factory team was reported to have entered. However, *Motorcycle Illustrated* listed only one Emblem rider, C.F. Jackson, who was not credited with completing a single lap.

Despite their belt drive, Emblem machines were somewhat advanced, or at least unusual. Their wrist pins were held in place by the lower wide piston ring, as can be seen in the accompanying photograph. Motor mounts were heavy horizontal frame lugs which linked up with the cast-in crankcase fittings. A single large cover could be unscrewed to reveal the timing mechanism, as opposed to the multitude of small timing cover screws typical of the period. The frame tubing was highly unorthodox, and consisted of a triangular cross-sectioned hollow beam within each hollow frame tube. Most prophetic of all was the 76.6 cubic inch (1256 cc) V-twin introduced in 1913. This machine predated by eight years the popular 74 inch models of Harley and Indian.

The Emblem never caught on in the USA, and domestic sales virtually ceased by 1918. However, a 32.4 cubic inch (531 cc) light twin was manufactured and exported to European markets as late as 1925.

An Emblem trademark was the use of a piston ring to secure the wrist pin. The employment of a single camshaft was typical of the period.   *(Earl Chalfant.)*   31

Excelsior/Super X

Until the advent of the Chicago-based Excelsior, the Indian marque had reigned unchallenged as the King of American racing. Since their 1907 birth, Excelsiors had featured the intake-over-exhaust valve configuration. This design was also variously described as ioe, F-head, and pocket valve, the latter being the most common term of the period. The theoretical advantage of the pocket valve engine was the situation of its relatively cool intake valve directly over the hotter exhaust valve, the two operating in a chamber or pocket to the side of the cylinder barrel. In view of the rather 'iffy' state of the era's metallurgy, such logic was probably sound, and therefore, the pocket valve arrangement was the standard of the day. In addition to Excelsior and Indian, the then obscure Harley-Davidson also employed the ioe arrangement.

Page's circa 1915 motorcycle maintenance manual (republished by Post Motor Books, 1971) acknowledged the theoretical disadvantages of the pocket valves, most notably their thermal inefficiency due to the heat loss through the valve pocket, and also the indirect paths of the intake and exhaust gases. However, in the low engine speed environment of the times, it was also noted that these theoretical problems appeared of no practical significance.

1911-1913

The 'X' didn't impress many people with its racing capabilities until the 1911 racing season. During the early part of the year. Excelsior's Joe Wolters was practically unbeatable, a situation which forced Indian's co-founder and chief engineer, Oscar Hedstrom, to withdraw to the drawing board and design the 8-valve Indian overheads. Appearing in Chicago, Illinois' Riverview Motordrome, Wolters twice defeated the famous DeRosier, now also an Excelsior factory rider after his firing by Indian. In these late August (1911) races Wolters set a new unofficial world record for two miles of 1 minute 22 2/5 seconds (87.3 mph), quite a stunning speed considering it required six laps on a tiny 1/3-mile oval. On August 26, also at Riverview, Wolters broke De Rosier's Indian-mounted record for one mile, burning up the boards in 40 1/5 seconds for an average of 88.9 mph. DeRosier had finished third in some of these August races, and having long been top dog in the United States, he complained to Excelsior management that he was being provided with inferior equipment. The press agreed with DeRosier, long their darling, and after narrowly defeating Wolters in the 'DeRosier Sweepstakes', Jake was shortly provided with a new machine.

Opposite: **In 1909, the Indian company and Jack Prince joined forces to build this unusual circular 1/3 mile Motordrome in Indian's home town. Most tracks were ovals of 1/4-1/3 mile. The track surface on all dromes was built from either 2 inch by 2 inch boards, or 2 inch by 4 inch boards, laid on edge. The height of Motordrome (short track) popularity was in 1912, but a handful of one-mile or longer board-tracks operated until the late twenties.**

(Motorcycle Illustrated.)

SPRINGFIELD TRACK TO BE THE FINEST OF ALL

Circular Speedway, Three Laps to a Mile, Will Be Ready Between Middle of July and First of August.

On September 17, 1911, DeRosier was his usual all-conquering self, not only winning the feature event, but also setting a new unofficial world record for the kilometer of 23 1/5 seconds (94 1/5 mph), the official record remaining in the hands of England's Charlie Collier (Matchless).

Before reviewing subsequent Motordrome events, it is appropriate to examine the design and construction of these uniquely American facilities. The accompanying photographs well illustrate the general layout. The frail-appearing narrow slat-like planks were only two inches wide, but their four-inch depth provided rigidity for the resistance of centrifugal force. Motorcycle board track racing had originally occurred on bicycle tracks, called Velodromes, which were banked about 25 degrees in the corners. Accordingly, the first Motordrome, in Clifton, New Jersey, was also banked at 25 degrees. Afterwards, the angle was increased to 35 degrees in Denver, Colorado and Salt Lake City, Utah, and then to 38 degrees in Chicago, Illinois, and New York City. This escalation process continued until, in 1913, the Cleveland and St. Louis Motordromes were banked at 62 degrees. Subsequent track construction in Detroit, Michigan, Cincinnati, Ohio, and elsewhere settled on 60 degrees, which became the standard.

Jake DeRosier was now a veteran of over 900 motorcycle races, having literally started his motorcycle racing career at the earliest possible time in 1898 (see the Indian section). His constant exposure to the ever-increasing speeds and risks, and the fact that other riders naturally singled him out in their race tactics, had resulted in his several accidents over the years. Jake's most serious fall had been at Gutenburg in October of 1911, but when he lined up for the match race with Charles Balke on March 12, 1912, it had been but two weeks since Jake's most recent brush with death. Balke was a hard-charging rider whose deliberate unyielding style was causing some people to refer to him as 'Fearless' Balke or 'The Fearless One'. During their match race, DeRosier crashed hard and so badly mangled his leg that he would never again race. On March 31, 1912, a special DeRosier Benefit race was staged, netting $600 for the injured star.

Coincident with DeRosier's misfortune, the Los Angeles board track racing scene fell apart. As the home of one of the earliest Motordromes, and now sporting two dromes, competition in the Los Angeles area had been unusually fierce. Consequently, as a result of a rider and referee row on March 24, 1912, both Excelsior and Indian factory and dealer support were withdrawn from the Los Angeles Motordrome. Thus, for the 'DeRosier Benefit', the riders had to resort to the use of borrowed machines, some of the Indians coming from the Los Angeles Police Department.

The final argument which precipitated the track's fall from favor was a dispute over fouling. Fouling, whether by crowding, bumping, or in some cases even swinging a fist, was a reality accepted by many riders as a stock in trade. Thus, neither of the accused riders, Graves and Balke, would file a protest against the other. The FAM's Competition Committee Chairman, Dr. Thornley, stated, 'There has never been anything but trouble in Los Angeles since motorcycle racing began.'

At the end of 1912, Excelsior's Lee Humiston secured for himself a permanent piece of history at the Playa del Rey Motordrome. Humiston turned the mile in 36 seconds flat, becoming the **first motorcyclist in the world to be officially timed at 100 mph by a sanctioning organization** (Curtiss' 1907 run was unsanctioned). That Humiston in fact 'turned the ton' is quite believable, as during 1912 speeds on the Motordromes had been steadily on the rise throughout the year, climbing from Hasha's Indian 8-valve speed of 90.9 set in March to Ray Seymour's 97.82 in May, also on an 8-valve Indian. To put Humiston's 100 mph performance in perspective, it should be noted that the then-current official world record was held by Britain's Charlie Collier (Matchless) at 91.23 mph, and furthermore, that Humiston's 'ton' would not be bettered under international sanction during the next eight years.

During the December 30 run, the Excelsior's one-mile averages were: 100, 97.8, 95.2, 94.7, 94.2, 94.2, 94.2, 93.7, 94.2, 94.2, 92.7, and 88.2 (broken manifold). The five laps at 94.2 mph would have required stopwatch errors on the order of 1.4 seconds each in order to have erroneously credited Humiston with a faster speed than Collier over each of these five one-mile intervals. Looking at it another way, operator stopwatch error would have exceeded 138 feet in terms of where the operator spotted the motorcycle when pressing the button.

American records were customarily not given FICM recognition, but there was concern that the new Excelsior-powered records would not even be recognized in the United States, as the previous difficulties at the nearby Los Angeles Motordrome had erupted into a virtual civil war within the FAM. President Patterson of the FAM had appointed a new west coast referee, Collins; and the new referee had submitted the official sanctioning request for Humiston's record run. However, the incumbent referee, Gates, refused to step aside and was supported by the FAM's Competition Committee Chairman, Dr. Thornley. This then raised the question of whether or not Humiston's sanction was legal. In the midst of the bickering, the Chairman announced that Humiston's records would stand, not wishing to penalize the Excelsior rider who was merely an innocent bystander in the legal morass. The whole episode is illustrative of the lack of effective organization which was largely responsible for the isolation of American motorcycle record breaking from the official international motorcycle scene.

For Chairman Thornley and the FAM, the outcome of their squabble was less pleasant and culminated in the suspension of Thornley, who was alleged to have been guilty of financial irregularities. Thornley waged a legal battle to the last and relented only when on the verge of being physically evicted from his New York office. All in all, the Thornley affair symbolized the sometimes chaotic nature of American motorcycle organization, a spin-off of which was the aforementioned isolation of some of the best motorcycling effort within the United States. In addition to the lack of official blessing to American efforts, there was an unfortunate tendency of British and Continental fans to completely disregard reports of American speed and the sometimes startling Yankee margin over official marks made such suspicion all the more easy. 35

On the American scene, the new Excelsior records for one through one hundred miles were a big blow to Indian, which was accustomed to holding over ninety percent of all FAM records. Indeed, in the previous year Indian had held all 121 FAM-recognized distance and time records. Excelsior's rapid emergence as a racing power, symbolized by their snagging of DeRosier from the Indian tribe, was now firmly documented in the American record books. Although no one yet suspected that Harley-Davidson was soon to be reckoned with, it was now clear to race followers that a new racing era was in progress. Indian could no longer assume success. Wolters, DeRosier, Graves, and Humiston had put the 'X' on the map.

Savannah, Georgia hosted the most prestigious race of 1913, the 300-mile Grand Prix road race over an 11 1/2-mile circuit. Despite a lengthy pit stop, Perry was credited with the win at a course-record 62 mph pace. In retrospect, it appears that Perry was erroneously given the Savannah win, as the Savannah Motorcycle Club later cited Maldwyn Jones (Merkel) as the winner. Both the Excelsior and Merkel factories laid claim to the victory in their advertisements. The hub of contention was whether or not Jones had been credited with all of his laps. Unfortunately, this lap-counting problem would continue to rear its head for a number of years in American racing.

A common racing sight prior to the Kaiser's War, that of a young rider and a stock Excelsior converted to a racer. *(Stephen Wright.)*

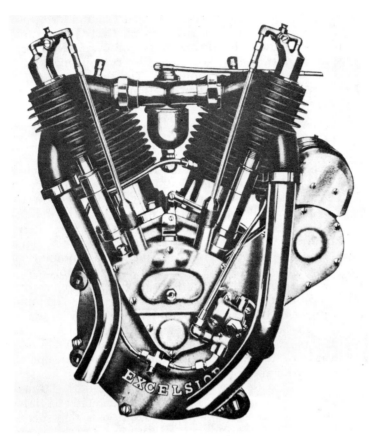

Closeup of the stock 'X' motor used in the touring bikes and early racers. Typical speed modifications for all makes included extensive drilling of pistons and rods. Some riders used an extra long skirt for the front piston to improve oil pickup. Rear cylinder oiling tended to be more effective, due to the natural slinging effect from the crankshaft. The oil line at the base of the front cylinder also serves the purpose of equalizing the oiling of the cylinders.

(The Antique Motorcycle.)

1914: Neck and neck with Indian

In the 1914 season, the Excelsior ioe twin proved equal to the 8-valve Indian in numerous race meets. In April, Bob Perry won a close battle for the 5-mile National Championship at Sacramento, California, with Indian's Charles 'Fearless' Balke in second spot. The following month Balke turned the table by beating Carl Goudy in the 5-mile pro event at Philadephia, Pennsylvania. However, Goudy then added to the confusion of the picture by taking the 10-mile pro event. Also in May, Excelsior's Bob Perry was described as 'invincible' in the strictly stock class of the two-day Chicago meet.

The inaugural Dodge City 300-mile National Championship was run on July 4, and proved an Excelsior disappointment. Carl Goudy came in third behind Indian's Glen 'Slivers' Boyd and Thor's Bill Brier. However, at the big St.Louis, Missouri meet two weeks later, Excelsior riders won half of the events including all three National Championships. The final big event of the year was the Oct. 8 FAM One-Hour Championship at Birmingham, Alabama, which Joe Wolters won.

1915: The High Point for the 'X'

The 'X's first big win of 1915 was at Madison, Wisconsin, when Bob Perry took the checkered flag in a 100-mile event. His rivals were Harley-Davidson's Irving Janke and Al Stratton. Perry used a little generalship in this race, for he ran out of gas at the 97th mile while leading Stratton by two miles. But scarcely had a couple of sloshes of gas been poured into his tank when Perry stopped the operation and rekindled his bike by furious pedaling. He then managed to beat Stratton to the wire by half a mile, or roughly the amount of additional time it would have taken for complete servicing of his motorcycle.

Relay races were a popular attraction in the teens. At the Boston 300-mile relay on June 19, Bob Perry and Carl Goudy won in 4 hours, 24 minutes. 1 1/5 seconds, an average of 68 mph over the dirt track. This event was the public debut of Excelsior's new big valved engines, in which the exhaust valves measured a whopping 2 1/4 inches in head diameter. The two non-ported big valves of Perry and Goudy were faster than the ported old style engine brought to the meet by Perry for the sprint events.

Perry had his best season in 1915. He won another 100-mile race at Madison in August, and a third 100-miler at Phoenix, Arizona in November, and although his three centuries were non-Nationals they were seriously contested by Harley-Davidson, Indian, and Cyclone. Perry's Phoenix victory was a record for the century on a circular flat track, as he averaged 72.5 mph, and bettered Morty Graves' previous Indian mark by almost two minutes. Perry's most prestigious win was on Oct.3, when he won the FAM One-Hour National Championship. He covered 64 3/4 miles on the Hawthorne, Illinois (Chicago suburb) dirt track, finishing ahead of Morty Graves (Indian) and Glenn Stokes (Excelsior).

But the 'X's largest share of glory was captured by Carl Goudy at the Speedway Park (Chicago) board track on Sept. 12. Goudy won the 300-mile event, breaking all previous 300-mile records. His time over the two-mile track was 3 hours, 29 minutes, 51 3/5 seconds, an average of 85.8 mph. Goudy led

Top right: **Closeup of the special racing engine, the 'Big Valve X'. The cylinders are completely different from those of the stock model.** *(The Antique Motorcycle.)*

Bottom right: **The most successful racing machine ever built by the Chicago firm was this 'short coupled' big valve model which was raced from 1915 through 1921. While the performance was continuously improved, the 'X' seemed always to be about a year behind Harley and Indian.**

(The Antique Motorcycle.)

the second-place Indian rider, Teddy Carroll, by four laps at the finish. However, the race also revealed the speed margin of Harley-Davidson over Excelsior as Otto Walker set a 100-mile record of 89.11 mph before experiencing problems on his 'Chicago Harley' as the latest pocket-valve Milwaukee motors were termed.

1916

There was but one National Championship for Excelsior in 1916, the 10-mile FAM title taken May 30 at Chicago by Glenn Stokes. However, the 'X' did win some other well-publicized races. Of these, the most meaningful was the one-two finish of Bob Perry and Glenn Stokes at the 100-mile flat track event on June 11 at Detroit. Their competition included Red Parkhurst and Bill Brier on the new Harley-Davidson 8-valves; and Indian's Ray Creviston, Lee Taylor, and 'Krazy Horse' Verrill.

At Dodge City on July 4, the Excelsior team flirted with success for the second consecutive year. In the 1915 300-mile classic, Bob Perry and Glenn Stokes had traded first and second places between the 44th and 46th miles, while Carl Goudy had made the best time in 1915 for 100 miles. In the 1916 affair, Joe Wolters finished with an elapsed time that was 7 minutes, 52 seconds better than the 1915 winner (Otto Walker, Harley-Davidson), but two minutes, 17 seconds slower then the 1916 victory of Harley's Irving Janke.

1917-1921: Bennett carries the 'X' flag

The United States' entry into the First World War accounted for a two-year drought in major motorcycle competition, with the mutual agreement of Excelsior, Harley-Davidson, and Indian to refrain from racing support. Motorcycle competition in 1917 and 1918 centred around hillclimbing, endurance runs and record setting. The 1917 Capistrano (California) hillclimb featured victories by C. Lambert in both the stock and free-for-all events. Three months later, Wells Bennett made the only perfect score in the twelfth annual endurance run of the Los Angeles Motorcycle Club.

During the five years of 1917 through 1921, Wells Bennett accounted for most of the favorable Excelsior publicity. In June of 1918, Bennett set a new record for the 302 mile trip from Los Angeles to Needles, Arizona, completing the rugged desert crossing at a 42.3 mph pace. This was a healthy average in light of the poor sandy pathways loosely described as roads. Two months later, Bennett set a Three-Flag record, a stunt so named because the journey was from Blaine, Washington (Canadian border) to Tijuana, Mexico or vice versa. Bennett's time for the 1,621 miles was 70 hours, the 23 mph average a testimony to the poor roads.

Bennett was involved in four unofficial record-setting runs during 1919, which was fortunate for Excelsior as they won no National Championships that year. Bennett and passenger Roy Jones lowered the Los Angeles to San Diego (132 miles) record to 2 hours, 44 minutes (48.3 mph). Other record times were posted for; San Francisco to Los Angeles, Los Angeles to San Diego by sidecar, and Los Angeles to Bakersfield by sidecar (sealed in high gear).

1920

In 1920, Bennett made another Los Angeles to Bakersfield sidecar record, again for a sealed-in-high-gear configuration, the time being lowered to three hours and seven minutes for the mountainous 126 miles. Likewise, Wells Bennett renewed his Three-Flag Championship with a time of 51 hours, 4 minutes for the 1655-mile trip. Incidentally, there was a flurry of Three-Flag activity during this period, with the record bouncing back and forth between Excelsior, Indian, and Harley-Davidson, and soon Bennett would do the trick on a Henderson Four. However, interest in further speed dashes over the public roads was declining because the M&ATA had announced in 1919 that no more intercity records would be sanctioned.

The overhead cam twin

The high water mark of Excelsior interest in racing was reached in January 1920. At Los Angeles, California, Ascot Speedway, Excelsior had four riders ready for the 100-mile (non-titled) race. These included team chief J.A. McNeil, Wells Bennett, Joe Wolters, and Bob Perry. Their machines were brand new overhead cam V-twins, designed by McNeil with the assistance of Perry, a recent graduate of the University of Illinois. Unfortunately, details of these machines are unknown, but their Cyclone inspiration is apparent. They were not, however, carbon copies of the Cyclone as was the forthcoming Reading-Standard ohc machine. The ohc Excelsiors had much larger exhaust ports which exited more to the right side of the machine than fore and aft.

During a practice run on January 2, Bob Perry spilled and slid into a fence post. He died from massive head injuries, and the 'X' team withdrew from the January 4 race meet. Perry was quite popular with the Schwinns and the fatal accident had a lasting impact on Excelsior, which never again sustained an all-out race program. A fable grew up over the years that Ignaz Schwinn personally smashed the overhead cam machines with a sledge hammer. However, these ohc motorcycles were seen at subsequent race meets over a year later. Moreover, Gene Rhyne, who became the company's top hillclimber during their 1929-1930 competition renaissance, recalls seeing three of these rare motorcycles gathering dust during his factory employment in 1930.

In any case, certainly serious ohc development effort ceased after Perry's death. For the April 200-mile Championship Marion, Indiana, road race, the 'X' team was mounted on pocket valve (ioe) twins, and the overhead cam's promise remained untested.

41

Bob Perry on the overhead cam Excelsior a few minutes prior to his fatal accident. Although inspired by the Cyclone, the 'X' cammer was not a carbon copy. The Excelsior's exhaust ports were much larger than those of the Cyclone, and the Excelsior's cylinder heads also differed considerably.

42   *(Ted Hodgdon.)*

1921

The Dodge City, Kansas 300-mile National Championship was frustrating for Excelsior. Wells Bennett's fastest lap of the two-mile course was turned in one minute and thirteen seconds, an average of 98.6 mph. Harley's Ralph Hepburn, the winner, had a fastest lap of one minute and fifteen seconds, which was 2.6 mph slower than Bennett's best. Bennett ran well during the race's second 100 miles, but was sidelined at the 164th mile with a broken intake valve rocker arm.

In September, Paul Anderson set half-mile track records for 1, 2, and 10 miles on an ioe 'half twin', i.e., a single built up on a twin's case but with one cylinder blanked off. His one-mile (two laps) time on the dirt was 1 minute, 2 4/5 seconds, a rate of 57.3 mph. At this point, a 60 mph one-minute mile over a half-mile dirt track was the goal of every half-mile rider.

Another view of the ohc Excelsior. Prior to this machine's appearance, J.A. McNeil had designed a push-rod ohv V-twin similar to the British JAP units. Six push-rod ohv engines were built, but disappointing performance led McNeil to develop this overhead cam design. The rider is Joe Wolters.　　　　　　　　　　　　　　　　　　　　*(Sam Arena.)*　43

Paul Anderson and the 30.50 cubic inch motorcycle he rode through a much publicized barrier, the first sixty second mile on a half-mile dirt track.   *(Ted Hodgdon.)*

1922: A new cylinder design

Bothered by heat distortion due to its offset valves during the 1921 season, Anderson's 30.50 cubic inch ioe single had failed to run long at peak efficiency. This was a characteristic that would become more commonly known in the forthcoming Class C sidevalve racing era a dozen years later. To attack the problem, Chief Engineer Arthur Lemon developed a new 'M' type cylinder, the main feature of which was the provision of a cooling air passage between the cylinder proper and the valve pocket.

Lemon put the new design to the test on the half-mile circuit, in the hands of Paul Anderson and the recently recruited Maldwyn Jones, formerly a Harley-Davidson racer. Lemon took the radical step of running the engines with only one piston ring in order to reduce friction. It was soon determined that the single-ring setup was sufficient for only 25 miles of operation, so careful planning was required to budget operating time for practice and each race meet's several events.

Although only two racing frames were constructed, three engines were 44 built in order to facilitate maintenance support. At Singac, New Jersey,

The 'M' type cylinder, showing the air space between cylinder and valve pocket.

(Ted Hodgdon.)

Anderson tied Gene Walker's (Indian) record for one mile over a half-mile dirt track. His time was 1 minute, 1 1/5 seconds, an average of 58.8 mph, and the elusive 60 mph one-minute-mile was drawing closer. On November 12, at Winchester, Indiana, Anderson turned the first one-minute-mile over a half-mile dirt track, and much was made of this in Excelsior advertisements. (As a matter of interest, Maldwyn Jones recalls that the Winchester track was steeply banked and that its surface was unusually hard-packed, so that the course more resembled a macadam circuit that a typical dirt track).

Owing to the success of the 'M' cylinders in flat tracking, Lemon adapted them to the factory hillclimbers. In the 1923 Capistrano, California climb, Ed Ryan took the 80 cubic inch free-for-all (combined professionals and amateurs) class. His machine used a metal tractor band instead of a conventional rear tire. The frame was extended several feet beyond the rear wheel in the manner of modern drag (sprint) racers, thus preventing end-over-end spills. Both features were shortly outlawed by the M&ATA. The success of the 'M'-cylindered twins at Capistrano gave rise to the term 'Capistrano engine'.

For the 1924 Capistrano event, the Excelsior factory showed a determination not seen for a decade. The company prepared three 'M' twins for each of the classes, the 61, 74, and 80 cubic inch (open) classes. Moreover, the Chicago works paid Wells Bennett's expenses for the journey from his Portland, Oregon home to the southern California meet, and likewise footed the bill for 45

Ed Ryan's travel from Colorado Springs, Colorado. (The third team member, Shorty Healton, was from the Capistrano area). Each of these riders won his event: Healton won the 61 event, Ryan the 74 event, and Bennett the 80 (open) event.

1925: The Super X arrives

Meanwhile, development work had been proceeding steadily on a new concept of American motorcycle, a 45 cubic inch (750 cc) sport model. During 1923, advertisements in the two leading British motorcycle magazines, *The Motor Cycle* and *Motor Cycling,* had proclaimed the advent of this model known as the Super X. Strangely, however, the arrival of the Super X on the American scene occurred one year later with its formal introduction via the catalog of 1925 Excelsior models. With the arrival of the Super X 45, the venerable Excelsior 61 was quietly dropped from production. The new Super X was destined to have a major impact on the evolution of American motorcycle sport, first in hillclimbing and ultimately in racing.

Specifications of the Super X were as follows: the bore and stoke were 3 inches and 3 7/32 inches. Roller and ball bearings were used throughout. Lubrication was by the total loss system as in contemporary Harley-Davidsons and Indians. The valve gear was typical ioe. The three-speed sliding gear transmission was built in-unit with the engine; that is, the gears were integrally housed in a common casting with the engine. There would not be another American-designed unit construction powerplant until the advent of the Harley-Davidson K series in 1952.

The primary drive was by helical gears running in an oil bath, as per Indian practice. A steel and Raybestos multi-disk clutch transferred power from the engine to the gearbox. The wheelbase was 56 1/2 inches. In general, the machine was of roughly similar size to today's 400 cc class motorcycle, but seat height was lower and the weight was about 100 pounds less. Despite the shortage of available rpms by today's standards, the relatively flat torque curve of the understressed 750 cc engine and the bike's light weight combined to give it, as Madison Avenue might say, a sparkling performance.

In club-level competition the Super X was an immediate hit. As there was as yet no 45 cubic inch class, the Super X was thrown against 61, 74, and 80 cubic inch machines in both hillclimbs and flat-track events. Nevertheless, the little 45 won often against these bigger motorcycles. On the 1 1/8 mile board track Laurel Speedway, near Baltimore, Maryland, Red Wolverton set three 45 cubic inch class unofficial records, turning the mile distance at 95.7 mph, 5 miles at 92.68 mph, and 10 miles at 91.05 mph.

1926: The first 45 inch competition

The ready acceptance of the Super X, together with the company's influence in the three-sided industry oligarchy, forced official recognition of the 45 cubic inch class effective with the 1926 season. Oddly enough, in the 45

46

The Super X steered American racing towards a new 45 cubic inch (750 cc) class.
(Del Duchene, author)

cubic inch class which the Super X had mandated, the Excelsior product did not win the first National Championship. That honor fell to Jim Davis on an Indian 30.50 single at Salem, New Hampshire, on August 21. However, the Super X acquitted itself well in a number of events. As this was the time when the board tracks were being boarded up, Joe Petrali set the all-time 45 cubic inch Class A board track records on July 2. His speeds over the Altoona, Pennsylvania course were: 1 mile, 107.65 mph; 5 miles, 103.60 mph; and 10 miles, 100.70 mph. Petrali also won a 10-mile 61 cubic inch class (non-national) race at Salem.

The performance of the Super X almost immediately steered Indian and Harley-Davidson in a new direction. Indian constructed twenty-six special 45 cubic inch overhead valve motorcycles in 1926, and Harley-Davidson followed suit a year later. Both proved effective against 61, 74, and 80 cubic inch rivals.

1927: 1928

Against the rival Harley and Indian overheads, the Super X was nevertheless successful during 1927 and 1928. Petrali set two 45 cubic inch board track records on March 15 at Culver City, traveling 50 miles at 82.3 mph and   47

The Super X was quite popular in hillclimbing. Outstanding features are its unit construction and the excellent engine protection afforded by its frame. *(Stephen Wright.)*

100 miles at 73.0 mph. At Milwaukee, on July 31, Petrali set a 10-mile dirt track record of 75.3 mph and a 15-mile dirt record of 75.5 mph. More importantly, 'Smokin' Joe' gave the Chicago brand its first National Championship title since 1916, winning the 10-mile 45 cubic inch title. However, Petrali continued to bounce back and forth between Chicago and Milwaukee, giving evidence of both Excelsior's and Harley's lack of total commitment to racing during this period. The Super X was also successful at the non-professional level. At the last Capistrano hillclimb on December 4th, 1927, Harold Mathewson won the 80 cubic inch novice class.

During 1928, Petrali was joined by Gene Rhyne as a factory hillclimber. Meanwhile, Petrali had developed a 61 cubic inch 'Big Bertha' hillclimber by mating the old 'M' type ioe cylinders on a Super X base. In June, Rhyne won the 61 inch class of the Vallejo, California, climb on Big Bertha. In July, Petrali rode Big Bertha to the 61 cubic inch class win at the prestigious Mount Garfield, Michigan, hillclimb. Between May 27 and July 15, Petrali won two (non-National) flat track races and shared six hillclimb wins with Rhyne.

Gene Rhyne on the 45 ohv hillclimber.   *(Herb Ottaway.)*

1929: The overhead valve Super X

Although the stock-based Super X 45 hillclimber and the special Big Bertha had given Excelsior more honors than typical of the 1920s, Ignaz Schwinn was not satisfied. Apparently his taste for victories, after the long Championship drought, had been whetted strongly. He therefore instructed Lemon's engineering successor, Arthur 'Connie' Constantine, to build a machine that would win the 45 cubic inch National Hillclimb Championship. The outcome was a set of fifteen overhead valve 45s that, along with the Big Bertha 61, would write the final chapter of Excelsior glory.

Details of the 45 ohv

The crankcases were standard Super X. The cylinders were of close-grained gray iron. Surprisingly, the engine was more 'undersquare' than the stock Super X. The stocker's bore and stroke were 3 inches by 3 7/32 inches but the overhead's dimensions were 2 7/8 inches by 3 1/2 inches, yielding 45.44 cubic inches (744.6 cc). The cylinder heads were truly hemispherical, as the valve   49 included angle was 90 degrees. The valve diameters were: intake, 1 3/4 inch; exhaust, 1 5/8 inch.

The intake valve port opening was 1 1/2 inch, and the exhaust opening was 1 3/8 inch. The intake opened 37 degrees before top dead center and closed 45 degrees after bottom dead center. The exhaust opened 52 degrees before bottom dead center and closed 14 degrees after top dead center. Valve overlap was consequently 51 degrees. The valve lift was 5/16 inch. Double chrome vanadium valve springs were used. Each cylinder had two exhaust ports. The compression ratio was 10:1. The horsepower of these overheads was 45, or one horsepower per cubic inch. As late as the 1950s this one-to-one relationship was considered highly satisfactory in modified stock twins. Moreover, two of the fifteen engines were custom-tuned to the 50 horsepower level. Incidentally, the fuel used in these Class A climbers was alcohol-benzol.

1929, 1930: Schwinn's swan song

The combination of Joe Petrali, Gene Rhyne, Big Bertha, and the 45 ohv motors, gave Super X the National Hillclimb Championships in both 1929 and 1930. These titles were earned at the Muskegon, Michigan climb. In 1929, Petrali won both the 45 cubic inch event and the 61 cubic inch climb. Petrali was the overall Hillclimb Champion and Rhyne was the runner-up. In addition, Petrali had the distinction of being the only rider who had ever put a '45' over the top of Muskegon hill. In 1930, the finishing order was reversed and Rhyne was the National Champion. Besides winning the 1929 and 1930 official titles at Muskegon, Petrali and Rhyne were highly successful in other hillclimbs. Petrali had been the first to conquer Mount Garfield and other impossible hills.

Despite these victories, the slumping American economy teamed up with family matters to bring down the curtain on Super X and Henderson production. Ignaz Schwinn was by this time about 75 years old. He and his son Frank held the controlling interest in over 50 businesses in the Chicago area, and the famous Schwinn bicycle business was booming. Long ago, the motorcycle operation had ceased to be critical to the Schwinn fortunes, but Ignaz Schwinn liked motorcycles and he was also a proud man who was reluctant to throw in the towel. His son Frank, however, was not a motorcycle fan. As it was time for Frank to take over operations, he was guided solely by the harsh realities of the economic depression.

Consequently, in March of 1931, Ignaz Schwinn assembled his key motorcycle personnel for a brief and stunning announcement, saying, *'Boys, today we quit'*. Close out operations began at once, and only a handful of machines were thereafter clandestinely assembled as personal mounts for a few employees. Many large orders were in hand, some of which involved commitments to municipalities for police motorcycles – but none of the back orders

Opposite: **The same machine on which Gene Rhyne won the 1930 National Hillclimbing Championship, after restoration by Herb Ottaway.** *(Herb Ottaway, author.)*

were filled despite threats of legal action. In a way, it was appropriate. The firm went out the way it had stayed in – boldly.

A cam linkage from the kickstarter mechanism automatically lifted the exhaust valves slightly, which made starting possible. *(Herb Ottaway, author.)*

The oil pump mounting on the rear of the primary drive necessitated a rather long oil line from the oil tank – not a good feature. *(Herb Ottaway, author.)*

Harley-Davidson

A slow starter in the racing game

Of all the motorcycle companies in the world, none has been a more steadfast supporter of racing than Harley-Davidson. Through boom and bust economic periods; while influencing America's racing rules, and at other times without political clout; through an era of technological leadership, and despite subsequent seeming obsolescence, Harley-Davidson has established an axiom well learned by all past and present racing foes: You can count Harley-Davidson 'down' but you can never count it 'out'.

Yet, it was not always thus. During its first ten years of existence Harley-Davidson virtually ignored motorcycle competition. Until 1913 the Milwaukee, Wisconsin, firm concentrated on methodical development of its original basic touring layout, a 1903 pocket valve (ioe) belt drive single, hand built by the original founders, William S. Harley and Arthur Davidson. During this period a host of better financed companies, often with designs which were better 'on paper' fell by the wayside, victims of poor reliability and poor management.

1913: Milwaukee flirts with racing

During 1913 Harley-Davidson revealed an increasing interest in racing when it ran full-page advertisements in the motorcycle press, advertisements which proclaimed several racing successes accomplished without factory support. One of these was a flat track record of 346 miles in 7 hours, turned by Ray Watkins and Ben Torres on December 8, 1912, for an average of 49.43 mph. The advertisement stated, 'As manufacturers we do not support racing and do not build racing machines. This new record came as a complete surprise to us. The contest was conducted entirely without our knowledge and the first we heard of it was a newspaper clipping sent in to the factory'. In the background, Harley-Davidson had hired William (Bill) Ottaway from Thor, where he had been the engineering brains behind Thor's racing attempts for several seasons.

Thoroughness of planning was the outstanding strength of Harley-Davidson during its first decade. It was, therefore, characteristic of the firm that its forthcoming racing commitment would be total and that its racing organization would surpass all others. When Harley-Davidson threw its racing hat into the ring, it was done with a relative financial commitment and a total seriousness of purpose which would not be paralleled until the rise of Honda, almost 50 years later.

1914: Racing for sure

Harley-Davidson's first major race occurred on July 4, 1914, at the Dodge City, Kansas 300-mile road race. This was in fact a two-mile flat track course   53

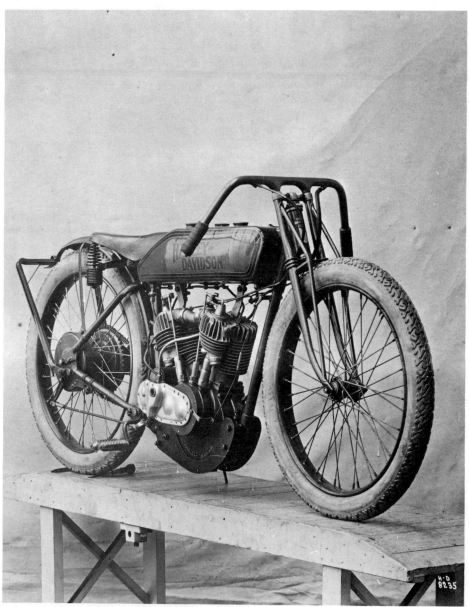

This ioe racer is labeled in the Harley-Davidson archives as a 1920 model. Later versions had a lower frame which necessitated cutaways in the right fuel tank in order to clear the overhead valves. The front fork is rigid. An external contracting band brake is contained in the right rear hub and is operated like a bicycle coaster brake by backward pressure on the appropriately positioned pedal, in this case the left pedal. *(AMF/Harley-Davidson.)*

of the typical American flavor, emphasizing straight line speed and acceleration. Glenn 'Slivers' Boyd won for Indian, and only two of the six pocket valve
Harley entrants were running when the checkered flag terminated the race.
These last two survivors were 40 and 64 miles short of the 300 mile distance.
One historian has described this first serious Harley-Davidson effort as a heavy
defeat, and doubtless it was in the eyes of the casual observer. Nevertheless, the
more discerning were presented with evidence that Harley-Davidson's potential was considerable. Indeed, at the 120 mile point Harley rider Walt
Cunningham was practically tied for the lead with Indian's Boyd, but
Cunningham was later sidelined with chain and spark plug problems after 180
miles. Both Bill Harley and Bill Davidson were in attendance and were very
much pleased with their motorcycles' speed. They suggested that they were
considering increased racing emphasis, but only through the support of
dealers interested in racing; no factory team was to be established.

During the balance of the year, Harley-Davidson won several shorter flat
track events against lesser competition, as well as a 100-miler in October at
Milwaukee.

Then, on November 26, 1914, Harley-Davidson made a dramatic move
which was eventually to alter the course of American motorcycling history. For
the Savannah, Georgia 300 mile National Championship road race, Milwaukee fielded its first fully factory-supported team. Irving Janke finished
third to Indian's Lee Taylor and Excelsior's Joe Wolters, the balance of the
Harley team suffering from repeated melting of spark plugs. Thus, at the end
of 1914, Harley-Davidson had established its desire to make American
motorcycle racing a three-sided contest.

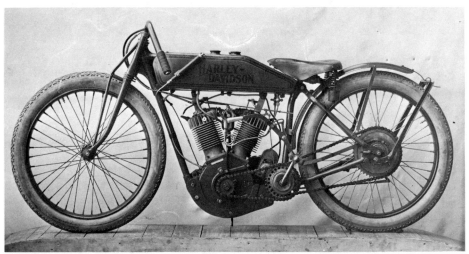

The serial number is 20Y14014. The clutch is contained in the rear hub of this single-speed
machine, and is actuated by the hand lever near the carburetor. An auxiliary oil handpump is
mounted on the gas tank side.   *(AMF/Harley-Davidson.)*   55

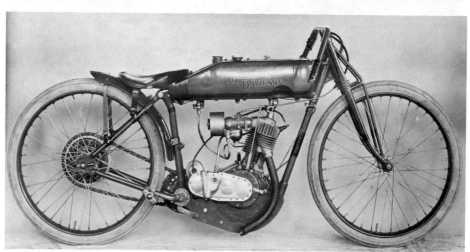

1915: A reputation begins

In Venice, California, near Los Angeles, Paul 'Daredevil' Derkum was demonstrating his promotional and construction talents. A former board track racer on both Reading-Standards and Indians, Derkum had also raced at the Isle of Man in the 1914 TT. Beginning about 1911, he had been an employee of promoter Jack Prince, and had supervised the design and construction of several board tracks. Derkum then went into the promotional game himself, and promoted several highly successful board track meets on the west coast. For Venice, Derkum had greased the appropriate political skids, achieving the co-operation of Venice city officials and the Mayor of Los Angeles, and enabling Derkum to lay out a road race course which used some of Venice's prominent streets. Included in the layout were three mildly banked wooden surfaced turns similar in construction to board tracks, as well as about three miles of newly laid concrete for the straightaways. In addition, the city of Venice relocated power lines and a railroad station to improve course safety. The race's big promotional build-up drew as strong a field as had ever been seen in any one American race, and included all the top stars of the big three, as well as the prominent Don Johns on a Cyclone, and other factory teams from Thor, Pope and Dayton.

Otto Walker won for Harley-Davidson, his time for the 300 being 4 hours, 24 minutes, 17 1/4 seconds, for an average of 68.31 mph, followed by team mate Red Parkhurst, and Excelsior's Goudy and Perry. Indian's top man, Fred Ludlow, was not a factory rider, and finished fifth on an 8-valve. Venice was Harley-Davidson's first big win and began a pattern of continual Milwaukee successes in the more prestigious long distance grinds. Under the jovial atmosphere that surrounded the 1915 Dodge City build-up, a serious struggle was in progress, the struggle between Excelsior and Harley-Davidson for second place in the industry's sales. The Dodge City 300 was now being given top importance by the motorcycling press and by the factories. Consequently, seven makers fielded factory teams at the July 4, 1915 race. These were: Cyclone, Emblem, Excelsior, Harley-Davidson, Indian, Merkel, and Pope. The Harley-Davidson entry consisted of eight pocket-valved motorcycles, while Indian challenged with eight factory riders on both pocket valves and 8-valve machines.

Left above: **Powerplant of the 37 cubic inch (625 cc) Sport model, introduced in the spring of 1919. Innovative features included a sidevalve unit construction, two cylinder engine, with gear driven primary transmission, and a wet plate clutch. Curiously, each innovation was abandoned by Harley-Davidson after the Sport's three-year life, yet each feature was later popularized by the Indian Scout and Chief. The integral casting of the intake and exhaust plumbing was supposed to aid fuel vaporization. The Sport was not as powerful as its rival, the Indian Scout 37.** *(Del DuChene, Sam Hotton.)*

Left below: **The model 22-S single, essentially half a twin. This is the same photo which was used in the 1922 competition catalog. The large fixture over the carburetor could be rotated, to act as a choke.** *(AMF/Harley-Davidson.)* 57

Harley's Otto Walker crossed the tape first at 3 hours, 55 minutes, 45 seconds, a new record, and was followed some three minutes later by team mate Harry Crandall, and Excelsior-mounted Carl Goudy. Harley-Davidson riders also finished 4th, 5th, 6th, and 7th. For Harley-Davidson, there were thousands of victories ahead, yet no single checkered flag has proved so important to their survival and prosperity, and no single race would more strongly impact the future of Excelsior and Indian. Harley-Davidson had arrived.

The 1915 IOE twins

The 1915 Dodge City Harley-Davidsons were yet another example of Milwaukee's policy of technical evolution. With a bore of 3 5/16 inches and a stroke of 3 1/2 inches, each engine's cubic capacity was 60.34 cubic inches (989 cc). The terminology of the times lends confusion, as the factory termed the engine an L-head with overhead intake valves, but over a period of time this

Freddy Dixon on an early 8-valve. Note the use of clip-on handlebars, a Dixon innovation. The carburetor box was used to hide the twin carburetors. Dixon won a number of races at Brooklands with this machine. On September 9, 1913 he used an ioe model at the Bois de Boulogne to take the World Flying Kilometre Record at 106.8 mph. *(AMF/Harley-Davidson.)*

ioe arrangement became referred to as the F-head or pocket valve type. Recent induction improvements included larger intake ports, intake manifolds, and intake valves.

Like Indian, Harley-Davidson's racers were equipped with four-row roller bearings on the crankpin. However, the bearing approach for Harley's crankshaft was different from Indian theory. The Milwaukee motors had a ball bearing drive side and a plain bearing timing side whereas the Indian 8-valve had plain bearings in each end. The crankpin was enlarged from 7/8 inch to 1 inch, while the crankpin bearing width was increased from 1 3/8 inches to 1 3/4 inches, netting a total bearing area increase of 46 percent.

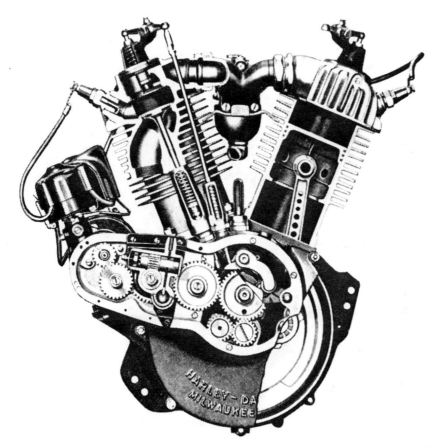

This 1926 pocket valve engine used a single camshaft, which had been both Harley-Davidson and standard industry practice since the beginning. Both the ioe and overhead valve Harley-Davidsons used this basic valve lifting mechanism until the advent of the 'two cam' design in the late twenties. The single cam configuration is distinguished by the cylindrical timing gear cover.

(The Antique Motorcycle.)   59

The complete machine was cataloged as the model 11-K and its specially tailored nature was evident from the following list of specifications.

Motor:	Air cooled, piston displacement not exceeding 61 cubic inches. Mechanical construction to meet any requirements.
Tanks:	Any shape, size or location desirable.
Lubrication:	Hand pump or mechanical pump, either or both, or any oiling system deemed advisable for the safety or convenience of the rider.
Wheels:	28 inches
Tires:	28 x 3 inches or smaller
Saddle:	Troxel or special racing
Transmission:	Roller chain with or without change speed mechanism.
Ignition:	Magneto
Wheel Base:	51 1/2 inches or optional

Clutch, brake, forks, handlebars, frame, finish and equipment optional. The right is reserved to change any feature without further notice whether listed above or not.

In September, at Chicago's Maywood Board Speedway, Excelsior's Carl Goudy took top honors in the feature 300-mile event, but along the way the latest pocket valve Harley of Otto Walker set a 100-mile record of 89.11 mph, a century average unsurpassed throughout the world. Consequently, these latest products of pocket valve evolution became known as the Chicago Harleys.

1916: The 8-valves

For the 1916 season, Bill Harley and his assistant Bill Ottaway completed development of the highly advanced 8-valve Harley-Davidsons. While Indian's Oscar Hedstrom had beaten Bill Harley by five years in developing an overhead valve racer, Harley-Davidson was actually with the advantage. Milwaukee was in a position to learn from the extensive aeronautical development spurred by the war in Europe. Consequently, the gray version employed a hemispherical combustion chamber with a sharply domed piston and a 90 degree included angle between the intake and exhaust valves. As with the firm's pocket valve racers, Harley-Davidson's catalog description provided for custom tailoring of these very special models. The quoted prices of the single and twin cylinder versions were astronomical for the era, being $1400 and $1500 respectively.

The single cylinder 30.50 cubic inch (500 cc) Harley was designed for the half-mile dirt track circuit, a racing venue which had been around from the first owing to the popularity of the horse racing for which the tracks had been built. In the agricultural midwest, the half-miles were especially prominent and the competition especially keen. The FAM had issued sanctions for these

60

events for a number of years, and while the half-miles lacked National Championship status, their popularity induced many of the top riders to join the fray. As the four-valve Harley was essentially but half a twin, and with abundant 'laboratory' opportunities afforded by the numerous half-mile events, Milwaukee entered their top riders on four-valves for several of the 1916 events. The lessons learned with the singles on the half miles would also apply to the 61 cubic inch (1000 cc) twins and the long tracks. On May 29, 1916, Irving Janke convincingly demonstrated the four-valve single by winning the 5- and 10-mile events at Cedarsburg, Wisconsin.

Ohio was a particular hotbed of half-mile activity, with frequent regular schedules at Toledo, Mansfield, Akron, Dayton, and Hamilton. Between rounds of the National Championship circuit, some of the more prominent riders began to enter the Ohio half-miles and they found the competition surprisingly tough. Harley-Davidson took a serious interest in the Ohio circuit, officially dubbed the Interstate Circuit, since there was also some action in Indiana and Illinois. Milwaukee's interest was both from the standpoint of 'laboratory' work and for the purpose of spotting new racing talent for their official team. Consequently, whether measured in terms of machinery or men, the Ohio circuit was top caliber.

The Jones special

Maldwyn Jones had been the Merkel factory's top rider, but with the failure of Merkel in 1916 he had transferred his allegiance to Harley-Davidson. The factory provided him with a four-valve for campaigning in Ohio and neighbouring Indiana, while off duty from his regular job as an aircraft engine tester. Jones was not only a talented rider but quite gifted mechanically, having previously converted an ioe Merkel into a potent overhead valve racer. In addition to his theoretical and practical knowledge, he was apparently a persuasive individual for he was able to convince Harley-Davidson to build him the interesting one-off special shown in the accompanying photograph.

The bike was basically a Harley four-valve engine mounted in Jones's custom Merkel frame, previously built to his requirements by Merkel. The handling was much improved over the standard Milwaukee layout which Maldwyn had raced in a few meets. Various configurations were experimented with and used by several riders. It can be seen that Jones's version used the rear half of a V-twin, but later configurations were built from the front half. The later versions also provided a slightly forward incline to the cylinder. An unchanging feature was the use of standard Merkel forks. Although they offered but scant travel, the telescopic Merkel forks steered dead true. Eventually, all the Harley-Davidson half-milers were so equipped.

In the third and last annual Dodge City 300 before the USA's entry into World War 1, Harley-Davidson entered a mixture of three 8-valve and four pocket valve motorcycles for the July 4, 1916 spectacle. Irving Janke and his 8-

61

valve won at an average of slightly under 80 mph. Excelsior's Joe Wolters finished second by some three miles, and while he had occasionally drawn close to Janke, the Harley-Davidson rider had pulled away at any time he chose. Ray Weishaar piloted a pocket valve to third.

1917: 1918 – A slowdown

In concert with the other manufacturers, Harley-Davidson backed off from serious racing support during the 1917 and 1918 seasons. However, record-setting activity continued, apparently supported on a local basis by a handful of dealers in Harley-Davidsons, Indians, Hendersons, and Clevelands. The Harley banner was carried by Alan T. Bedell in April of 1917 at the Ascot one-mile dirt track in Los Angeles. Bedell broke both the 100-mile and the 24-hour marks.

At the Sheepshead Bay, New York board track, Red Parkhurst broke the solo 24-hour record on July 26, besting Cannonball Baker's 24-hour mark, 500, and 1000 mile times. Otto Walker and Carl Lutgens broke the sidecar mark.

Meanwhile, the old rider-organized FAM died off, the victim of political infighting, mismanagement, and a general decline in motorcycle interest. In its place, the motorcycle industry set up the Motorcycle and Allied Trades Association (M&ATA), which took over competition effective with the year 1919. With the new organizational setup came new rules, the most significant of which was the banning of the motordromes, i.e., the banked board tracks of less than one mile in circumference. Another important change was the elimination of ported engines from all forms of competition. Half-mile dirt tracks were limited to 30.50 cubic inch (500 cc) motors and no National Championship titles were awarded for the half-mile events.

Above right: **Maldwyn Jones and his Merkel-framed 4-valve special. Jones is believed to be the first to use a steel-soled shoe. The braced handlebars were designed by Jones, while just beneath the left brace can be seen the inner telescopic member, over which the external girder-like portion of the forks could slide about one inch. Part of the serial number is obscured by the crankcase breather line, which hopefully aimed helpful amounts of oil mist on the primary chain. The portion which is readable is M402J.** *(Maldwyn Jones.)*

Below right: **In the mid-twenties a new two-camshaft gear was introduced on the racing models, and subsequently was offered as an option on the 1929 road models, the last year of ioe production. This 'two-cam' machine was purchased in England. The serial number is 17 8V 1, indicating that some previous owner had mated the timing side crankcase to a 1917 left-side. The transmission is non-standard.** *(John Cameron, Sam Hotton.)*

1919: The game renewed

With the summer of 1919, motorcycle racing returned full bore to the United States, the first big event being the 200-Mile National Championship on June 22 at the Ascot Park (paved 2-mile oval) Speedway in Los Angeles. Harley riders swept the top five positions, the winner being Ralph Hepburn. A typically demanding race for machinery still in evolution, only eight of the sixteen starters in the field finished; but Milwaukee had only one non-finisher.

One key to victory was the outstanding performance of the Harley-Davidson pit crew, headed by Dudley Perkins of San Francisco. For example, Hepburn was serviced with gas and oil and had a rear tire change, all in 38 seconds. The average of all Harley riders for this service was less than 50 seconds.

To this point Harley-Davidson had shown little interest in long distance intercity road records, leaving that sphere of the sport to Indian, Excelsior and Henderson. However, the Milwaukee brand entered the intercity record books three times during 1919. Hap Scherer, an advocate of smaller motorcycles, was the perpetrator of two records on the 37 cubic inch (600 cc) opposed twin Sport model. In June, he set the Three Flag record for middleweight motorcycles at 64 hours, 58 minutes. The Three Flag was so named because it consisted of the ride from Blaine, British Columbia to Tijuana, Mexico or vice-versa. On August 27 Scherer lowered the middleweight time for New York to Chicago, using 31 hours, 24 minutes to cover the 1,012 miles. The last of the three records was another Three Flag ride, Walter Hadfield collecting the solo honor at 51 hours, 22 minutes (subsequently broken in 1919 by Paul Remely, Indian).

The premier road race of the year was a 200-miler at Marion, Indiana on September 1. Red Parkhurst won at a 66.6 mph pace, followed by Harley-Davidson teammates Hepburn and Otto Walker. The course was a five mile affair bordered by farm houses and plowed ground, the dirt roads about 1 1/2 lanes wide by today's standards, full of dips, rises, and bumps.

The most important race meet of 1919 occurred on October 11 at the Sheepshead Bay Speedway in Long Island, New York. Four National titles were contested, the 2, 10, 50, and 100-mile Championships. Indian won the 10-mile title, but the balance belonged to Harley-Davidson.

The year 1919 was tremendously successful for Harley-Davidson racing. In all they accumulated 552 miles of National titles to Indian's 67 miles, while Excelsior failed to grab a single Championship.

1920: Racing interest grows

Motorcycle racing activity increased significantly during the 1920 season, when approximately twice as many race meets were held as in 1919. Although Indian improved their relative status with 191 miles of racing titles, Harley-Davidson again dominated the overall picture with 513 miles of National

Championships, 500 of which were annexed in just two races, the Dodge City 300 and the Marion 200. Indian seemed to have better speed than Harley-Davidson, but could not stand up as well as Milwaukee in the punishing long prestige races. Strangely, this was a situation that was to continue for another generation.

In a move to enhance their speed image, Harley-Davidson dispatched Red Parkhurst, Bill Ottaway, and a technical crew to Daytona Beach, Florida. Parkhurst set 61 cubic inch (1000 cc) 8-valve records for 1, 2, and 5 miles as well as a 61 cubic inch 8-valve sidecar record. He also used a 68 inch ioe motorcycle to better the 61 inch speeds, but the recorded speeds were not recognized by the M&ATA, which refused to acknowledge records by machines over 1000 cc displacement.

There was increasing interest in sidecar racing, so much so that some race meets listed the sidecar finale as the feature event of the program. While the sidehack speeds were, of course, much slower than solo efforts, the antics of rider and passenger, the full power drifting with copious wheel spin, and the peculiar excitement afforded by the Flexi sidecars which predominated, all combined to provide high spectator appeal. The Flexi sidecar was a banking unit built in Ohio which was unbeatable in half-mile and mile dirt track racing. During 1920, Harley-Davidsons copped seven sidecar records, six occurring during mile and half-mile flat track events, the other being Parkhurst's Daytona straightaway blast. The most outstanding Harley-Davidson sidecar operator was Jiggs Price.

The pre-war Dodge City 300 classic was revived on July 5, and Milwaukee again dominated. Jones set new 100 and 200-mile records before a spark plug lead became disconnected in the 234th mile, and an attempted restart failed to light off his motor. The fastest laps were turned by Hepburn on a pocket-valve Harley and Burns on a big base 8-valve Indian, both turning 1 min 20 sec laps of the two mile oval, for an average of 90 mph. However, when it was all over the winner was Jim Davis on a pocket-valve Milwaukee missile. Harley-Davidson philosophy was now in favor of the pocket-valve design, and all seven Harleys entered were pocket valves. Indian entered three 8-valvers with five side-valvers. Davis' winning time was some five minutes better than the 1916 record, giving him an average of 80.1 mph and a four minute edge over 8-valve Indian-mounted runnerup Gene Walker.

Milwaukee added to the long distance monotony by again taking the Marion 200, this time in the hands of Ray Weishaar, whose elapsed time was 18 minutes faster than Parkhurst's 1919 time. Harley-Davidson seemed to be about one year ahead of its rivals in power development. The fifth place finish of Excelsior's Paul Anderson, although some 5 minutes faster than the previous year's Harley-Davidson winner, was 13 minutes back of Weishaar. Somehow, Messers Harley and Ottaway had built a 1920 motorcycle that was 7 mph faster than its 1919 ancestor.

In England, Marvin and O'Sullivan established 1000 cc sidecar records for distances of 100 to 600 miles and for times of two to twelve hours. Incidentally, Marvin was a one-legged man. The pair alternated as rider and passenger each 65 two hours. Their various records were recorded at averages ranging from 50.4 to 53.3 mph.

1921: Harley-Davidson wins 'em all

As if Harley-Davidson's long-haul supremacy of 1915-1920 wasn't enough, the Milwaukee brand really outdid themselves during the 1921 season. Harley-Davidson riders won **every** National Championship, these being the 1, 5, 10, 25, 50, 100, 200, and 300-mile titles. All but the 1 and 5-mile races were won at record speeds.

However, perhaps the most impressive of all victories was a non-title race, when a big meet was scheduled on Washington's birthday, Feb. 22. Otto Walker continually lapped the Fresno, California one-mile board track at over 100 mph, finally winning the 50-mile feature in 29 minutes, 34 4/5 seconds, an average of 101.4 mph. As things turned out, Walker's speed that day was to remain on the books as the **all-time board track record for the 50-mile distance.** Otto's ride was **the first motorcycle race in the world to be won with an average speed over 100 mph.**

Opportunities for maximum speed trials in Britain were essentially limited to England's Brooklands concrete track, and even at Brooklands top speed was impacted by the extreme roughness of the course. Consequently although sanctioned 100 mph speeds had been accomplished in the USA as far back as 1912, as of early 1921 no motorcycle had yet reached the three-figure mark in Britain. On April 28, at Brooklands, D.H. Davidson *first exceeded 100 mph in Britain, establishing a British record* of 100.76 mph. Davidson, who was not related to *the* Davidsons, used a single-speed ioe twin. He beat by 24 hours Bert LeVack's Indian effort to turn the first 100 mph speed.

An interesting aspect of Ralph Hepburn's win in the last of the classic Dodge City 300s was the return of the 8-valve. In 1919 Hepburn had turned down an 8-valve Harley in favor of the more reliable pocket valve for the Dodge City event, while in 1920 Harley-Davidson had not offered its riders a choice, entering only pocket valve machines. In both a personal and company reversal, Ralph Hepburn won the last 'real' Dodge City title on an 8-valve Harley-Davidson.

Hillclimbing was continuing to grow in popularity, particularly on the West Coast. The biggest of California's several slant runs occurred each spring on the Capistrano hill in Santa Ana, where in April of 1920, 13,000 spectators had witnessed the event. At that meet, San Francisco's Dud Perkins flamboyantly wagered Colorado's Floyd Clymer the then healthy sum of $100 that Perkins would win the free-for-all event, which he did. Just one year, Perkins was again the star on his Harley-Davidson, beating his 1920 time over the top of the 500-foot hill by 10 seconds and playing before an estimated 30,000 fans.

Hillclimb victories were big in the advertising strategies of the motorcycle manufacturers, and accordingly, many of the better track racing stars did double duty on the slopes. In later years, the customary local-area hillclimbing modifications to stock machines were done at the three surviving factories. For the benefit of non-Yankee readers, it should be understood that hillclimbing in the United States was not a steep climb on a public road over a mountainous course. Instead, Yankee hillclimbing was a quick blast up a 45°–60° roadless slope of some 200-600 feet in length, the rougher the better. Riders were judged on their amount of forward progress, it being assumed that most would not make it over the top. Stop watches were also used, but times obviously did not matter except as tie-breakers. Huge rear sprockets and tire chains were the order of the day, while the literally rough and tumble action was not unlike the bareback bronco riding event at western rodeos.

1922-1925: Milwaukee loses interest
1922

As a tribute to their all-conquering 1921 season, Harley-Davidson decided that they had established a sufficient reputation to allow them to withdraw from factory sponsorship effective with the 1922 circuit. Instead, they concentrated on making available their production racers. Just nine years before, Indian had seemed beyond serious challenge, but now, Harley-Davidson was the consensus speed bike. Former Harley factory riders continued to race their mounts, which were made available by Milwaukee either by loan or by sale. But gone were the days of salaried pit crews and elaborate signaling of riders during long events. Nor was the famous Bill Ottaway at trackside to manage the mounts. It was not surprising, under the circumstances, that Indian had things their own way during 1922. To further strengthen Indian's hand, Ralph Hepburn switched to the Redskins, and Jim Davis divided his efforts between Indian and Harley-Davidson.

1923

Likewise, 1923 was dominated by Indian. However, Jim Davis won the 25-mile 30.50 inch crown at Milwaukee, and an 'unknown' rider, J. Branson, copped the 100-mile 61 inch board track title at Kansas City, Missouri. In the April 26 issue of *Motorcycle and Bicycle Illustrated,* a staff writer penned a remarkably prophetic article concerning the difficulty of defining the term 'stock machine'. Intended to be a look backwards at recent troubles, the article unknowingly outlined the fundamental instability of the Class C concept which was to define American motorcycle racing a decade later. As much of the story of Harley-Davidson was destined to be written under the stock machine concept, the following words are quoted.

"... *In 1911 a 'stock' machine was one of which 25 or more were regularly made and cataloged by the manufacturer. It was thought that no factory would go to the expense of making specials in such quantities, but the FAM rule-makers guessed wrong. I have here in front of me a list of 'stock' models from various factories of that period; it is interesting to read, for it contains the motor numbers of 26 eight-valve machines, 34 stripped-stock machines (practically racers in touring frames), and numerous short-coupled models with special motors. One catalog of the period simply lists the piston displacement of the motor and the wheelbase and brake equipment. The rest of the 'stock model' was built to order.* 67

You can realize from this what value could be given to the word 'stock'. Anything of which 25 or more were made was thus defined."

1924

The year 1924 was distinguished by the absence of any 61 inch solo Championship events. an action taken to counteract the growing safety problem. Harley-Davidsons returned to their former habit and won most of the Nationals, still without a big factory commitment. In the solo 30.50 inch class, Jim Davis was practically the whole show, winning three of the six National Championships, while fellow Harley rider Paul Anderson won another, and Indian took two crowns. Hepburn won two of the three 61 inch sidecar Nationals. Harley-Davidson stalwart Ray Weishaar was killed at an Ascot Park race meet. Besides having won a lot of races, he was a very popular rider. There was increasing editorial comment on the need for slowing down the pace of racing.

1925

Several record rides were made by Harley-Davidson riders during 1925. On July 4, on the 1 1/2-mile board at Altoona, Pennsylvania, Joe Petrali set the **all-time 100-mile board track record,** averaging 100.36 mph for the distance on a 61 inch pocket valve. On the same day, Bill Minnick won the 50-mile sidecar National at a rate of 79.85 mph on a 61 incher, which was the **all-time board track sidecar record.** As this was near the end of board track racing, three more all-time records were made by Harley riders before the year was out. On the 1 1/8-mile Laurel, Maryland boards, Petrali made the **fastest 10 miles ever,** at 111.18 mph, and the **all-time best 25 miles** at 106.08 mph. In Fresno, California, Jim Davis ran the fastest 20 miles ever at a pace of 101.32 mph. It was another good Harley-Davidson year, as Milwaukee won nine of the fourteen National titles.

1926 The Peashooter Nationals

A new class of championship racing debuted in 1926 with the introduction of 21.35 inch (350 cc) National Championships. The Harley-Davidson 'Peashooter' had been unveiled in August of 1925 at a Milwaukee race meet, and was unchallenged by Indian, which still had their 'twenty-one' on the drafting tables. The write-up of *Motor Cycling* for August 19, 1925 described peashooter racing as '... *practically as fast as our 30.50 stuff and a hundred percent safer',* a bit of double talk, characteristic of the era.

During 1926, Harley-Davidsons won six of the fourteen National titles, Indian taking the other eight. The 'iffy' nature of Milwaukee's racing commitment was evidenced by Joe Petrali, who spent most of the season campaigning on Super X machines before straddling a Harley in September.

1927

Another popular rider was fatally injured in 1927, Harley racer Eddie Brinck. When Brinck's front tire blew in a 21.35 inch National, he was hit by Joe Petrali, whose serious injuries included a fractured collar bone and severe facial cuts. Incidentally, Petrali had been continuing his habit of switching back and forth between Super X and Harley-Davidson. Harleys won but three of the nine National Championships, all in the 21.35 inch class. In the famous Capistrano, California hillclimb, Finnegan Speer finished first, and Tom Sifton second, in the 61 inch free-for-all event. Much more would be heard from Sifton in later years as a builder/tuner.

1928, 1929

Indian riders won *every* National Championship in both 1928 and 1929. About the only bright spot for Milwaukee in this period happened on July 21, 1929 at Pittsburgh, Pennsylvania. This was the competition coming-out party for Harley-Davidson's special overhead valve 45 inch V-twin, and Bill Ottaway was at this hillclimb to look after his machines. John Grove won the 45 inch expert event, the first significant Harley 45 victory. With Ottaway in attendance, it appeared that Milwaukee was once again ready to do serious battle.

Two of the earliest 45 overheads were provided to Dud Perkins and Windy Lindstrom in California, and did not perform well at first, as they tended to run out of gas. Subsequent testing at the factory resulted in the use of larger fuel lines and establishment of a procedure for purging the lines of all air prior to events. Although a 1930 model is illustrated, the configuration is essentially the same as the earliest machines. Sometime after 1930, a new double tube frame and more conventional-appearing fuel tank were devised. During this period, the factory also continued limited production of the ioe hillclimbers, as well as a number of Peashooter variations.

1930

In flat tracking, Harley-Davidson and Indian competed on equal terms during 1930. Milwaukee's most consistent performers in the strictly 21.35 inch Class A races were Walter Stoddard and Andy Hader.

The factory produced two road racing models during 1930, a V-twin (probably a 45) and a 30.50 single. Details of these machines and the exact number produced are unknown. Apparently, serious consideration was given to the 30.50 single as a production roadster, for Red Wolverton recalls testing such a machine in the early thirties while visiting the Milwaukee works. Wolverton later had to cancel two orders he'd taken for customers, orders placed by them solely on the basis of Wolverton's enthusiastic verbal description. The overhead valve single was championed by the second generation of Harleys and Davidsons, but was vetoed by the founding fathers as it was considered too competitive with the 45 sidevalve twin. And speaking of the second generation, none other than William H. 'Bill' Davidson won the 1930 National Championship Endurance event, the Jack Pine 500-miler through the Michigan woods.

69

The serial number of this 8-valve is not completely legible, but the first two digits read '27', indicating a 1927 model. *(AMF/Harley-Davidson.)*

A 1927 two-cam pocket valve racer. From 1914 through 1934 all Harley-Davidsons used a tapered cylinder bore. Early cylinders had a 0.003 inch taper, meaning that the top of the cylinder bore was 0.003 inch smaller than the bottom of the bore. Later, a 0.007 inch taper was used. Fitting of pistons to these taper bored machines required careful use of a micrometer to obtain proper mating of pistons and cylinders. Measurements were taken 1/2 inch below the top of the bore. The advent of cam ground (elliptic) T-slot pistons in the early thirties allowed Harley-Davidson to adopt untapered bores in 1935. *(AMF/Harley-Davidson.)*

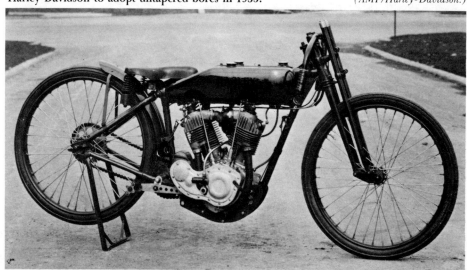

Hillclimbing in the USA bears no resemblance to the European tradition of riding up mountain roads. An ideal hill was 300 to 600 feet long, sloped at 45 degrees or more, and untoppable.

(Stephen Wright.)

Although this is a posed shot, Dud Perkins could stay aboard such nearly vertical machines. Perkins was one of the more successful Harley-Davidson dealers for over fifty years. He sponsored a number of top riders, including former Grand National Champion Mert Lawwill.

(Motorcycle Illustrated.)

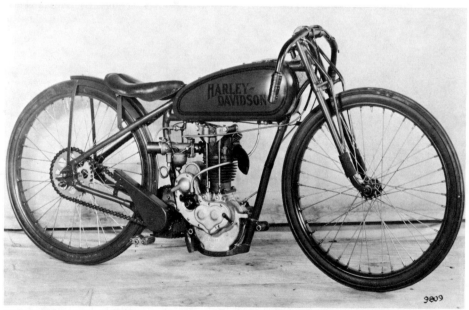

The original 21.35 cubic inch (350 cc) 'Peashooter'. The machine first appeared at a Milwaukee race meet in August of 1925.

(AMF/Harley-Davidson.)

Peashooter racer specifications included: 28 x 2 1/4 (2 1/4 x 24) clincher wheels and tires, 185 pounds, 56 1/2 inch wheelbase. Oil was pressure fed to all bearings except the connecting rod upper end. The exhaust valve was sodium-cooled. *(AMF/Harley-Davidson.)*

The late model Peashooter series. The most obvious changes are to the fuel tank and upper frame structure. Additional finning is provided on the cylinder head, which now includes a long cast-in intake manifold. Both the primary and final drive chains are of smaller pitch than in the earlier series. *(AMF/Harley-Davidson.)*

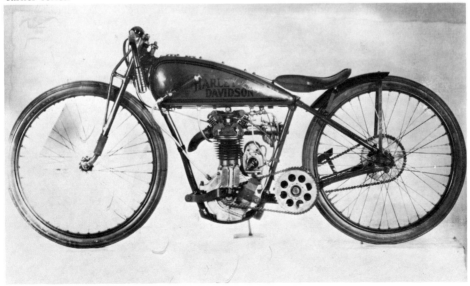

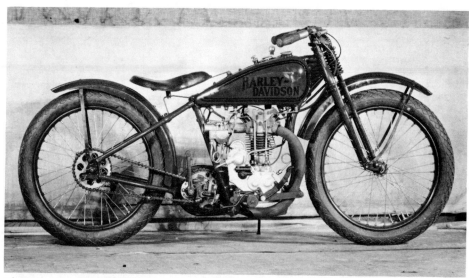

The cast-in intake manifold is more obvious in the TT/road racer version. The ground clearance has been increased and the engine moved forward, as compared to the flat-track configuration. The right-hand clutch control and footpegs suggest this machine was destined for an overseas market. *(AMF/Harley-Davidson.)*

The serial number of this twin port TT/road racer is 28SA531, the 'SA' indicating the use of a Schebler barrel type carburetor. As there were no visible obstructions in the carburetor throat at wide open throttle, it was popularly believed that the barrel type was a better racing carburetor than the butterfly valve unit. However, Maldwyn Jones, chief carburetor designer for Schebler, says the barrel unit did not perform one iota better than the conventional carburetor. *(AMF/Harley-Davidson.)*

A 1927 factory ioe hillclimber, serial number 271BAD. Principal modifications included a longer rear structure with extra bracing. *(AMF/Harley-Davidson.)*

A handful of 45 cubic inch (750 cc) ohv hillclimbers were built for the 1929 season. Limited production was continued at least through 1930, at which time these trailing link forks were introduced. The oil line to the crankcase provides a supplementary supply from the hand pump on top of the right tank. The oil pump on the right-side was for the total-loss system. An external contracting band brake is fitted. The serial number is 30DAH507.

(AMF/Harley-Davidson.)

Later versions of the 45 ohv hillclimber used a double-tube frame and a smaller and more conventional looking fuel tank. The rider is Herb Reiber. *(AMF/Harley-Davidson.)*

Closeup of a 1930 two-port racing engine, serial number 30SF505. Many racing models were numbered in the five hundreds, but the year this practice began is unknown. Dry sump oiling is used, although not introduced on road models until 1936. The carburetor is a Schebler barrel unit. Cylinder head design is completely different from the Peashooter series, and resembles the 1930 ohv hillclimbers, V-twin ohv racers and 500 cc ohv single racers.

(Pete Smiley, Sam Hotton.)

A 1930 road racer built for the European market, serial number 30CAF302. Similar machines were used in hillclimbing beginning in 1930.   *(AMF/Harley-Davidson.)*

A 1930 V-twin roadracer, probably a 45 cubic inch (750 cc) engine, serial number 30DAB521. Both the left-side exhausts are mounted high. Lubrication is dry sump, the oil supply being carried in a cast aluminum tank. Two extra spark plugs are mounted behind the handlebars.

(AMF/Harley-Davidson.)

1931-1933: The low ebb of motorcycle sport

Due to the terrible economic conditions and the lack of rider identification with the unrepresentative Class A motorcycles, motorcycle sport reached an all-time low during this period. As the United States was V-twin country, the spectator appeal of the relatively small 21.35 inch singles was decreasing. The largest spectator turnouts were for the hillclimb meets, where the V-twin still reigned supreme and where interest was spurred by the intense factory-supported competition of Harley-Davidson and Indian.

When Excelsior/Henderson folded in March of 1931, Harley-Davidson managed to pick off Joe Petrali, National Hillclimb Champion of 1929 and runner-up in 1930. Petrali was a distinct plus in advertising value for he was uniquely skilled and interested in both track racing and hillclimbing. In 1931, he set a record for half-mile dirt tracks, circling the Cincinnati, Ohio oval in 24.65 seconds (73 mph). The following year, he was both the National Dirt Track Champion and the Eastern United States Hillclimb Champion based on his cumulative records.

Meanwhile, European-style speedway racing, introduced by Rudge exponent Sprouts Elder, had displaced traditional half-mile and mile track racing as the most popular racing event. Accordingly, Harley-Davidson brought out their 30.50 inch model CAC short tracker, and also experimented with an alternate frame design. In the end, however, it was the Rudges and later the JAPs which took over in this briefly popular type of racing.

The extreme difficulties of the sport were evidenced in the discontinuance of two traditional motorcycle publications at the end of 1932. One of these was the house organ of Milwaukee's rival, *Indian News*, which reappeared in 1934. The other and more significant loss was the collapse of *The New American Motorcyclist and Bicyclist*. Originally known as *Motorcycle Illustrated*, this was one of the first American motorcycle publications and dated back to January 1906. Its publisher had founded several other magazines over the years and had operated the motorcycle periodical at a loss for quite some time for sentimental reasons. At its peak in the 1911-1912 time frame, the bi-weekly magazine was about 3/8 inch thick. By 1931, its successor was published monthly and averaged about 1/16 inch thickness, a drop in coverage of over 90%. The last surviving American Motorcycle periodical was the *Western Motorcyclist and Bicyclist,* and it too was ready to fold when the AMA stepped in and offered financial assistance. With the new setup came a new title, *The Motorcyclist.*

In the March 1933 issue of *The Motorcyclist,* AMA Executive Secretary, E. C. Smith, editorialized in favor of the 1933 racing rules which were designed to provide more equitable competition by restricting equipment modifications. However, the riders were still grouped into either Class A or Class B during 1933. In Class A events, the special factory 21.35 inch ohvs and 45 inch ohvs were still allowed for racing and hillclimbing respectively, while in Class B, the racing and hillclimbing jobs were 45 inch and 80 inch pocket valves. Smith went on to say that previous racing rules had stifled competition, since dealers were more interested in protecting their individual tuning secrets than in helping new riders compete.

79

1934: The Origin of Class C Racing

The Class C events, hinted at in the 1933 article, became a reality in 1934. As Class C racing is still nominally the American system, an understanding of the Class C concept is vital to the study of racing history in the United States.

The basic purpose of Class C racing, as originally conceived, was to put racing into the hands of amateurs. The rules were deliberately designed to discourage factory involvement. To this end, the cornerstone of Class C was the limiting of the flat track and road race events to the 45 cubic inch sidevalve design. These engines were considered to be near the peak of development and not subject to the apparently unending escalation of compression ratios and engine speeds of the overhead valve designs. The 45 inch sidevalve design constraint and the requirement for using normal pump gasoline were expected to hold speeds well below the old Class A 61 inch events. With the de-emphasis on machinery, it was argued that racing would now be a truer and more equitable test of rider ability. To insure that special modified jobs did not violate the spirit of amateur competition (a sort of Olympic ideal) encompassed by Class C, there was the requirement that all competing machines had to be owned by the men who raced them. Additionally, there was even the stipulation that each competitor had to ride his own machine to each event.

Almost as an afterthought, it was agreed that 30.50 inch ohv bikes could compete in Class C, provided that such machines were in fact stock road-going motorcycles. The insurance of this road-going requirement for all Class C competition machines was the measure of producibility. The original Class C setup called for a minimum of 25 identical motorcycles to be produced by the manufacturer to qualify each of his various models as stock road jobs. This producibility requirement has remained to this day,, although the minimum figure has varied from time to time, including 25, 50, 100, and 200 units.

The 'afterthought' nature of the 30.50 inch ohvs' inclusion was due to their insignificance. Except for New York's Reggie Pink, who imported various British bikes throughout the twenties and thirties, there wasn't a noteworthy USA dealer in foreign motorcycles. Class C inclusion of the relatively low numbers of British 61 inch (1000 cc) bikes was obviously out of order. The next size down was 30.50 inch (500 cc) aside from a few off-beat types, and these 'thirty-fifties' would 'obviously' be outclassed by American 45 inch sidevalves. There was nothing particularly sinister about the rules, even though they were self-serving for Harley-Davidson and Indian, for the foreign marques were not a perceived threat to continued Harley and Indian dominance.

A classic case in mislabeling is the term TT. Originally TT referred to Britain's Isle of Man events which measured the 'tourability' of competing motorcycles by limiting their fuel capacity and by other techniques as well as by comparing their speeds. In time, all the Isle of Man requirements except

Opposite: **The model CAC, 30.50 cubic inch (500 cc) speedway racer. The small oil tank under the seat is the supply for the chain oiler. Note the extra longitudinal frame strut to resist frame flexing on the drive side. The serial number is EX1320, probably meaning it's a 1932 model.**
(AMF/Harley-Davidson.) 81

speed were dropped, and the classic TT motorcycles became increasingly different from standard touring machines. Nevertheless, the term TT hung on.

The Americans added another degree of inappropriateness by devising a type of racing originally referred to as the 'miniature TT'. Indian's advertising staffer, Ted Hodgdon, originally popularized the idea in a 1931 issue of *Indian News*. The requirements then, as now, were simple. There had to be at least: one right turn, one left turn, and one jump, the latter feature doubtless derived from the exciting photos of Ballig Bridge action in the Isle of Man TT. The 'miniature' modifier came from the restriction of course lengths to about 1/2 mile. The scheme provided for good spectator viewing as well as the added excitement of the right turns and jump. Moreover, these miniature TTs were easier courses to lay out than flat tracks, an important feature in the club-oriented American sport.

When Class C rules were originated, both TTs and hillclimbs included classes for the 61 inch V-twins, as speeds would not be prohibitive in either the climbs or the TTs. The inclusion of these 'heavyweight' TTs in the Class C calendar continued until the mid-sixties. Another distinction of the TT events was the permitted use of brakes, as opposed to flat tracking which barred the binders until 1969.

In conclusion, Class C racing was a distinct break with the evolution of American motorcycle sport. It must, therefore, have been considered an experiment at the outset of the 1934 season.

The 1934 Season

In the 1934 Class C wars, there was not yet a circuit of individual Flat Track Championships, for a flat tracking circuit already existed for the Class A jobs and Class C had yet to prove itself. The establishment of various lengths of Class C flat track titles on half-mile and one-mile tracks was to occur in 1939. As far as National titles were concerned, the Class C experiment was confined to a 200-mile National TT Championship and a 6-hour National. Arthur 'Babe' Tancrede won the TT title at Keene, New Hampshire on a 1932 VL 74 inch sidevalve twin. Howard Almond won the 6-hour crown at Macon, Georgia on a 1931 model DL 45, while other 45 twins finished second and third. A 200-mile road race at Jacksonville, Florida, won by Bremen Sikes, was well publicized but was not billed as a National Championship. It was not yet apparent, but American motorcycling's new stars were coming up through the Class C ranks. Some, like Babe Tancrede, would be around for many years.

Meanwhile, Class A racing continued. The old established stars, riding the handful of fastest machines, had things all locked up – which was precisely the reason for the new Class C experiment. Joe Petrali finished second in the overall seasonal Class A flat track standings behind Harley stable-mate Louis Balinski. The increasing prominence of JAP-powered machines was evidenced by the winnings of former Harley star Andrew Hader, who won three Nationals at the big Syracuse, New York meet. In hillclimbing, Petrali won the 45 inch Class A and Expert (Class C) National Championships at Bethlehem,

Ray Tursky, after winning the 1934 Jack Pine, Harley-Davidson's 10th consecutive Jack Pine victory. The bike is a 1934 74 twin. The cowbell was the traditional 'trophy' for the event, loaned to the victor for publicity purposes and returned to the clubhouse afterwards. Previous winners' names are inscribed on the bell. *(AMF/Harley-Davidson.)*

Pennsylvania. Ray Tursky won the Jack Pine 500-mile enduro in Michigan, Harley-Davidson's tenth consecutive victory. Goldie Restall won the Eastern Short Track Championship on a CAC.

1935: The Petrali peak

Joe Petrali reached the pinnacle of his flat track career in the 1935 Class A wars, winning *every* National Championship for these 21.35 inch machines. In addition, Petrali was also the season's top hillclimber in both the 45 inch Expert and Class A categories.

Earl and Dot Robinson set a transcontinental sidecar record of 89 hours, 58 minutes. Dot was later to become famous as the President and chief spark plug of the women riders' organization, the Motor Maids. She also remained highly competitive for a number of years as a sidecar enduro pilot.

83

1936

Petrali again was the seasonal Class A flat track Champion, and he also copped the 45 inch National Hillclimb Championship at Muskegon, Michigan. Oscar Lenz, one of the all-time great enduro riders, won his second consecutive Jack Pine 500. The almost forgotten Three-Flag record custom was revived by Fred Ham, a Pasadena motorcycle patrolman and successful off-road rider. Ham's new mark, made on a 1935 74 inch sidevalve twin, was 28 hours, 7 minutes, Bill Connelly and Fred Dauria set a transcontinental sidecar mark of 69 hours, 46 minutes, which was to remain the fastest motorcycle crossing until 1959. All of these long distance marks were unofficial by the AMA rules, but well publicized by the factory.

1937: Two Model 61 ohv records

Indian was doing better than Harley-Davidson in the evolving Class C competition, but the Milwaukee brand grabbed the limelight with two interesting early season record runs. In March, Joe Petrali piloted one of the newly developed 61 inch overhead valve twins to a new American record of 136.183 mph, a two-way average. While this speed was over 30 mph down from the world record BMW, Petrali had clocked the fastest sanctioned speed

Joe Petrali on the 1937 61 cubic inch (1000 cc) streamliner, which reached 136.183 mph at Daytona Beach. Poor handling necessitated the removal of the fancy streamlining, yet the press releases implied the bike set the record as shown. A special timing case and gears were built to drive the magneto, as stock 61s used battery ignition. *(AMF/Harley-Davidson.)*

yet achieved by an unsupercharged motorcycle. More importantly for Harley-Davidson, Milwaukee had erased Springfield's eleven year old American record of 132 mph set by Johnny Seymour on the same beach.

The Muroc Dry Lake, now a part of the huge Edwards Air Force Base and NASA space center, was a popular speed site in the twenties and thirties. It was here that Fred Ham rode a standard 61 inch ohv job to a new 24-hour record, covering 1,825 miles for an average of 76.02 mph. Ham's record, for which he did all the riding, broke a record set in France by a team of four riders. The effort also earned forty-three new AMA records from 50 to 1,800 miles and from one to twenty-four hours.

1937 was also notable for the retirement of Jim Davis. His twenty-one-year career on Harleys and Indians gave him the distinction of being the **only rider to have won National Championships under each of the United States' sanctioning organizations:** the FAM, the M&ATA, and the AMA.

1938: Class C takes over

The transition in American racing, which had been underway since 1935, continued to its conclusion during the pivotal year of 1938. 'C' racing, in effect introduced for the 1935 season, had continued to gain in popularity at the expense of the old Class A game. During the decline of Class A interest, the once truly national circuit had shrunk to somewhat isolated and regional affairs, and while the term 'National Championship' was legally alive in Class A, the dwindling crop of riders and hard economic times had robbed the 'A' championships of their former luster. Indeed, by 1938 the only prominent Class A meet was the annual Syracuse, New York, shoot-out held at the season's end.

Meanwhile, Class C racing had perhaps proven more popular than anticipated. The establishment of this 'poor boys' class immediately multiplied the field of competitors ten-fold; moreover, every neighborhood motorcycle shop could now provide racing hardware. Even at this early stage of the Class C game there were talented men who were beginning to bridge the gap between tuner and engineer, moving the boxstock class inevitably towards a hybrid battle and leaving the casual tuner behind. In this process, the term 'tuner' was to become increasingly less descriptive, and the author prefers the term 'builder' as a label for the more dedicated preparers of racing iron. The earliest Class C events were heavily dependent on local riders. It was therefore considered a novelty when Rhode Island's Babe Tancrede journeyed across the continent for the Hollister, California 100-mile TT National Championship for 1938. The other riders, in keeping with the custom, were west-coasters, and one of these, Milton Iverson, powered his Harley-Davidson to this National Championship on May 30. Coming shortly after Ben Campanale's National road race title at Daytona Beach, the Hollister affair seemed to restore Harley-Davidson's racing parity with Indian which had the better of it during 1937.

Returning to the subject of 'builders', probably the best of these non-factory engineers was Tom Sifton of San Jose, California, Even at this early

85

stage of his technical career, he was a man apart.

Consider the 1938 Oakland, California 200-mile Pacific Coast Championship, run on the one-mile oval. Although not billed as a National contest, this November event drew many of the top riders from all over the country. During the year, Tancrede's Hollister precedent had become the rule, and 1938 thus marked the beginning of a genuine National Class C circuit. As the biggest race in the nation, Oakland drew the best riders from all over the country, the most famous at that time being Class A star Joe Petrali. Sifton's rider was Sam Arena, whose talents were well respected locally, but Arena was something of an unknown to the eastern fans.

Class C racing motorcycles were still in the early stage of evolution and had not developed much reliability, particularly if all the common racing tricks were employed, such as raising the compression ratio. In the strategy of the times, builders and riders treated a long event on a mile track as if it were a continuous series of drag races (sprints) connected by the turns. Consequently, adjustments were made to the oil pumps and (on Harley-Davidsons) to the timing of the crankcase breather valves, while piston ring design was closely studied, all with a view towards increasing the oiling while the engines were shut off during the turns. Shutting off in the turns was, therefore, essential to nurture the somewhat oil-starved engines and to reduce the problem of overheating, always a threat to the eccentrically laid out sidevalve designs.

Sifton figured otherwise. Feeling that the repeated on-again-off-again throttling and lubrication were an inherent problem rather than a solution, he deliberately set up Arena's bike to 'over oil' on the straights. Sifton then instructed Arena, a remarkably talented and cool rider, to hold the throttle on during the turns, otherwise the spark plugs would be fouled out from the consequent increased cylinder oiling during shut-off. The result was phenomenal: Arena broke the 200-mile Class C flat track record by 19 minutes, 20.6 seconds!

Coinciding with the rise of Sifton was the decline of Joe Petrali. Joe won his last National title in 1938, finishing first in the seasonal over-all Class A hillclimbing points race, but significantly he failed to finish in the top four at the big Muskegon climb which capped the season. Moreover, in Class A flat-track racing he was no longer competitive. Whereas in 1935 he had won every Syracuse event and National Championship, in 1938 his results in the five Syracuse Nationals were: one second-place finish and two third-place finishes. Petrali never adjusted to the new Class C mode, and in any case, even the greatest have to hang up their spurs.

Somewhat symbolically, the end of Petrali's dominance was also the end of Class A racing. In the last Class A Championship meet held, Fred Toscani took two of the five 21 inch Syracuse titles on a JAP speedway bike, and finished the season as the high-point Class A rider.

Before closing discussion of this truly pivotal year of 1938, mention should be made of another glimpse of things to come. At the Jack Pine 500-mile enduro, Ted Konecny carried Harley-Davidson's colors to its now traditional win, giving Milwaukee its 14th consecutive Jack Pine win. The futuristic glimpse was in the form of Bob Dickieson, who piloted his Norton to the **first foreign machine finish of the Jack Pine.**

1939

Harley-Davidson's outstanding racing success for 1939 was the Daytona 200. Ben Campanale became the first two-time winner of this event, again setting a new record on the beach course.

The balance of the year was rather typical, with Harley-Davidson losing out to Indian in many of the shorter events, but with Harleys doing well in the longer runs. Jack Cottrell won the Oakland 200, now rightfully termed a National Championship. Charles Daniels won the Laconia 100-mile National TT, the fourth consecutive Harley-Davidson win in this event. At San Pedro, California, Ernie Holbrook won the 50-mile national TT. At Muskegon, Michigan, Willard Bryan won the 45 inch Class A hillclimb title and finished the season as the 45 inch Class A Champion, while placing second (to Indian's Howard Mitzell) in the seasonal 'Expert' standings. Apparently, there was some embarrassment being caused by hillclimbers who were winning club events on the ioe 'J' series 74 inch Harley-Davidsons, out of production since 1929 but capable of bettering the current 61 inch over-head 'E' series Harley-Davidsons. Consequently, the 1939 AMA rules prohibited motors of over 61 inch displacement having overhead inlet valves, in effect outlawing the 74 inch 'Js'.

An event of note was the **first major Class C win by a foreign motorcycle.** Robert Sparks captured the Langhorne 100 on a Norton International, a signal of forthcoming increased British bike competition to America's racing motorcycles, Harley-Davidson and Indian.

1940

As the successor to the model WLD, Harley-Davidson brought out the WLDR in 1940. Besides featuring aluminum cylinder heads, these WLDRs also had incorporated several minor reliability and speed improvements, the latter including optional flat cam-followers (valve lifters) in order to save reciprocating weight. Horsepower had gradually climbed over the years from near 30 horsepower in 1935 to about 35 horsepower on the run-of-the-mill WLDR in 1940, though the best privateer builders such as Sifton, and the factory 'breathed-on' jobs, were always good for a little more suds. Still, the WLDR was pretty much a touring machine, which the racer was obliged to strip down himself, adding whatever factory accessory or home-brewed speed parts he chose, except that in the latter case there were only a few authorized deviations from standard such as tires and handlebars.

Arthur 'Babe' Tancrede was the standout Harley-Davidson rider of 1940, winning both the Daytona 200 road race and the Laconia 100 mile National Championship, now termed a road race instead of a TT. The latter event was notable for the second place finish of Triumph rider George Day of Verdun, 87

Quebec. Two other English-built bikes figured prominently, an Ariel in fourth and another Triumph in fifth. Willard Bryan was Milwaukee's top hill-climber, garnering both the Class A and Expert National Championships for the season, and wrapping up these titles even before the Muskegon finale.

At Oakland, Louis Guanella won the 200-mile National using a spare motor built up by Sifton in less than a week. Guanella's record average over the 200-mile was 84.64 mph, the highest average speed yet maintained in a Class C race, regardless of the race length.

1941: A milestone motorcycle

Class C racing continued to move away from the original 'box-stock' concept and passed another milestone in 1941. To this point both Harley-Davidson and Indian had maintained a party line that had become increasingly fictitious, namely, that the motorcycles being raced to National Championship titles were merely stripped-down versions of the same 45 inch touring models available from any dealer's show room. In terms of the skeleton and skin of the machines, including the external portion of the engine, this was true. But, the natural process of tuning and building had proven the impossibility of supervising any but the most basic aspects of design. The controllable features consisted of parts visible to the naked eye, together with easily checked factors such as displacement and compression ratio.

As Tom Sifton related to the author, the development of more racing reliability and more usable racing horsepower essentially boils down to better valve movement and improved porting, together with extending the reliability of all the motorcycle's individual parts. Under Class C rules, tuners and builders experimented continually with all manner of pistons, rings, rods, bearings, cam-followers, and so on. The two American factories participated in the process, both as innovators and as copiers of the better privateer ideas. Gradually the notion of what constituted a 'stock' motorcycle for Class C racing purposes evolved into descriptions of the skeleton and skin.

The milestone in question for the year 1941 was the introduction of the Harley-Davidson model WR. Whereas the original Class C concept had envisioned and had even required that each competing motorcycle must be ridden to the event, all such pretense was now abandoned. The WR, then, marks the acceleration of the transformation of Class C racing from its original, almost Olympian ideal, into what ultimately would evolve into a replay of the Class A theme – the same song but with different lyrics.

The influence of the WR on American racing was profound. The WR was the mainstay of Harley-Davidson racing for the eight seasons of 1941, and

Opposite: **The 1941 model WRTT in road racing trim. The 1941 WR series were the first Harley-Davidsons equipped expressly for Class C racing. Previous W-series machines had to be stripped of road equipment in order to be made race-ready.** *(AMF/Harley-Davidson.)*

1946-1952, and was the precursor of the 'K' series which dominated racing in the USA for the seventeen seasons of 1953-1969. The WR, then, merits a close look.

The WR model

The WR's cylinder barrels featured larger ports than its predecessors; moreover, the valves were moved closer to the cylinder bores. The bore was 2.745 inches, and the stroke was 3.8125 inches, a slightly more undersquare ratio than in the Indian Sport Scout. While modern theory would immediately term this bore/stroke ratio undesirable, these dimensions offered the compensating advantage of permitting a higher/usable compression ratio. The standard compression ratio was 6.1:1, but over the years this figure varied to some extent, never going above 6.25:1 in the most successful machines.

The WR intake valves were 1 13/16 inch diameter, compared to the Sport Scout's 1 5/8 inch. Like the Scout, the WR also had 1 5/8 inch exhaust valves. Valve timing was highly experimental, the factory setup being considered a point of departure by the more adventurous builders, the more successful of whom sometimes had the factory following their lead. Generally, however, best results for most riders were obtained by sticking to the factory figures. A representative set of figures is as follows: intake opens at 37 degrees before top dead center (stock) and closes at 68 degrees after bottom dead center: exhaust opens 66 degrees before bottom dead center and closes 35 after top dead center. Consequently, the valve overlap was 72 degrees. Actuation of the valves was by four camshafts working on flat cam-followers (valve lifters, or tappets) instead of the road model's roller followers, the idea being to reduce reciprocating weight. In contrast, the Indian Sport Scout valves were operated from only two camshafts.

The pistons were of dow metal and cam ground (i.e., eccentric) to provide for the irregular growth resulting from the eccentric combustion chamber. There were two compression rings and one oil ring for each piston. Lubrication was dry sump, with a baffle cast into the front cylinder well to achieve increased oiling. The baffle provided more vacuum under the piston during the upstroke, assisting in the pickup of oil. No baffle was needed for the rear cylinder, due to the natural action of the crankshaft's rotation in slinging oil to the rear cylinders walls. A gear-driven rotary crankcase breather valve was employed, and its proper timing was critical because the crankcase was relatively small. Improper breather timing could result in either inadequate cylinder lubrication or excessive oiling and plug fouling. Again as a matter of interest, the rival Sport Scout used a comparatively crude disk flutter valve for crankcase pressure control. However, crankcase ventilation was less critical on the Sport Scout owing to its larger cases.

The WR mainshaft had ball bearings on both the timing side and drive side. The connecting rod big end had 3/16 inch rollers and the little ends had bronze bushings. The primary drive was by a two-row chain under a sheet metal housing, inferior to Indian's cast aluminum oil bath. Conversely, the

90

WR's three-speed transmission was more modern than Indian's three-speed, the WR having constant mesh gears instead of the Scout's sliding gears. Another contrast between these two classic rivals was the transmission mounting, with the WR gearbox bolted to the frame and the Scout's bolted to the crankcase.

WR wheels were available in either 18 inch or 19 inch sizes; tires were either 4.00 x 18 or 3 1/4 x 19. The frame was chrome molybdenum, and the wheelbase 57 1/2 inches. Total weight was about 300 pounds for the brakeless flat track version.

Horsepower was in the upper thirties, as delivered, sufficient to produce speeds up to 110 mph. However, good mid-range performance was not sacrificed to attain a slightly higher top speed, since there was only a three-speed transmission. Moreover, shifting these hand-operated devices was impractical (if not impossible!) during flat track turns. (Incidentally, to either equalize Harley and Indian's chances against the foot-shifted British bikes, or to wantonly discriminate if you prefer, shifting gears during a flat track race was illegal for a number of years in the AMA. British-bike riders got away with it often, however, as it was difficult to see the offense with their footshift layouts, or hear the evidence when in a pack of several riders).

As usual, Daytona was the first major event of the season. Harley and Indian fans were upset when the USA's premier motorcycle race was captured by Canada's Billy Mathews on a Norton International. Thereafter, things returned to normal, with Harley-Davidson and Indian getting a roughly even split of racing laurels.

Two 100-mile events fell to Harley-Davidsons, Jim McCall winning Laconia and Tommy Hayes copping Langhorne. Langhorne was typically grueling; only 12 of 35 starters managed to finish and eight were Harley-Davidsons. In the season's last big race, McCall and Hayes were killed at Oakland.

A new Sifton motor

After Oakland, there were no more American championship races for the next four years because of the United States' entry into the war. However, during the closing months of 1945, local interest racing was resumed. Sifton and Arena immediately took up their winning ways against formidable opposition on the California flat tracks.

Besides some familiar names from the previous Class C days, the immediate post-war California scene included Wilbur Lamoreaux. 'Lammy,' along with the Milne brothers, Jack and Cordy, had continued riding speedway in the late thirties, while most of their peers turned to Class C racing. Competing in the British speedway circuit they finished 1, 2, 3 in the World Speedway Championship of 1937. None of the three was accustomed to being beaten by anyone outside their trio, and their JAP-powered 30.50 inch bikes were thought to be invincible by their sidevalve competition. 'Lammy' put on   91 his spurs again early in 1946 and would have indeed been invincible in California racing, except for Sifton and Arena.

With the slowdown in motorcycle business caused by the war, Tom Sifton had found the time to devote some extra thought and methodical attention to the 1941 WR Harley-Davidson. Sifton's previous experiments with larger intake valves had reduced rather than increased horsepower, and he was curious as to why. He made a plaster of paris mold of a combustion chamber and noted that the area around the intake port was 30 percent larger than the cross-sectional area between the valve chamber and the cylinder bore. Consequently, it made little sense to worry about improving flow through the intake ports when the process was in effect being strangled later by the restricted flow from the valve chambers to the cylinders. Like most smart men, he did the 'obvious' thing, but it was only obvious to others much later. Sifton cut away the excess metal in the 'floor' between the valve chamber and the cylinder bore. He removed about 3/16 inch of metal down to about 1/32 inch above the top piston ring, so that the piston protruded above the valve-side of the bore by about 5/32 inch. The end result was about 4 more horsepower.

The first time out with this '46-Arena' motor, Arena ran away from the field, including the bewildered Lammy, Ed Kretz, Jimmy Kelly, and Bruce Pearson. This Sifton motor carried Arena through the abbreviated 1945 season and the full seasons of 1946 and 1947, with Sam winning **every** main event and heat race he entered in the busy California circuit over a 2 1/2 year period. The masterfulness of Arena was somewhat unappreciated outside of the West Coast area, for he didn't ride the National circuit of championship races. However, the fact remains that Arena's victims included many of the top riders in the country.

1946

The traditional series of National Championship races was somewhat abbreviated in 1946. The Daytona 200, always held early in the year to take advantage of the Florida tourist off-season, could not be organized in time. The mustering out of military men was in progress and the consequent problems of becoming resettled had a slowing effect on the revival of motorcycle sport in general, as well as on the renewal of racing interest. Many of the more prominent races had been promoted by individual motorcycle clubs, and the clubs were not yet revitalized. Nevertheless, some well known events such as Langhorne, Laconia, and the Jack Pine were staged.

Harley-Davidson winnings were light in comparison to earlier years, but the results are more indicative of the struggle for reestablishment of motor-cycling than of any Harley-Davidson weaknesses; i.e., Indian didn't win much either. In September, Harley-Davidson's Jack Pine streak was ended at seventeen. Claude Goulding won the event on a BSA 350 single, **the first foreign bike to win the prestigious Jack Pine.** Harley and Indian riders shared roughly equal numbers of wins in lesser events during the year, but with the

Experimental footshift WR with double tube frame. Rider: Jimmy Chann. Date: August, 1946. Place: Milwaukee State Fair track.
(AMF/Harley-Davidson.)

Leo Anthony on another experimental 1946 WR. *(AMF/Harley-Davidson.)*

increasing prominence of British motorcycles serving as a warning to both Milwaukee and Springfield.

1947

Racing was in full swing by 1947. On Jan 5, Dick Page won the Big Bear, California Enduro, one of the oldest, toughest, and most prestigious events in the nation. Page's 74 ohv was a near swansong for the big rigid framed V-twin as a cross-country bike, though it may not have yet been apparent that British bikes would soon take over the cross-country field. Harley rider Ray Tanner was second, and was to figure several more times in important races over the next few years.

1948

Nineteen forty-eight was an extremely successful year for Harley-Davidson. Harley riders took nineteen of the twenty-three National titles, the others falling to Indians. The biggest wins were Joe Weatherly's 100-mile road race title at Laconia and Jimmy Chann's second consecutive Springfield 25-mile Flat Track Championship. At Laconia, Harley-Davidsons took all of the top ten places except third. An oddity was the 10-mile National for half-mile tracks at Atlanta, Georgia. In this race Billy Huber (Harley-Davidson) and Bobby Hill (Indian) finished in the **only tie ever awarded by the AMA**.

After Sam Arena retired from track racing at the end of the 1947 season, he became one of the top hillclimbers for over twenty years.

(Tom Sifton.)

Hillclimbing, while no longer of much interest to the factories, remained fiercely competitive. Harley-Davidson riders took all Class A honors at the Detroit, Michigan climb. At San Jose, California, Windy Lindstrom continued his many years of hillclimbing success by winning the 80-inch National Class C Championship. Sam Arena, a brand new retiree from racing, won the 45 inch National Class C. Sam would remain one of the best climbers over the next twenty years.

1949

Nineteen forty-nine was another good year for Milwaukee. Although failing again to win the Daytona 200, this time the property of the Francis Beart-tuned Norton of Dick Klamfoth, the WR was the predominant winner in the season's flat track events. At Laconia, New Hampshire, Harley-Davidson riders crushed their opposition in the 100-mile road race, taking all of the top ten spots but the 9th place. Joe Weatherly won for the second consecutive year, making it three in a row for Harley-Davidson riders. In the past three Laconia races Harleys had won a cumulative total of twenty-seven of the top thirty places. (For Indian, the 1949 Laconia was a catastrophy, as all twelve of their new vertical twins expired).

Jimmy Chann repeated his previous years' wins at the Springfield, Illinois 25-miler. The Springfield mile was considered the ultimate test of the dirt track-dominated National circuit, and accordingly the winner was awarded the honor of the No. 1 plate. Chann, therefore, won the number one tag for the third consecutive time. (Incidentally, while there have been other 'brother acts' in American motorcycle racing, Jimmy, Pete, and Steve Chann were the only successful trio). Despite Norton's Daytona win, the AMA raised the maximum allowable compression ratio for 1950 from 7 1/2:1 to 8:1.

1950

The early 1950s were characterized by the increasing prominence of builders (in common and undescriptive language, tuners) none of whom was more successful than Tom Sifton. In 1950 his two protégés were expert class rider Larry Headrick and a young amateur class rider named Joe Leonard. Headrick won the Milwaukee 15-miler (1/2 mile track) and all three mile-track Nationals. The miles were the category most impacted by the builders' capabilities due to the combined needs for horsepower and midrange torque as well as reliability. By winning at Springfield, Headrick earned the right to the number one plate.

Although losing Daytona to Dick Klamfoth and his Manx Norton, Harleys captured two other prestige races in 1950. Bill Miller won the Laconia road race, and Billy Huber won the Langhorne 100-mile flat track event, only 50 percent finishing. In the Jack Pine, Jerry McGovern rode a Harley 125 and was the **first rider to ever complete this 500-mile enduro on a 125 cc machine.** Roger Soderstrom scored double wins in the Peoria TT. A harbinger of things to come, Sody's 80 inch win was less than 1 1/2 seconds faster than his 45 inch title. The end was drawing nigh for the TT reign of the rigid-framed big twins.   95

The 1950 model WR flat-track racer. The magneto could be mounted either horizontally as on earlier models, or vertically, as shown here. The WR frame always included a vertical brace on both sides of the rear frame structure, unlike the WRTT or road models.

(AMF/Harley-Davidson.)

1951

Nineteen fifty-one was another downturn for Milwaukee, as they lost both Daytona and Laconia. Harley-Davidson's biggest win was Billy Huber's Langhorne 100, a race which was halted after fifty miles due to rain and re-run in its entirety the day following. Huber finished in front both days and the press termed him the winner of a race and a half.

1952: The Model K

The Model K Harley debuted in 1952 and was the most extensive design effort ever undertaken by Milwaukee. True, the sidevalve configuration was retained along with the W-series bore and stroke (2 7/8 inches by 3 13/16 inches), but the K was a new concept in Harley-Davidsons. Its unit construction and swinging arm rear suspension were radical departures for Milwaukee, while its footshift and telescopic fork features completed a dramatic change from the nineteen-thirtyish W-series.

In addition to a road model, the K generation was offered as the KRTT road racer/TT model and the KR rigid-framed flat tracker. Predictably, however, the competition versions got off to a gradual start. For the third time Dick Klamfoth took Daytona on a Norton, making this the fourth consecutive Norton win and the seventh consecutive Daytona Harley-Davidson had failed to win. All Harley entrants were WRs, the racing KRs not having been

A late 1950 or 1951 WR, once campaigned by Floyd Emde. The timing cover has been changed and no longer provides room for an optional horizontal magneto mounting.

(Bob Tryon, Sam Hotton.)

completed as yet, and the top Harley came in 17th. This was Harley-Davidson's low point in the beach classic, now becoming somewhat of an embarrassment. By August the fledgling KRs were ready and Everett Brashear rode his to victory at the Sturgis, South Dakota 5-mile National (half-mile track). A WR finished second and other KRs rounded out the top five.

1953

The 1953 Daytona provided a momentous victory, as Paul Goldsmith won on his K at a record 94.45 mph average. The new design was now in full stride, and once again Milwaukee dominated.

A new off-road competition model was offered, the KRM. Spark timing in the Wico magneto-powered ignition was advanced five degrees over stock. The cam action was quicker and opened the valve 1/32 inch higher. The intake valves were also 1/32 inch larger in diameter than in the street version. There was a skid plate to protect the engine's bottom and other detail modifications.   97

The 'K' series engine. The double-decker cylinder head fins are reminiscent of sidevalve BMWs of the thirties, and Harley's World War II copy, the shaft driven XA. To avoid power loss, it was

critically important that the exact subtle internal shapes and contours be maintained. 'Tuners' who experimented with the factory setup almost always reduced performance.

(AMF/Harley-Davidson.)

The 1953 KRTT, for TT events and road racing. Principal differences from the stock road model included Wico magneto ignition, elimination of lights, a bobbed rear fender with pillion pad, and a sheet metal primary cover.

(AMF/Harley-Davidson.)

However, the KRM was some fifty pounds heavier than competitive British twins. Harley-Davidson was interested in stopping British domination of California desert racing and put out feelers to several riders. Bud Ekins, the noted rider of TT and cross-country events, declined an offer of financial support to campaign the KRM and stuck with his Matchless. However, another top off-road rider, Del Kuhn, gave up British-bike riding for the KRM. In the long run, the KRM did not fare well against the 650 cc vertical twins and 500 cc singles in California desert racing.

The low point of 1953 was the death of Billy Huber. Billy died from heat prostration while leading in the last half of the Dodge City 200-mile race. Billy had always been a crowd favorite for his sportsmanship as well as his skill. His post-war career was very successful, perhaps reaching a peak in his 1951 'race and a half' win at Langhorne.

Perhaps the most important individual in the history of Class C, Tom Sifton, is shown sharing the joy of his rider's victory. Joe Leonard is the rider, who has just won the 1953 Bay Meadows mile-track National Championship.   *(AMF/Harley-Davidson.)*

1954

The mid and late fifties blended into a steady stream of Harley-Davidson victories, giving rise to increasing criticism of the Class C rules which pitted Harley's 750 cc sidevalves against 500 cc overhead valve competition. In 1954 there was a notable exception, promoting brief hopes by British bike fans that technology had finally left the 750 cc sidevalve hopelessly behind. BSAs took the top five spots in the 1954 Daytona, a feat not duplicated until the rise of Yamaha some twenty years later, but it proved to be a flash in the pan. Joe Leonard went on to win eight National titles, including the Laconia 100, proving himself a winner in the mile, half-mile, TT, and roadracing events. Accordingly, Leonard was proclaimed the Grand National Champion based on his cumulative season record and awarded the No. 1 plate for the following season. Joe Leonard was **the first such No. 1 rider,** the previous year's honors going to the Springfield, Illinois, winner. Harleys captured 13 of 18 Nationals.

The story of Leonard's 1954 season is a story of great natural riding talent backed up by probably the greatest single leap forward ever made by a private builder – Tom Sifton. Despite Sifton's long successful record as a racing engine builder, his building efforts had always been a night-time and Sunday affair. As a motorcycle dealer in San Jose, he had always insisted that work on customers' street machines had priority over all racing work. In August 1953, Sifton fulfilled a promise made several years earlier, and completed a handshake deal with Sam Arena, turning over the San Jose Harley-Davidson agency keys to Sam.

Early in 1954, Walter Davidson approached Sifton, requesting his help in building up a good motor for Joe Leonard. Having unloaded the responsibility of the dealership, Tom was now able to concentrate his efforts on racing and try some techniques that he had been turning over in his mind. In February, Sifton started the Leonard project, perhaps his greatest work as an engine builder.

Sifton's 1954 'Leonard' engine

The keys to horsepower are porting, good cam action, and good value springs, thought Sifton, and he attacked each aspect in earnest. Porting had been a Sifton forte predating his 1946 Arena motor, and his efforts in this area were not radical, being a continuation down a familiar path. Before doing any cam experiments, Sifton believed he needed better valve springs for more positive control, and he got these from Tim Witham, the noted Triumph builder who had started his own valve spring business. For the 1954 'Leonard' engine, Witham provided a set of double springs for each valve, for which Sifton had to make special collars to adapt them to the KR engine. The valve springs were stronger than standard Harley-Davidson issue, and were expected to hold this margin of strength. A side benefit was the extremely tight packing of the springs, which precluded the valves from opening too far in the event of overrevving.

This machine is a typical flat-tracker in appearance, but not in performance! Joe Leonard, behind the rear wheel, relinquishes his No. 1 plate to Brad Andres at the end of the 1955 season. The number 11R motorcycle, built up by Tom Sifton, was raced by Leonard in 1954 and won him the No. 1 plate. Brad Andres' father purchased the machine for Brad to race in the 1955 season, and Brad dethroned Joe with it.   (AMF/Harley-Davidson.)   103

Alabamian Millard Reynolds amid the challenge of the 1952 Jack Pines. The photo typifies a bygone era when big men on big motorcycles could be competitive. *(AMF/Harley-Davidson.)*

Sifton was concerned about overheating of the exhaust valves, both with respect to reliability and with respect to power loss. Much has been made of the ability of valves to conduct heat away through their stems, and to this end the aircraft industry and certain motorcycles, notably the Velocette, have employed hollow-stemmed exhaust valves filled with sodium. While sodium-filled valves are beneficial in improving heat transfer, most heat transfer occurs through the valve seats. This being the case, the eccentric sidevalve engine combustion chamber posed a special problem, since the portion of the exhaust valve nearest the cylinder bore was invariably hotter than the remainder of the valve head. This led to a vicious cycle of valve warpage, reduced contact with the valve seat, higher valve temperatures, further warpage, etc., and had much to do with the fact that sidevalve racers typically slowed down after the first few laps of racing, since any valve warpage results in lost compression.

Again, Sifton did one of those 'obvious' things which had been so unobvious to others. He installed rotating valve lifters from an International-Harvester truck, which produced six degrees of valve rotation with each valve lift.

To check cam action, Sifton built a test engine-simulator, consisting of a right crankcase containing all the valve gear together with two cylinder barrels housing the valves. To drive the cams he attached a variable speed electric motor. A strobe light was then employed, so that he could observe the actual relationship of the cams, lifters and valves. He found that stock racing cams

104

and valve springs produced a considerable amount of valve float, particularly if the springs had seen even a few laps of racing duty. His Witham springs, already tested in another motor, were installed in the simulator and cured the valve float problem.

This led to concern that the cam action was too slow, as the valve springs were no longer being challenged. Sifton felt that cam action would be improved if greater attention were given to the problem of accelerating and decelerating the movement of the valves at either end of their travel. Using a trial and error process, he devised a set of cams which would lift the valves as fast as possible without the valve losing contact with the cam and lifter combination. (From this approach he developed a technique for cam profile generation which he later used in his own cam business.)

As a result of his cam work, new valve springs, and continual porting updates, Sifton found that the factory-specified figures for valve openings were no longer optimum. The factory called for the intake valve to move off its seat at 37 degrees before top dead center, but Sifton found that opening the itake valve later, at 33 degrees before top dead center, produced a gain of 2 hp, a tribute to the cam design and valve movement, since ordinarily one would expect a fall-off in maximum horsepower under these conditions. More predictable was the ultimate outcome, when Sifton settled on an intake opening starting at 59 degrees before top dead center, a combination which netted a 4 hp increase over previous Sifton motors. Why the middle setup (i.e., intake opening at 37 degrees) should have produced less power (than either the 59 or 33 degree openings) is still a puzzle. The end result was an engine producing about 50 hp at the rear wheel. By comparison, the 1952 stock KR racers put out about 44 hp.

Sifton used chrome-plated stainless steel piston rings, reground to size. These rings proved unbreakable, produced less friction at the outset and picked up less microscopic abrasives. For cam followers, he had switched to a roller setup in 1953, as he had gotten the weight of these down to that of the factory-supplied flat followers; and the factory followed his lead a year later.

Regarding compression ratios, he found that every improvement in porting of his sidevalve racers had the coincidental result of lowering the compression ratio. The compression ratio in the 1954-'Leonard' motor is beyond memory, but Sifton recalls that his last Harley-Davidson KR was producing 54 hp at the rear wheel on a 5 1/2 to 1 compression ratio.

Pistons and cylinder barrels received special attention on the Sifton motors. Pistons were taper-turned, with the top diameter 0.004 inch smaller than the bottom. Cylinders were never bored out during overhauls, since this would have removed 20 to 30 thousandths of metal and could only have been accomplished two or three times without going over the displacement limit. Since the cylinder castings also contained the valve ports which had been painstakingly perfected, any cleanup of the barrels was accomplished by honing, which removed only about 0.0005 inch of the surface. Consequently, Sifton was able to get three to four years of racing service from his cylinders.

Another Sifton modification was the use of 5/16 inch big end rollers in lieu   105 of the standard 3/16 inch rollers. This modification, later adopted by the factory, was accomplished because the slower moving 5/16 inch rollers were expected to be more reliable. Another reason was that the larger rollers were more likely to keep the connecting rods and flywheels parallel, since occasionally the 3/16 inch rollers would allow the rods to rub against the flywheels.

Gear ratios were naturally highly variable, and tailored to the requirements of each race course and even to the style of each rider. Maximum horsepower was achieved at 6400 rpm, but near maximum power was reached at 7000 rpm, while valve float occurred at 8000 rpm. Accordingly, Sifton set up his gear ratios for 7200-7400 rpm at the end of the straights.

Sifton's 1954-'Leonard' engine had come none too soon, as he now admits that the Indian Sport Scouts of Bobby Hill, Bill Tuman, and Ernie Beckman had a horsepower edge on the Sifton Harleys in late 1951 and throughout 1952 and 1953. Harley fans were doubly lucky, for the 1954-'Leonard' motor coincided with the collapse of Indian at the end of 1953. From now on there would be only one serious 45 inch sidevalve challenger – Harley-Davidson.

A prelude to controversy

The March AMA Bulletin, published in *Cycle* for May 1954, outlined the requirements for Class C eligibility of motorcycles. These requirements included the following:

a   For a machine to be eligible to be used in Class C competition, all 7 members MUST vote yes; one dissenting vote can bar a machine.

b   The motorcycle to be approved MUST be basically the counterpart of a standard production model, sold for everyday use.

Besides clearing the bureaucratic administrative hurdles somewhat typical of *any* large organization, obtaining Class C eligibility was an 'iffy' process due to the veto power of any single member of the Technical Committee. Provision b, the standard production model requirement, was particularly subjective. There was obviously the opportunity for an aggressive manufacturer to build as few as 25 highly specialized racing machines, provided the manufacturer went through the sham of installing road equipment on these 25 machines and including these 'everyday' motorcycles in company catalogs.

Practically speaking, the AMA was now well along in its journey from the 1934 amateurish ideal to a racing program admittedly based on specialized equipment. However, while practices had changed, ideology had not changed. There was still the widely-held idea that American racing had to be protected from evolving into the European situation. The European game was one in which less than half a dozen riders were competitive in most races, and it was a game in which no serious competitor could afford to own his personal racing mount. The latter condition was abhorrent to many Americans. The true workings of AMA racing were in fact approaching the European scenario because of the special racing expertise of the Harley-Davidson Racing

Department in their monopolized sidevalve field, and because of the quantum difference in the capabilities of a few builders/tuners of British motorcycles compared to the 'shop on the corner'.

Nevertheless, the AMA ideology was appealing, for even as many young Americans enjoy the idea that they can become the nation's President, many young motorcyclists liked the *apparent* open road to their racing success. While there was more than a little logic and sincerity to the AMA position, it is also true that the AMA's oligarchic nature and the stakes of the game hardly promoted objectivity. Moreover, even with a Technical Committee of angels, it would be impossible to return to the 1934 environment or even to maintain the status quo. No set of rules could maintain the idealized shop-on-the-corner character, for there was too much inherent pressure on Harley-Davidson and the British-bike distributors. The pressure forced them to stay fully immersed in the racing game, to cut every possible corner, and to bend the rules to the breaking point.

In summary, the AMA racing program was a combination of wishful thinking, unintended but inevitable 'creeping professionalism,' and downright political intrigue. As for explaining the motivation behind the rules maneuvering, it is doubtful whether all the key players could even explain to themselves why they took various courses of action. Certainly the AMA of the fifties and sixties will be a favorite subject of bench racers for years to come.

The end of Norton as an AMA power

The AMA's most one-sided racing era was symbolized by the organization's January 1955 bulletin which announced the Class C rejection of the Norton Manx Models 30M (500 cc) and 40M (350 cc) in featherbed frames. Two months later, when the Technical Committee's decision was appealed to the full Competition Committee, the decision was confirmed by a vote of eighteen to seven. The major hangup was the fact that the Manx double overhead cam model was never intended to operate with full road equipment. Norton, of course, could have constructed and cataloged 25 make-believe roadsters, but apparently felt the effort was not worthwhile.

Meanwhile, the single overhead cam Norton International had been left behind by progress. In America, as in the Isle of Man's Clubman TT, the pushrod BSA Gold Star was proving to be more powerful than the classic Norton. The International, never a big seller, had fallen from even limited favor as a roadster because of the new Norton vertical twins, while Norton racing development had been confined to the double overhead cam Manx machines.

The combined effect of Norton's inattention to American racing and the AMA's domination by Harley-Davidson was the death of Norton as a serious proposition in American racing. No Norton had won an AMA National Championship since Bill Tuman's mid-season win of the Dodge City 200-mile track race in 1953, in contrast to the marque's glory days as the only threat to   107

Harley-Davidson and Indian. The remnant of the Indian company, formerly the Norton distributor, was now exclusively in the business of marketing so-called Indians, which were cosmetically altered Royal Enfields. Norton motorcycles were thus without a vigorous distributor network to promote needed development and the necessary votes in the AMA's inner circle to look after politics. Sadly, a Norton would not win another AMA National until 1973.

1955

At the end of the 1954 season, Tom Sifton was persuaded to sell his 1954-'Leonard' motorcycle to Leonard Andres, who had been Sifton's traveling companion during the 1954 circuit. Andres, a fellow Harley-Davidson dealer, was the father of Brad Andres who was facing his rookie year in the Expert class the next season.

The 1954-'Leonard' engine was next seen at the 1955 Daytona 200, where the 19-year-old Brad Andres won the 200-miler at the record pace of 94.57 mph. Incidentally, thanks to Sifton's work, Andres' KR turned its last lap as fast as any other. Joe Leonard was crowded during 1955 by both Everett Brashear and Brad Andres, the latter winning not only Daytona but two other road races as well, the Laconia 100 and the Dodge City 75. Andres also won the Langhorne 100-mile 'speedway' title. Brashear won five flat track nationals on both mile and half-mile tracks. Leonard took three titles, the Peoria 45 inch TT and two flat tracks. Andres emerged as the winner of the No. 1 plate chase and is the only 'rookie' expert class rider to have done so. Harley-Davidsons won fifteen of the seventeen National Championships.

Owing to the continual criticism by British-bike fans, in November the AMA raised the maximum allowable compression ratio for the next season from 8:1 to 9:1, a move which did not affect Harley-Davidson's KRs, operating at around 6 1/2:1.

1956

The time trials at the 1956 Daytona 200 proved that Harley-Davidson had come up with yet another increase in horsepower during the off-season, and that the new 9:1 compression ratio allowance, a concession to British-bike interests, was no immediate threat to Harley-Davidson. The top Harley KR was ridden by Brad Andres at 126.31 mph, while Joe Leonard qualified at 124.13 mph. The top qualifying foreign bike was Dick Doresteyn's Triumph at 121.62 mph. Johnny Gibson won the big race after favorites Paul Goldsmith, Brad Andres, and Joe Leonard were all sidelined, the latter two having magneto failure.

Although Joe Leonard won only two Nationals, the Bay Meadows 20-miler and the Peoria 80 inch TT, he regained his No. 1 plate. Leonard's feat was to become more common in subsequent years as the AMA Grand National Series scoring system put a big premium on consistently high finishes as opposed to outright wins. Another factor was the greatly reduced number of championship races, there being but seven title runs during the year.

An amusing but nevertheless significant event was the 1956 Jack Pine. Leroy Winters powered a model 165 to the **first overall win by a lightweight.** Winters' 165 had a special home-grown swinging arm rear suspension in contrast to the stock rigid rear end. Harley-Davidson's magazine advertisements, of course, managed to hide the special rear end.

Harley-Davidson riders won *every* Class C National in 1956, an unprecedented situation in Class C and one not duplicated since then, which prompted the following comment in the November 1956 issue of *Cycle* magazine.

'*It is apparent in light of Springfield and other events throughout the US this season, that the increased 9:1 compression ratio gift to the British ohv Camp by the AMA is not enough to offset the 50 per cent increase in displacement allowed the flatties, especially when the Harley-Davidson factory mounts are entered. The imported brands need more horsepower – but it is obvious that the best efforts of the Triumph and BSA tuners cannot offset those 15 cubes, and those superlative H-D riding stars and machines which were responsible for the Milwaukee clean sweep this season.*'

A motorcycle which could have changed the course of American racing, the mid-fifties experimental model KL high camshaft ohv unit. According to William H. Davidson, time simply ran out on the KL development program, so the Sportster series was launched in 1957 instead of the KL.   *(AMF/Harley-Davidson.)*   109

1957

Joe Leonard won half of 1957s eight Nationals, including his first Daytona 200 win as well as the Laconia 100; plus the two mile-track Nationals, the San Jose, California, 20-miler and the Springfield, Illinois, race, now a 50-miler. Carroll Resweber first emerged as a key player in 1957, finishing fourth in the points chase and winning two half-mile track Nationals, the Columbus, Ohio, and St. Paul, Minnesota, events. BSA gave the circuit some semblance of competition by winning two of the eight title races, and Beezer rider Al Gunter finished a close second to Leonard in the points standings.

Hank Syvertson retired as Harley-Davidson's race boss, a post he'd held since the beginning of the W-series era. He was replaced by Dick O'Brien. Criticism of the 'mixed bag' rule continued, despite a gradual improvement in the British position owing to increases in the maximum allowable compression ratio, first, from 7 1/2:1 to 8:1 in 1951; and then, from 8:1 to 9:1 in 1956.

1958: Sifton's swan song

The Carroll Resweber reign began in 1958, when he edged Joe Leonard, 36 points to 35 points, for the number one plate. Leonard's two wins were: his second consecutive Daytona 200 and the Springfield, Illinois, 50-miler. Resweber's wins were less prestigious, these being the Duquoin, Illinois, 20-miler (one-mile track) and the St. Paul, Minnesota, 5-miler (half-mile track). Leonard missed half the season because of injuries, so Resweber's consistency won him the title. Of the ten nationals, British machines won five, so that the season 'score' was: Harley-Davidson, 5; BSA, 4; and Triumph, 1. This was the **first year in which American motorcycles failed to win a majority of the National titles.**

Tom Sifton was by this time somewhat of a living legend for his nearly thirty years of Harley-Davidson speed work. He was also a member of the in-crowd of the AMA, so to speak, serving as a member of the much cussed and discussed Competition Committee. In addition, he was much more than acquainted with the Harleys and Davidsons, several times being a house guest of one or the other. It was said that Walter Davidson, the second generation's most visible racing supporter, got as big a kick out of a factory Harley beating a Sifton Harley as he did from beating the British machines.

As a member of the Competition Committee, Sifton had grown tired of the constant bickering over the mixed-bag 750/500 rule, a rule he sincerely believed fair. He was also a little piqued at the implication voiced by British motorcycle supporters, namely that all Harley-Davidson victories were tainted by an unfair rule. Referring to this period, Sifton termed it to be '....*during one of my falling outs with Walter Davidson,*' but he said it with a smile, indicating that the Sifton/Davidson problem was temporary and long dismissed.

So, to defend his integrity, to satisfy his strong curiosity, perhaps to show Harley-Davidson just how good he was, and to have the last laugh on all

The amazing Carroll Resweber, four times consecutively the Grand National Champion. During his best five years, 1957 through 1961, Resweber won exactly half of the thirty flat-track National Championships. No other Class C rider has come close on a percentage basis.

(AMF/Harley-Davidson.)

concerned, Tom Sifton built up a BSA Gold Star for Everett Brashear to ride in Sifton's home town National, the San Jose mile. Formerly a Harley-Davidson racer himself, Brashear gave the situation somewhat the look of a vendetta.

In the time trials, Brashear turned the mile in a record 43.49, breaking the Joe Leonard's one-year old track record by 0.36 second. Later, both Carroll Resweber and John Gibson set new qualifying track records on their Harleys, the best time being Gibson's 43.31 seconds. In short, the speed capabilities of the Sifton-Gold Star and the best Harley-Davidson KRs were just about identical. In the Championship Race, Brashear won a closely fought 25-mile battle with Resweber and another Harley rider, Don Hawley. Sammy Tanner, also BSA-mounted, finished second.

The point of all this is to provide another perspective on the 750/500 rule. In his swan song as a builder/tuner, Sifton felt he'd proved his point. To this   111 day, Tom Sifton says the 750/500 rule was a fair one. His 1958 Gold Star produced 58 hp at the crank, about the same as his latest XR. But he finally advocated elimination of this rule he considered fair. Why? Because he felt it was a bad rule politically; it promoted, in his view, excuse-making and hard feelings.

1959-1961

The years 1959-1961 blended into a familiar pattern of Harley-Davidson supremacy, distinguished from earlier years mainly by the rise of Carroll Resweber. He won the No. 1 plate in each of these years, giving him the No. 1 plate four consecutive times. Joe Leonard finished second to Resweber in the points battle in both 1960 and 1961, being barely nosed out for No. 1 in 1960. Nevertheless, Resweber was the dominating rider of this period. He improved with each passing year, hitting his peak form in 1961, when he won a personal high of five National Championships. Of the five types of Nationals; i.e., road racing, short tracks, half-mile, mile, and TT; Resweber won championships in every category during his career except TTs. His four-time No. 1 plate honor has not been duplicated since and the fact that he was number one in four consecutive seasons makes it all the more remarkable.

Harley-Davidson's competition during this period consisted mainly of BSA Gold Stars, which won two titles in each of these three years. In 1959, Dick Mann won the Peoria 45 inch TT on a BSA 650 cc twin, only the second twin-cylinder BSA National title in the past five years. (Moreover, the Beezer twin would not win another AMA National until 1967, when Mann would again claim the Peoria TT!). The only other non-Harley win over the last three Resweber years was Sammy Tanner's 1959 8 mile title, taken on a Triumph at the Ascot Park, California, half-mile track. Meanwhile, Harley-Davidsons had captured 26 of the 34 championships during the three years, a title-race winning rate of 78 percent. Resweber was the big winner, capturing eleven titles in the three years.

Brad Andres was generally the man to beat in 1959 and 1960 road racing, capturing his second and third Daytona 200-mile wins, as well as the 1959 Laconia 100 and the 1960 Watkins Glen, New York, 150-miler. Andres' 1960 Daytona title was the nineteenth and last of the classic beach course races, as the 1961 event was destined to be held at Daytona International Speedway. The 1960 Daytona was also the last in which an Indian competed.

A significant event occurred in October of 1961. Three American firms handling the importation and distribution of foreign motorcycles were admitted as AMA corporate members. These companies were: BSA, Inc.; The Triumph Corporation; and The Indian Company, now dealing in AJS and Matchless machines. There had been representation of British motorcycle interests prior to this move. However, such representation was limited to a minority of individual riders and dealers of the Union Jack marques and to the efforts of the previous Indian regime whose basis of power was its role as a manufacturer, not its growing interest in British machines. Now the British

Action from the 1962 Indianapolis road race, showing optional seat, front and rear brakes, and 7 1/2 gal. gas tank. With the optional rear brake, the mechanism was moved to the left-side, eliminating the cross-over shaft from the left-mounted pedal.   *(AMF/Harley-Davidson.)*

motorcycles' major distributors were officially on the inside of the AMA governing bureaucracy and a process of evolution had begun, a process which would eventually doom the mixed-bag rule.

1962

In 1962, the Daytona 200-mile Championship was won by Don Burnett on a Triumph, thus ending a string of seven consecutive Harley-Davidson 200 mile titles.

At the Lincoln, Illinois 5 mile-National Championship in September, Resweber was in his customary late-season points lead, by 44 to 40 over Markel, and it appeared likely that Resweber would bag a fifth consecutive number one plate. However, Jack Goulsen, Dick Klamfoth, and Carroll Resweber went down during a practice lap in the heavy dust. Goulsen was killed instantly. Resweber was so severely injured that he would never race again, and Klamfoth decided to retire.

113

With Resweber now out of the picture, Markel went on to win the No. 1 plate, thus ending the dramatic competition between the two which had lasted almost four full seasons.

Mention should be made of Dick Mann, who'd won his first National in 1959 and was to prove a thorn in the Harley-Davidson flesh for another eleven years. In one of his best victories, Mann lapped the field of the Laconia 100 on his Matchless G50 ohc single.

Harley-Davidson's eleven wins in fifteen Nationals yielded a healthy 73 percent win-rate for the year, still down from its 83 percent (10 for 12) records in both 1960 and 1961.

1963

Nineteen sixty-three was a downer for Harley-Davidson. After nine successive No. 1 plates, the steady riding Dick Mann dethroned Milwaukee, using a combination of Matchless and BSA machines. Also, for the second time in the modern Grand National Series (post 1953), Harley-Davidson failed to win a majority of the title races, breaking even with the Union Jack brands at seven wins each.

Harley-Davidson's biggest win was Ralph White's Daytona 200 title. This was the **first AMA Daytona race in which European style fairings were permitted.**

An insight into the political nature of the AMA was provided at Daytona by the refusal of AMA officials to approve Dick Mann's Matchless G50, equipped with a 'special' road race frame. The frame was 'special' in the sense that it was not the standard touring frame into which the minimum of 25 Matchless ohc engines had been stuffed to make them barely legal in AMA racing. Since Class C racing was theoretically still a stock machine game, these 25 Matchless G50CSRs were fully equipped, including touring frame, battery, generator, and lights. These road-going electrical accessories were, of course, instantly removed by the professional racers who were the exclusive purchasers of CSRs. Still, the Matchless G50CSR was hardly any further from the ostensible purpose of Class C racing than were the Harley-Davidson KRs, as Milwaukee hadn't built touring sidevalves since 1956.

Moreover, Mann had been permitted to race his 'special' Matchless G50 during 1962. He therefore naturally assumed that the bureaucratic indecision about whether his motorcycle had already been approved in 1962, as he and some members of the Competition Committee argued, would be resolved in his favor. Meanwhile, Mann was mistakenly reported by a local newspaper as trying to get a court injunction to halt the Daytona 200. That was enough to insure his doom, and the AMA refused to overlook the 1962 procedural shortcuts which had led to the 1963 situation's development.

From a strictly technical point of view, the AMA position was defensible, especially as Mann and other Matchless G50CSR owners had been notified *in February* that only the touring type frame had been approved. From a moral point of view, however, Mann emerged as the innocently wronged party as far as most British-motorcycle fans were concerned. Less than one month's notice was hardly adequate for G50 owners to do frame swap-outs. The whole scene was symbolic of what British-motorcycle partisans had been saying for years, namely that the AMA was a Harley-Davidson club. However, fans of the Union Jack marques had a way of overlooking that the AMA official who brought the matter to a head was Rod Coates, a longtime Triumph supporter as a racer and business man.

In short, by 1963, AMA Class C racing had long since lost sight of its stated purpose of 'standard' motorcycle competition. Mann's bike was disqualified on the basis of the letter of the law, not the intent, for all parties were racing specialized motorcycles. The evolutionary process, however, was more a matter of inevitability than of covert intrigue. After all, what set of rules and what mortal technical inspectors could hold back the ingenuity of individual riders, tuners, and builders, let alone the factories? For their own part, the technical inspectors had gradually been overcome by varying shades of gray, as each new idea but slightly stretched the former bounds of acceptability, and in turn became a precedent for a redefined norm. The situation was analogous to that faced by today's traffic patrolmen, who must resort to selective enforcement of the USA's 55 mph speed limit because it is universally violated. Unfortunately for Dick Mann, he was one of the selected 'guilty'.

Harley-Davidson's winning 'loyal opposition' consisted of Gary Nixon and Sid Payne on Triumphs; Dick Mann on BSA and Matchless; and two other BSA riders, Jody Nicholas and Al Gunter. Gunter practically owned the Ascot Park, California half-mile, taking his third Ascot half-mile National in 5 years. Harley-Davidson, dominant all over the country in flat track racing, couldn't buy a title at Ascot. For several more years, Ascot would remain BSA Gold Star territory.

The growing popularity of small motorcycles, a made-in-Japan phenomenon, had sparked interest in National Championship status events for the 250 cc lightweights. The 1963 Peoria TT was the first such 250 cc National Championship, and the **first visible impact of Japan on AMA championship racing.** Bart Markel won the event on a Harley Sprint.

The 1963 Harley-Davidson KR-TT

Detail improvements had continued on the KR series Harley-Davidsons ever since their 1952 introduction. Much of what had been going on was in the matter of porting, a critical aspect invisible outwardly, derived through trial and error, and impossible to fully communicate through the written word. The August 1963 *Cycle World* included a road test of the KR-TT and the 250 cc Sprint CR-TT. The KR-TT's obvious evolutionary changes included, as accessory equipment, a six-gallon fuel tank and larger light alloy (drum) brakes, the front brake having a wicked-looking large inlet air scoop.

Horsepower was a claimed 48 at the rear wheel, which would be about 53 at the mainshaft. This compares to a 1952 power output (at the crank) of about 44 horsepower, according to Tom Sifton, and demonstrates the effectiveness of   115 continuous combustion chamber experiments over the dozen-year period. With suitably juggled gear ratios, the *Cycle World* test crew rode the 385 pound KR-TT through a standing-start quarter-mile in 12.7 seconds, with a terminal speed of 103.4 mph.

By comparison, just three months earlier the same magazine had coaxed the 390 pound Triumph 650 cc Bonneville TT Special to a quarter-mile in 13.34 seconds and an even 100 mph. The Bonnie, which did not benefit from a wind-cheating road race fairing as did the KR-TT, was cited as having 52 horsepower. Assuming consistency of test data, the Bonneville TT Specials 12:1 compression 650 cc power plant put out about 57 horses at the mainshaft, or about 10 percent more than the claim for the KR-TT 6.3:1 750 cc sidevalve engine. As already discussed, about 58 hp or more was in fact a typical figure for the fastest KRs. The similar power outputs of the Bonnie and KR engines can naturally be interpreted in either of two extreme ways – either Harley-Davidson had done a remarkable job of development, or the KR's near equivalence with a contemporary hot 650 cc revealed how unfair the AMA's 750 cc sidevalve/500 cc overhead valve rule was. The reader has his choice. *Cycle World* put it this way in the August 1963 issue:

'Race favorites come and go, except for Harley-Davidson, who were hard to beat 10 years ago (or 20 for that matter), are hard to beat right now, and it looks as though they might be hard to beat 10 years hence. The reason behind their success is not as straight forward as it might seem. Many people credit their performance to the fact that, in Class C competition, they have a 50 percent displacement advantage—that margin being allowed for flathead engines running against those overhead valves. This is, in part, correct, but had Harley-Davidson not been willing to spend the time and money to develop their flathead to a level that would have seemed impossible a few years ago, they certainly would not be winning races today.'

A 1964 KRTT, this motorcycle is basically the 1952 KRTT with an optional larger fuel tank (probably a 6 gal. unit) and a fairing. The use of a fairing was first permitted at the 1963 Daytona 200. *(AMF/Harley-Davidson.)*

The 1965 KRTT, campaigned by Mert Lawwill, sports a fibreglass fuel tank and seat base, and has a left-side brake mechanism. However, the front brake is the old style.

(AMF/Harley-Davidson.) 117

1964

Although Roger Reiman won but two Nationals in 1964, compared to Dick Mann's (BSA/Matchless) four victories, one of Reiman's successes was the Daytona 200. Moreover, the AMA's emphasis on consistency, which had given Mann the 1963 overall Championship, now worked against Mann. Therefore, Reiman finished first, and Mann second in the points chase. Of the season's top ten racers, seven rode Harley-Davidsons, a rather typical statistic throughout the Grand National Series history to this point.

An unusual aspect was the first 250 cc road race National Championship, won by Larry Schafer at Nelson Ledges, Ohio. Dick Mann's 50, 150, and 175 mile road race titles, and Sammy Tanner's Ascot 8-mile and Springfield 50-mile Championships, robbed Harley-Davidson of most of the prestige wins. A strangely missing ingredient was the traditional Laconia 100, cancelled due to troubles with the hoodlum element of motorcyclists.

1965

Harley-Davidson's even split of the 1958 and 1963 Nationals was a preview of a new era firmly launched in 1965. Roger Reiman won his second consecutive Daytona 200 in March, and Bart Markel followed this with two half-mile track titles in early June, so that it looked like a typical Harley-Davidson year. However, British motorcycles won eleven of the next fifteen Championships and Harley-Davidson finished the year with only six of the eighteen titles, **the first time Milwaukee had garnered less than half the prestige races.** Triumph, which had won but seven Nationals in the previous five years, won five Championships during 1965 and was definitely on the move. A bit of history was Dick Mann's 250 cc road race National win at Nelson Ledges, Ohio. Mann rode a Yamaha which became the **first Japanese motorcycle to win an AMA National Championship in the Grand National Series.** This was also the **first two-stroke win of an AMA National.** Paradoxically, although the Union Jack marques dominated the circuit, Bart Markel rode his Harley-Davidson to the No. 1 plate. Markel, Mann, and Ralph White had three wins each, while the remaining eight British-motorcycles titles were shared by seven riders.

Whatever the technical merits or demerits of the 'mixed bag' 750 cc side-valve/500 cc overhead valve rule, the AMA was finding it a continual political problem. For Harley-Davidson, the handwriting was on the wall. The AMA was reported to be planning on a straight-out 750 cc rule effective with the 1967 season.

Regarding the 'mixed-bag' rule, there was enough difference of opinion to permeate the *Cycle World* staff. The following two different slants were taken in the June 1965 issue:

Publisher Joe Parkhurst reported, *'As we fully expected, Harley-Davidson's 50 percent displacement advantage took them over the top at the Daytona 200-mile national road races.'*

AMERICAN RACING MOTORCYCLES

Technical Editor Gordon H. Jennings was somewhat more laudatory and stated, *'Given an engine with fewer built-in disadvantages, this much development effort at Harley-Davidson could give them a 30.5 cubic inch engine that would offer an even greater edge in Harley-Davidson horsepower than the one now provided by the irksome 50 percent displacement advantage.'*

The Harley-Davidson Sprint

After experimenting with the Nelson Ledges and Peoria 250 cc Nationals in 1964 and 1965, the AMA abandoned the lightweights as formal competitors for the Grand National Series. Nevertheless, the 250 cc road races had proven popular with motorcycle fans in general, most of whom did not actually attend the Nationals but followed racing through the written word.

Although Daytona's combined Expert/Amateur road races had never been granted championship sanctions, these well publicized races had provided and would continue to provide some of the most exciting and technically interesting racing in the country. Consequently, Dick Hammer's 1963 100-mile 250 cc victory on a Sprint and his duplication in 1964 had been a source of considerable satisfaction to Harley-Davidson. However, eight of the first ten 1965 Daytona 250 cc finishers were on Yamahas, the Harleys taking only fifth and sixth. After the 1966 Daytona Expert/Amateur 250 cc race, it was apparent that the Harley-Davidson (Aermacchi) Sprints were falling behind Yamaha's increasingly fast and reliable two-strokes. The top three Sprint riders at the 1966 Daytona were: Reiman, 2nd; Markel, 7th, and Rayborn, 11th.

One reason for Harley-Davidson's interest in Expert 250 cc racing, which it originally dominated, was the possibility of a new 350 cc class replacing the 'mixed-bag' rule. The January 1966 issue of *Cycle World* reported that the AMA was considering such a rule change.

Harley's Sprints, although fading out as road racers, continued their hold on Expert Class short track (1/4 mile) racing. Aside from Triumph's Gary Nixon, who'd won the 1963 and 1965 short track Nationals, most short track glory was Harley-flavored. In 1966, Bart Markel gave Harley-Davidson its fourth short track National title in the six year history of this event. More importantly, the numerous non-National short track meets held throughout the nation saw more Expert Class wins from Harley-Davidson than from any other Marque. On the other hand, at the Novice Class (entry level) the less expensive Japanese bikes provided the bulk of the entries, and hence most of the winners.

Although *Foreign Racing Motorcycles* covers the road racing Sprints under their parental Aermacchi banner, the Aermacchi-Harley-Davidsons raced in the United States' short track meets were unique to the American environment.

On October 21, 1965, George Roeder piloted a streamlined 250 cc Sprint to a new Class C record at Bonneville, Utah. Using the same streamliner ridden to a 1964 record of 156 mph by Stormy Mangham, Roeder upped the 250 cc Class C mark to 176.817 mph. A similarly streamlined Sportster experienced

119

handling problems, twice crashing in the 180 mph vicinity without establishing any records.

1966

Nineteen sixty-six was similar to the previous season, with Markel again winning number one, but Harley-Davidson owned only five of the fourteen Nationals. As in 1965, there was a healthy Triumph showing, the vertical twins winning six Nationals. At Carlsbad, California the winner of the 75 mile road race was Calvin 'Cal' Rayborn. This was Rayborn's first National Championship, but he was to become known as the outstanding American road racer of his time.

The AMA's flirtation with 250 cc National Championships was now a thing of the past, as there were no such events in 1966. However, it was announced that consideration was being given to a 350 cc formula to replace the 750 cc/500 cc rule. Harley-Davidson's five wins were its lowest in the Grand National Series' history, nor has any subsequent year produced so few titles for the marque. Its winning percentage of 36 percent was slightly better than 1965's 33 1/3 percent, Harley's all-time low at the time. In horsepower, Harley-Davidsons were very much still in the hunt, as Cal Rayborn had been the fastest qualifier at Daytona, turning the outside oval at a rate of 134.148 mph. Triumph's Buddy Elmore won the Daytona 200, however, and Triumph was on the verge of its most successful two-year period.

1967, 1968: Triumph gets serious

The years 1967 and 1968 were characterized by the increased strength of the Triumph marque, a continuation of a trend begun in the 1965 season. In the first eleven years of the modern Grand National Series, 1954 through 1964, Triumphs had won but fifteen of the 139 National Championships, for a winning rate of eleven percent. In five of those years, Triumphs failed to capture any titles. During the same period BSAs had won twenty-four titles for a seventeen percent share, almost all wins coming on Gold Star singles. Harley-Davidson, of course, had dominated from 1954 through 1964, taking 98 crowns at a win-rate of 70 percent.

From 1965 through 1968 Triumphs won 22 more National Championships, which amounted to over 30 percent of the Grand Nationals for the period. The outstanding vertical twin riders were: Eddie Mulder and Skip Van Leeuwen in TT events, and Gary Nixon in road racing and flat tracking. Nixon was the most successful. In 1967, he copped both the prestigious (although non-titled) 250 cc and the 200-mile big motor National races at Daytona Beach, plus four more National Championships, and he finished number one in the seasonal standings. In 1968, Nixon won only two Nationals but again finished number one for the year after a thrilling season finale at the Ascot Park half-mile National pushed him over Harley's Fred Nix in the seasonal points chase.

Fred Nix, the top mile-track rider of the mid-sixties, is seen here after winning a preliminary event at a 1967 short-track meet in Montgomery, Alabama. His Aermacchi-built Sprint would be a stranger on European shores.   *(T.J. Ragan.)*

The most significant Harley-Davidson happening of 1967 occurred in August at the Indianapolis, Indiana 110-mile road race Championship. Soon after Gary Nixon's 1967 record-setting Daytona-200 win on a Triumph, Dick O'Brien began a serious update program on the KRTT. The first results of this project were the motorcycles raced at Indianapolis by Cal Rayborn and Mert Lawwill. These machines sported a completely new 'low boy' frame which was 2 1/2 inches lower at the steering head, and lowered the seat height from 30 inches to 27 1/2 inches. They were also equipped with Ceriani front forks, as used on the 250 cc Sprint, but with heavier springs and fork oil. The rear suspension was a new and more conventional-appearing nearly vertical unit, with British-made Girling shocks. The front brake was a Ceriani double-leading-shoe unit. Rayborn won the 110-mile National and Lawwill finished third.

On a larger scale, the most far-reaching news for the sport as a whole was an announcement concerning the AMA's principles of government. After study by a special committee and balloting of the association's corporate members, the AMA announced that the Technical Committee system would be replaced by a Competition Congress. The Congress would consist of two representatives

121

from each manufacturer or distributor; one AMA member from each of the AMA's thirty-six districts to be elected by the clubs within that district; six licensed professional riders from each region, to be elected by the professional riders of that region; the Executive Director, who would serve as the chairman of the Congress; and the Director of Competition. Democracy had at last arrived.

When Gary Nixon repeated as number one in the 1968 standings, it was a bitter disappointment to Harley-Davidson's Fred Nix, who had outslugged his rival in individual titles by six to two. Nevertheless, the 1968 season was a splendid one for the Harley sidevalves. After failing to win any of the first nine annual Ascot Park half-mile Nationals, a Harley-Davidson finally prevailed under the grip of Mert Lawwill. The 1968 season was one of transition in Harley flat track equipment, as the first experiments in rear suspension were accomplished. More importantly, 1968 was destined to be the last year of the 34-year old mixed-bag rule.

The 1968 KRTT

After much talk in the American motorcycling press about Triumph's supposed Daytona invincibility, Dick O'Brien and the Harley-Davidson Racing Department had put in their hardest year of development on the KRTT road racer, and the results were outstanding. In recalling the 1968 development program, Dick O'Brien related to the author that he considers this effort the most satisfying experience of his many years as Harley-Davidson's racing boss. Not only were the 1968 results outstanding but the 1969 season was to prove an even more impressive showcase for the venerable sidevalves.

To take full advantage of the new late-1967 low boy frame, Dick O'Brien sought out the well known Wixom Brothers firm of Long Beach, California. The Wixoms were commissioned to design and build new fairings and fuel tanks, and their work was tested in the wind tunnel of the California Institute of Technology at Pasadena. Surprisingly, the Wixom's first attempt at a new and narrower fairing proved to be less slippery than the old KR fairing and the final product was a modified version of the old type. While retaining many of the curves of the old KR fairing, the final Wixom version was much smaller overall. A total of ten fairings and ten seat/tank units were built, which included three extra sets and the complement of seven sets for seven factory riders. Each of the primary seven tanks and seats was individually custom fitted for a rider, according to a basic design originated by Wixom's LeGrande Fletcher.

Additional horsepower was also a goal, and to achieve this, the 1968 KRTTs were equipped with twin Tillotson diaphragm carburetors. Intake valve timing was unchanged from the 1966 KRTT engine, with the intake valve opening at 66 degrees before top dead center and closing at 66 degrees after bottom dead center. The exhaust valve timing was changed somewhat, and provided five more degrees of duration to the opening. The exhaust valve opened at 65 degrees before bottom dead center and closed at 40 degrees after top dead center. The cam design was a compromise between top speed and acceleration requirements. Because of the new twin carburetor setup, it was necessary to reshape the combustion chambers, after which the design compression ratio reached an all time low of 5:1. The 1967 single carb engines had developed 52 horsepower at the rear wheel at 7,000 rpm, and although O'Brien wouldn't publicly reveal the 1968 horsepower figure, he acknowledged that there was a definite improvement in power output.

The 1968 Daytona qualifying trials, run strictly on the outer oval in those days, were illuminating. Triumph had essentially made no progress since the previous year's 200-miler, as their best speed had risen from 135.746 mph to 135.931 mph. On the other hand, both Harley-Davidson and Yamaha had added considerable speed. Harley's one year of progress amounted to 8 mph, and Roger Reiman was the fastest qualifier at 149.080 mph. Meanwhile, the amazing 350 cc Yamahas had upped their best pace from 132.772 to 147.347! Every one of the top ten bikes, eight Harleys and two Yamahas, qualified at a pace faster than the 1967 record!

In the race Cal Rayborn went on to lap all but second and third place riders by the end of forty laps, and became the first rider to win the Daytona 200 at an over 100 mph average. Meanwhile, his six teammates had retired. Rayborn also won the other two road races on the calendar, Louden (Laconia) and Indianapolis.

Late in the season, the Sacramento 20-mile National provided an interesting sidelight. Dick Mann forsook his regular BSA Gold Star for a borrowed bike, and his chosen mount was the only competitive BSA in the field. Mann's bike was Everett Brashear's old rigid-framed Goldie built up in 1958 by Tom Sifton! Mann finished ninth, as Fred Nix won his fourth consecutive mile track National.

A time for strategy

In November, the AMA's newly established Competition Congress, meeting for the first time, made a momentous decision. Effective with the coming season, the old 750 cc sidevalve/500 cc overhead valve setup was to be replaced by a simple 750 cc displacement limit.

With so little notice, Harley-Davidson's strategy was largely dictated by the criticality of time. A smaller version of its 883 cc Sportster was in order, but 200 of these would have to be built, and a testing program was also essential before turning these machines loose on the tracks. Consequently, the Racing Department adopted a three-phase approach. During the coming 1969 season, if a destroked Sportster could not be readied by then, Harley riders would continue to campaign on the sidevalve KR series. Its proven reliability and level of performance were considered reasonable offsets to the expected developmental problems of the enemy camp, which would either field their traditional 650 cc machines or risk reliability problems with any overnight 750 cc versions. There was also at least a fair chance of having an overhead valve engine ready for 1969.

123

The second phase of Milwaukee's strategy was, of course, the 750 cc Sportster, to be accomplished by destroking the 883 cc engine from 96 mm to 82 mm. This model, the XR, would be intended for one or at the most two years of competition. The Racing Department was well aware of the racing limitations of the iron-barreled Sportster, whose design represented the state of the art for touring motorcycles of the mid-1950s.

Consequently, phase three would be an all-new aluminum alloy engine. The envisioned extensive development program would run concurrently with the campaigning of the stop-gap small Sportster, the iron XR.

1969: The KRs' last hurrah

The AMA did not approve Harley-Davidson's ohv hurry-up destroked sportster prepared for the 1969 season. The reason for the disapproval was the AMA's insistence that Harley-Davidson actually have ready for sale the minimum 200 motorcycles required by the rules. Milwaukee had assured the AMA that sufficient components had been manufactured to assemble 200 machines, but this was not good enough. It seemed that the AMA was partly motivated by a desire to prove at long last their freedom from Harley-Davidson dominance. Consequently, Harley-Davidson would campaign its sidevalve KR series against 750 or 650 overheads during 1969. Triumph and BSA fans were jubilant, for they felt certain that their brands would reek havoc on the hopelessly outclassed primitive sidevalves. Their revenge for the 'old rule' would be sweet, they thought.

Things proved otherwise. Mert Lawwill became the new number one rider and Harley-Davidson riders won over half the 1969 National Championships, with wins in all four major categories, the half-miles, miles, TTs, and road races. Moreover, their two road racing wins were both of the prestige events, Daytona and Louden (Maconia). Most of their competitors were on Triumph and BSA 650 twins; however, the sidevalve Harleys also defeated the ohv British triples in road races and at Nazareth, Pennsylvania. Nazareth was a big 1 1/8-mile dirt oval, at which the threes made their dirt track debut. The theory was that 650s were better for half-miles and TTs, but for road racing and mile tracks the triple's horsepower would be decisive. The theory was wrong.

At Daytona, much of the decisive action was in the hands of mechanics. The 200-miler was delayed for one week because the riders didn't want to run on the rain-soaked course. The delay was a godsend for Harley-Davidson as it had inexplicably showed up with motorcycles which were some five mph slower

Right top: **The last of the species, this 1969 KRTT, is one of only eight built to team specifications and is almost the same as the 1968 versions. The front forks and brake are Ceriani units. A larger Fontana front brake unit was later used on the unsuccessful iron barrel XRTT.**

Right bottom: **Owner Stephen Wright illustrates the much smaller size of the last generation KRTTs as compared to the original layout. The eight 1969 KRTTs were the only ones equipped with megaphone exhausts. Harley-Davidson was the first to use the streamline shaping at the rear of the seat.** *(Stephen Wright, Sam Hotton.)*

than the previous year's. The Milwaukee team was beset by a myriad of problems, most serious of which was erratic carburetion caused by varying diaphragm spring tension on the new racing Tillotsons.

With an additional week's grace, the pit crew was able to sort out most of the problems, and Cal Rayborn won his second consecutive 200-miler. His competition from second-placer Ron Grant, Suzuki, and the several Yamaha riders was intensfied by the AMA's recent allowance of five-speed gearboxes.

Both Daytona and Louden were also tributes to the incomparable Cal Rayborn, while Nazareth was the property of the sport's premier mile-track rider, Fred Nix. It was arguable that both Rayborn and Nix could give up bags of horsepower within their respective specialities and still remain masterful. Nevertheless, *Cycle World* was sufficiently moved to reverse its long-standing editorial slant.

In the August 1969 issue, *Cycle World* staffer Dan Hunt said:

'In terms of development of a given design, they (Harley-Davidson side valves) are no less sophisticated than a Honda six or an MV three, and they (H-Ds) were now holding their own against the inherently 'better' ohv designs.....It is general knowledge that the Milwaukee concern puts more money into racing, which in the end produces results. Riders in the opposing camps say they have no reason to believe that this pattern will not continue. So Harley may be able to withstand the pressure of a season that is truer to the spirit of Class C than ever before.'

Two years later, Hunt allowed himself a backwards glance to put Harley-Davidson's former sidevalve racing into perspective. After almost three seasons of experience with the new rules, Hunt remarked (in the October 1971 *Cycle World*), *'Harley didn't dominate with their KR only because they were 750s running with a pack of 500s. They won because they backed a team of good riders with consistent factory support.'*

An Editorial

Over a dozen years have passed since the end of the old 750 sv 500 ohv rule, and during this period two additional considerations have arisen which could influence one's opinion of the old rule. First, there was the collapse of the British motorcycle industry. It has become increasingly apparent that among the British industry's managerial mistakes was a lack of attention to the American market.

In this respect, the termination of BSA's Gold Star production at the end of 1963 must surely have been one of the biggest mistakes ever made by motorcycling management. During the thirteen years of 1955 through 1967, BSA twins won a total of three AMA National Championships, while Gold Stars won twenty-four titles, and Triumphs won twenty-eight. Despite the BSA Star Twin's dominance of the 1954 Daytona 200, a continuous and serious factory development program would have demonstrated the superiority of the older Gold Star singles over the twins.

America's Tom Sifton, and later, C.R. Axtell, prepared the most powerful 500 cc BSAs ever raced. Sifton's 1958 'Goldie' produced 58 hp, and Axtell's singles of the early 1960s were doubtless operating in the same hp area. These two builders were left to their own resources, a fact which speaks volumes for factory disinterest. Given a reasonable amount of factory support, one can but wonder how much better BSA's American racing experiences would have been, and whether there would have been so much perceived unfairness in the 750 sv/500 ohv rule.

The Triumph and Norton situations were analogous. For the 1966 Daytona 200, the Triumph factory demonstrated its first visible interest in the American circuit. Triumph's serious commitment produced numerous innovations from the factory and rewarded them handsomely with back-to-back Daytona wins in 1966 and 1967, and No. 1 plate honors in 1967 and 1968. Prior to 1966, the AMA's Triumph riders got their horsepower gains through either the American distributors or by dealing with a number of small-scale private American businesses which constituted a mini-industry aimed at making the USA's Triumphs faster than they ever were in Britain.

Norton, admittedly the victim of the worst part of the AMA's history, can hardly be excused for quitting forever after 1954. When its American competition program ended, Norton dropped out of sight in the USA market.

In addition to the British industry's lack of factory development, a second 'happening' of the past dozen years is relevant to a consideration of the old Class C mixed-bag rule. This second factor is the complete dominance of the Harley-Davidson XR in today's flat track racing, a dominance completely nondependent on special treatment in the rule book. It will be recalled that *Cycle World's* Gordon Jennings had postulated a theory in 1965 which was apparently not shared by his boss; namely, that Harley-Davidson would be even more dominant under a rule with a single displacement limit regardless of engine type. Jennings' theory has been proven by the XR Harleys.

In summary, the 750 sv/500 ohv rule was originally intended in 1934 to de-escalate the level of factory racing involvement in the depression years. In the economically disastrous 1930s, neither Harley-Davidson nor Indian felt any threat from British motorcycles, technically or on the sales front. Consequently, inclusion of 500 cc overheads in the Class C formula was more academic than defensive. By 1938, Milwaukee and Springfield found it impossible to stay out of racing. By 1941, the Class C game was essentially a re-established Class A program, in that competitive motorcycles were significantly different from their touring counterparts.

In the mid-1950s, Harley-Davidson virtually assumed control of AMA racing due to the decline of Indian. During this period, the continuing improvements in 500 cc ohv performance motivated Milwaukee to assume a defensive role via the rule book. Harley-Davidson's hold on the AMA was evidenced by the banning of the Manx Norton. Norton, in a way, was kicked out for doing a better job of building specialized racers than its competitors. On the other hand, the Norton firm seemed to lack a reasonable interest in its American fortunes.

By the late 1950s, Harley-Davidson was probably surprised at its own success, as the 750 cc sidevalves were producing about twice the power of their

1934 progenitors. Milwaukee continuously ran a full-time factory racing organization. Meanwhile, technical development of British motorcycles for the AMA circuit was in the hands of their American distributors and independent small-scale American speed equipment concerns. Moreover, the BSA and Triumph distributors never supported a whole stable of racing stars as did Harley-Davidson. Consequently, the 'real world' difference in potential between the 750 sidevalves and the 500 overheads was clouded over by the difference in factory support.

The foregoing paragraphs give the author's interpretation. Interestingly, Ed Kretz and Dick Klamfoth related nearly opposite views on the fairness of the mixed-bag rules. Kretz, who raced both sidevalve Indians and overhead valve Triumphs, said the AMA tried to keep things fair. Continuing, he said the compression-ratio limits were necessary to keep the 500 cc overheads from dominating. Klamfoth, on the other hand, said there was a basic imbalance. Dick went on to say that he never had enough horsepower on his BSA flat-trackers to match Harley-Davidson. In any event, two issues are debatable: the advisability of mixed-bag rules, and the specific formula for combining different designs into one class.

Somehow, long ago, the Olympic ideal got lost in the shuffle. Harley-Davidson helped to kill it by racing sidevalves long after these machines were extinct in the street market. But in the end, the 750/500 rule's death was not so much a matter of logic as it was a matter of politics. There was a new balance of power, for BSA and Triumph were now corporate AMA members. There was also the democratization process of the Competition Congress. Did this 'new order' restore the Olympic ideal? Hardly, for today's AMA racing machinery is further removed from 'standard' street motorcycles than ever before. But that is a story which will unfold in the coming pages.

The iron barrel

For the 1970 season, Harley-Davidson was ready with its stop-gap model XR flat tracker. The frame was based on the late-1967 KR roadracing layout, and was built from one-inch diameter, 0.065 inch wall 4130 chrome moly steel. The swinging arm was made of 1.5 inch diameter, 0.095 inch thick 4130. To minimize flexing, the swing arms were mounted in large pre-loaded Timken bearings. The front forks were Cerianis, and the rear shocks were Girlings.

The bore and stroke were 3.005 inch (76 mm) by 3.291 inch (82 mm). The intake valve was 1 5/16 inch and the exhaust valve was enlarged to 1 3/4 inch. Initially, the standard compression ratio was 9.5:1, but this was subsequently lowered, first to 9:1, and then to 8.5:1 because of overheating problems. A single Tillotsen diaphragm carburetor was employed. The power band was quite broad, 4800 to 7800 rpm. The engine pulled well from 3000 rpm, unlike the old KR sidevalves which were reluctant to operate below 4000 rpm. When

The 1970 iron barrel XR racer was virtually a destroked Sportster engine in a new frame.

(AMF/Harley-Davidson.)

the XR was introduced, Dick O'Brien stated that the horsepower was 62 at 6200 rpm, but he would not disclose the maximum power, in keeping with a long-established company policy.

Overheating became so severe that as many as four oil coolers were installed on the factory team machines! A contributing factor to overheating was the minimal to non-existent finning near the base of the cylinders. For the factory team, an ugly makeshift dual carburetor setup was devised, with the rear cylinder getting its induction from the left side and the front cylinder breathing from its right. The rear cylinder on these twin carb models was apparently an adapted front jug, with extensive welding around the intake port resulting in a homemade appearance.

1970: The low point

For the first time in the Grand National Championship series, a Harley-Davidson rider didn't finish in the top five slots of the seasonal standings. Moreover, only two Harley riders were among the top ten, Mert Lawwill and Mark Brelsford in the sixth and seventh spots. Harley-Davidson's share of the 1970 Championship races was seven out of twenty-five, or 28 percent, the lowest it had ever been. BSA was the top brand, with ten titles, six of them at the hands of Jim Rice. Other marque win totals were: Triumph, 5; Suzuki, 1; and Honda, 1.

Daytona was a particular disappointment for Harley-Davidson. Their best rider, Cal Rayborn, qualified his overhead valve XR at 145.091 mph, which was a slower pace than his 1969 sidevalve qualifying trial. The fastest Harley qualifier was Bart Markel, whose 147.540 earned him the 15th spot. Milwaukee's seasonal wins included four half-miles, two short tracks, and a TT; races in which horsepower and overheating were not so dominant as in the miles and roadracing.

At Bonneville, Cal Rayborn piloted an 89 cubic inch Sportster-based streamliner to a new American and International record of 265.492 mph, and erasing Don Vesco's recent Yamaha mark of 251 mph. The 700-pound machine had an 88 inch wheelbase and rolled on 5.50 x 15 tires. The bore was 3.38 inches, and the 5 inch stroke restricted engine speed to 6000 rpm. Nevertheless, piston speed was near 5000 feet per minute. The fuel was 70 percent nitromethane and alcohol. The record run was accomplished despite three previous serious crashes which had necessitated considerable repair work.

Gene Romero, Triumph, won the No. 1 plate. A missing rider was Fred Nix, who was fatally injured in an off-season dune buggy accident.

1971: Drifting along

In 1971, the venerable Dick Mann put BSA in the limelight by annexing the Grand National Championship. About the only bright spot for Harley-

Davidson was Mark Brelsford's winning of the Louden 100-mile road race, but Louden was a short twisty circuit where horsepower was not so crucial as in more typical road races. As things turned out, Brelsford's Louden ride would be the only road race title taken by the stop-gap iron XR.

The iron XRs did perform better than generally anticipated at the 1971 Daytona – that is while they were running. Qualifying runs were now accomplished over the full road race course instead of the outer banking only. Rayborn and Brelsford qualified in the number two and three spots at 105.678 mph and 105.613 mph. Improved acceleration in the infield was the key, as their 146-148 mph runs on the big oval were seven to nine mph slower than the BSA and Triumph triples. The enhanced performance was attributed to the twin Mikuni carburetor setup, with the 36 mm units bored out to 37 mm. Although relatively heavy at 340 pounds, their low center of gravity contributed to good handling. A large fiber glass air box was installed over the two carburetors, both of which were now mounted on the right side.

In the 200-miler, Rayborn experienced a rare failure of the gearbox selector mechanism. Brelsford's engine blew up, and Mert Lawwill crashed after getting a flat tire. Roger Reiman, on a self-prepared XR, finished fourth, although he had qualified well down, in 27th spot.

1972: The alloy XR

The problems of the iron barrel XR were fully anticipated and required more than a simple switch to aluminum alloy jugs. The original XR engine was a souped-up mid-fifties touring motor, and in the new Class C scheme of things – a contemparary state-of-the-art touring design would be inadequate for racing. The Class C environment not only permitted but even necessitated a top-to-bottom redesign if Harley-Davidson were to stay competitive. Dick O'Brien and other Harley staffers had closely followed trends in engine design concerning porting and connecting rod geometry, and the Racing Department was determined to incorporate the latest thinking into the new XR series. Moreover, fundamental strategy decisions had secondary spin-off effects on components not originally targeted for rework. The end result was a completely revamped alloy engine which, despite its similar appearance, had little in common with its iron predecessor.

The design of the new alloy XR engine was an evolutionary process which reflected the joint efforts of several key personnel. Working with O'Brien were: Peter Zylstra, who had raced motorcycles in his native Holland, project engineer Matt Kroll, Clyde Denzer, and John Pohland.

On first thought, the effect of connecting rod length on power characteristics might seem unimportant, but this is not so. For a given stroke, the acceleration and deceleration pattern of a piston is determined by the length of its connecting rod. For example, on the power stroke a shorter rod will produce greater acceleration away from top dead center than would a longer rod. Likewise, the shorter the rod the quicker the deceleration of the piston   131 near bottom dead center during the end of combustion and the beginning of the exhaust stroke. Consequently, the shorter the rod, the more time the piston spends traveling near its maximum speed.

There is an inertial resistance to accelerating an intake charge and to expelling its exhaust gas remnants, and the significance of this 'drag' effect accounts for valve overlap in all four-stroke engines. Because the piston of a short rod engine spends less time 'hovering' near either end of its travel and more time moving significantly, it is feasible to open the intake valve earlier because the effective cylinder vacuum occurs sooner.

A short rod engine also places less stress on the main bearings and rod bearings, since angularity between the crank and the rod occurs sooner. The quicker angularity hastens relief of momentary stress at and near top dead center of the combustion cycle, when the rod and crank are in alignment and the piston in effect tries to push the rods and crank down through the bottom of the crankcase.

A disadvantage of the short rod engine is the increased sideloading on the piston and cylinder barrel. Nevertheless, the Racing Department was convinced that shorter connecting rods were needed.

From studies of other high performance engines, a rod-to-stroke ratio of near 2:1 was considered ideal for the new engine, whereas the iron XR's rod-to-stroke ratio was 2.3:1. To obtain the target 2:1 ratio with the tentatively selected 75.5 mm stroke, 6 inch rods would have been required. However, due to the 45° V-positioning of the cylinders, the piston skirts would have collided near bottom dead center. Furthermore, even if the piston skirts were shortened to accommodate a pair of 6 inch rods, the cylinders would have to be shortened too much, for as the V-disposed cylinders were brought down they would also come closer together. This closer placing of the cylinders would have sacrificed cooling fin area and would have complicated the already difficult job of arranging inlet and exhaust plumbing. The final judgment was a compromise rod-to-stroke ratio of 2.15:1, resulting in a rod length of 6.438 inches, an inch shorter than the iron XR's rods. As new rods had to be fabricated, the opportunity was taken to lighten them and improve reliability by eliminating the old stress-inducing practice of pressing in the big end bearing's outer race. Instead, the bearing was allowed to run directly against the rod.

With these decisions out of the way, the seemingly simple task of cylinder barrel design could at last be finalized. When the alloy XR project was begun, nothing had been certain except that alloy cylinders were mandatory. As a testimony to the complexity of cause-and-effect engine design relationships, the apparent starting point had been deferred until well into the engineering task.

In addition to the changeover to aluminum alloy cylinders, the cooling problem was tackled by increasing the cooling fin surface area. Although the alloy barrels were over an inch shorter than their iron predecessors, the number of cooling fins was increased from 11 to 12. In addition, the fins were larger in diameter. Whereas the iron barrel finning was largely nonexistent near the base, the new jugs had effective fin surface from top to bottom. Another significant cylinder change was the switchover to long hold-down studs which extended through the cylinder heads. In the old engine, the shorter studs secured only the barrels and the heads were bolted to the cylinders. The new setup lowered the loads on the base of the cylinder. Finally, where the cylinders and heads joined, the gas seal was accomplished by lapping the cylinder and head together using a fine grinding compound. The cylinder head gasket was dispensed with.

As improved flow characteristics were a high priority, O'Brien secured the services of C. R. Axtell, well known for his development of the BSA Gold Stars successfully campaigned by Sammy Tanner and others. An outcome of Axtell's work was the decision to scrap the traditional 90-degree included angle between the intake and exhaust valves, and change to a 68-degree angle. The classic 'hemi-head' with its high-domed piston had been the hallmark of good design for a generation, but the ever increasing engine speeds in racing had stretched flow demands beyond the hemi-head's capabilities.

The 90-degree hemi-head theory counted among its attributes the ability to use larger valves than would be possible with a lesser included valve angle, but this advantage had gradually become offset by other problems. In the first place, the trend to higher compression ratios had necessitated radically domed pistons with large reliefs for the valve heads. While fine for moderate engine speeds, the old configuration produced a valve-masking effect at higher revolutions, and in a sense the classic 90-degree layout choked on itself. The final irony was the proof that maximizing the valve sizes, the very object of the 90-degree included angle, was in fact detrimental to *optimum* racing performance in the new heads!

The term 'optimum racing performance' is more appropriate than 'maximum racing performance' since the strategy was to provide good power over a broad range of engine speeds. Consequently, the staff sought to maximize flow through the midrange of valve lift rather than to maximize flow at maximum lift. The valve sizes were continually reduced until optimum flow characteristics were achieved. The outcome was a pair of valves unusually small for each 375 cc cylinder head. The new XR exhaust valve was 1.380 inches at the head, a reduction of 3/8 inch compared to the iron XR exhaust valve, and providing 21 percent less valve head area. Likewise, the new intake valve head was smaller than the iron XR's 1.650 inches compared to 1.937 inches a drop of 15 percent in intake valve head area.

Although the alloy XR pistons had a much flatter dome, the compression ratio was upped to 10.5:1 from the old XR's maximum of 9.5:1. To seal the combustion, two compression rings were used with one oil ring. The rings were cast iron with molybdenum-filled outer edges for contacting the cylinder bore.

Intake valve timing of the new engine was the same as in the iron XR. Measured at 0.053 inch of tappet lift, the intake opened at 33 degrees before top dead center and closed at 53 degrees after bottom dead center. However, the exhaust timing provided an additional 11 degrees of duration, opening at

65 degrees before bottom dead center and closing 16 degrees after top dead center.

Twin Mikuni carburetors were used. The Mikunis were sized at 36 mm for short flat tracks and TTs, and up to 39 mm for mile-track racing. Originally, ignition was solely by Fairbanks-Morse magneto, but subsequently a dual ignition system has been provided. By flipping a switch, the rider can select either magneto or coil ignition, and each system has its own plugs. The dual setup is, of course, a tribute to the historical problem of magneto reliability, although O'Brien said that the magnetos were working better than ever in 1980.

The remaining new XR modifications were aimed primarily at reliability. New right and left flywheels were one-piece forgings which included the mainshafts, rather than having the shafts welded in. The new crankpin was hollow, considerably larger in diameter, untapered, and pressed to fit, each characteristic a change from iron XR practice. The right crankcase had metal added around the main bearing support. The main bearing size was increased to 2.04 inches. The beefed-up cases required the shortening of the camshafts in order to retain the original timing-side cover. Additional metal was also provided at the front and rear of the crankcase halves in order to provide extra strength for the cylinder mounting studs.

1972: Number One again

Mark Brelsford returned the coveted No. 1 plate to the Milwaukee brand at the end of 1972, by winning the Ascot TT and two half-mile races. Although Harleys won but seven of the twenty-four Nationals, they were still the top brand as five other marques split the other titles.

In the 'horsepower' events, the mile-track races and road races, the new alloy XR proved capable. Cal Rayborn won the Indianapolis 125-mile and Monterey, California 125-mile road races. Canada's Dave Sehl won the Atlanta, Georgia 25-mile title on the one-mile track.

An oddity was Harley-Davidson's absence at the 1972 Daytona 200. The company had been unable as yet to assemble the minimum of two hundred alloy XRs required for Class C eligibility, although it had sufficient parts on hand to do so. While the AMA home office had provisionally agreed to declare the aluminum XR eligible, the AMA Executive Committee vetoed this plan. Thus, 1972 clearly marks the **end of Harley-Davidson dominance of the AMA.**

Among the 'loyal opposition' for 1972, a significant event was what proved to be Dick Mann's last National Championship. Mann went out like he came in, by winning the Peoria TT, the same event that started his collection of 24 championships back in 1959. A remarkable aspect of Mann's career was his versatility. When he won the 1972 Chicago mile-track National, his next to last title, he had completed a thirteen-season quest for a unique honour. He became the **first rider to have won National Championships in all five**

categories; short track, half-mile, mile, road racing, and TTs. A popular bench-racing topic during Mann's long career was the question of how well he might have done if he had linked up with Harley-Davidson. It's still an interesting question.

1973: The lowest win-rate

The low point of Harley-Davidson's Class C racing history as measured in winning percentages was the 1973 season. In 1973, the Milwaukee motorcycles won six of the twenty-four titles, or twenty-five percent. However, AMA racing was now a five-sided affair, so a twenty-five percent rate was hardly a poor showing. In addition to Harley-Davidson, other marques winning National titles and their numbers of wins were: Yamaha, 7; Kawasaki, 5; Triumph, 3; Suzuki, 2; and Norton, 1. BSA was now essentially out of the picture because of their financial collapse, and another five years would pass before the next BSA title.

The most spectacular accident in Daytona's history had much to do with finishing Mark Brelsford's brief but successful career. Brelsford and teammate Larry Darr collided and Brelsford's machine instantly became a huge sphere of flame. Daytona was a complete disaster for Harley-Davidson, whose top finishers were Dave Sehl and Mert Lawwill in 16th and 17th positions. Lawwill would have done better except for losing a gas cap and paying for it with extra time in the pits. Rayborn spilled after his engine momentarily froze and then freed itself. Oddly enough, Rayborn, Brelsford, and Darr had been the three fastest qualifiers.

Kenny Roberts was the top points rider for the season although he won only three of the twenty-four Nationals on his Yamaha. A notable non-Harley victory was scored by Dave Aldana in the mid-season Ascot TT. Aldana's ride was the **first Norton AMA title in twenty years.**

1973 marked the departure of two of Milwaukee's finest, Bart Markel and Cal Rayborn. Markel announced his retirement. Since fracturing his pelvis in the 1972 Denver, Colorado mile, Markel had run an abbreviated schedule. His record of twenty-eight National titles was not surpassed until Kenny Roberts won his twenty-ninth in 1980.

Calvin Lee Rayborn, obviously the premier American road racer of his time, was killed in New Zealand on Dec. 19 while racing a Suzuki. During his peak years of 1968 through 1972, he won over 40 percent of the AMA's National Championship road races. He amassed this record despite lack of top notch equipment in 1969 and 1970, when Harley-Davidson had been caught by the new AMA rules. Rayborn was also quite popular in Britain for his 1972 and 1973 appearances in the Trans-Atlantic Match Race Series, during which he proved himself capable of beating the best British riders. Rayborn's last National title was his July, 1972 victory in the Monterey, California 125-mile road race. As of this writing, this is also the last Harley-Davidson road racing National Championship.

1974: Whatever happened to Harley-Davidson dominance?

A new fan in 1974 would have wondered about stories of Milwaukee racing dominance, and then would have passed such stories off as pure nostalgia. Through 1974 eyes, the racing fan would have seen that Harley-Davidson's win rates over the past five seasons of 1970 through 1974 were: 1970, 28 percent; 1971, 29 percent, 1972, 29 percent; 1973, 25 percent; and 1974, 35 percent. As of the 1974 season's end, Harley-Davidson's five-year cumulative average win-rate was 29 percent.

The big story of the 1974 season was not a Harley-Davidson one; it was Kenny Roberts. Roberts won six Championship races, at least one of each type except the half-mile, and grabbed the number one plate.

History was made at Daytona. For the first time in the event's thirty-five years. Harley-Davidson *deliberately* did not field a team of riders. The track was now too large and the horsepower too small to compete with the big two-strokes.

Other notable 1974 events involved Gary Scott and Mark Brelsford. Scott won the 250 cc non-titled road race at Louden, held in conjunction with the annual 100-mile big motor title. Scott's win on an Aermachi-built two-stroke twin was Yamaha's first 250 cc expert road racing defeat by a Harley-Davidson since 1964.

A bench mark was the mid-season Leguna Seca (Monterey), California 75-mile road race. Only three four-strokes competed in this National Championship: a Kawasaki Four, a BMW, and a lone Harley-Davidson piloted by Gary Scott. Although Scott rode very well, his alloy XR was hopelessly behind in horsepower compared with the field of big two-strokes. *Cycle World* described Leguna Seca as probably the last appearance of the roadracing XR Harley-Davidson. The prophecy was indeed correct and it was the end of an era. Meanwhile, the BSA and Triumph triples, which had been all-conquering a scant three years before, were also things of the past.

1975: Consistency over brilliance

After finishing second for three consecutive seasons, Gary Scott benefited from the AMA Grand National formula. Although he won only two Nationals compared with Roberts' six, Scott's more consistent performance gave him the No. 1 plate at the season's end.

Nevertheless, it was Yamaha-mounted Kenny Roberts who made a bigger name for himself in the history books. It will be recalled that as of 1972, Dick Mann was the only rider to have won titles in all five modes: short track, half-mile, mile, road racing, and TTs. To accomplish this distinction, Mann had labored through thirteen seasons. In 1975 Roberts pulled off the amazing feat of winning all five types in a single season!

The Terre Haute, Indiana half-mile on August 17 was a turning point in Harley-Davidson racing. **For the first time in Class C racing history, the** 136 **starting lineup for a National Championship event was a one-brand show;**

every finalist was on a Harley-Davidson. During the year, Harley's win-rate climbed from its lately customary thirty percent to forty-five percent, but this was mainly due to the now two-sided scope of Class C racing; i.e., Harley-Davidson versus Yamaha. The latter equaled Milwaukee's nine wins, and Triumph riders copped two events.

Significantly, only three road races were on the 1975 calendar, less than half the average over the previous five years. Moreover, the five future seasons of 1976 through 1980 would yield a total of only twenty-three road race Championships, compared with a total of thirty-three for 1970 through 1974. This shift in emphasis, the continuous improvement of the XR flat trackers, Yamaha's lack of success in flat track development, and the disinterest of other Japanese-bike factories and distributors, had laid the foundation for a return of Milwaukee dominance.

1976: Springsteen takes over

Although Yamaha had matched Harley-Davidson in total wins during 1975, a closer examination of the 1975 results brings into focus the problem Yamaha faced in 1976. In the previous season, Harley had outscored Yamaha by nine to two in half-mile and mile-track championships, the backbone of the Grand National Championship Series. Accordingly, the Yamaha factory invested $50,000 in the development of a special 750 cc vertical twin engine for Robert's 1976 campaign. It produced a total of twenty-five engines, the then-current minimum.

However, the results were disappointing, as Roberts failed to win any of the first seven Nationals entered with the special engine, dubbed the OW72. He finally managed two flat track wins, the San Jose and Terre Haute half-miles, but Harley's Jay Springsteen outscored Roberts by seven wins to four wins, and Springsteen was number one.

1977, 1978: Things get one-sided

Jay Springsteen was the seasonal points leader in both 1977 and 1978. He thus was the only rider other than Resweber to have won three consecutive number one plates.

As the National circuit was now dominated by flat track events, and with the stagnation of the OW72 program, Milwaukee returned to its former role as the majority 'shareholder'. In 1977, Harleys won 61 percent of the Nationals. and in 1978 they garnered 57 percent of the titles. Roberts saw better 1978 opportunities on the European Grand Prix circuit, and with his departure Harley-Davidson riders occupied all of the top ten spots in the 1978 standings.

Another distinction of the 1978 season was the emergence of former Grand National Champion Mert Lawwill as a builder/tuner. Lawwill's approach was to set up the XR Harleys for higher rpms, which was unpopular with the factory because of resultant extra demands on Milwaukee for the manufacture   137 of replacement parts. Harley-Davidson was now in a position where it should have been able to relax somewhat, emphasizing reliability over speed, as it would dominate in any case now that the OW72 had been left behind. It was therefore ironic that the next evidence of Class C's fundamental instability would come from the privateers. At the May 1978 San Jose half-mile, privateer Garth Brow won over a field composed entirely of other Harley-Davidson privateers, the machines having been set up according to Mert Lawwill's theories and using Mert Lawwill speed components.

The 1976 team. *Left to right* they are: Jay Springsteen, Corky Keener, Rex Beauchamp, Gregg Sassaman, and Mert Lawwill. Mert has since become a successful builder/tuner, specializing at first in the XR Harleys, but more recently on Yamaha dirt-trackers. *(AMF/Harley-Davidson.)*

138

The XR's crowded exhaust plumbing is evident in this photograph taken in the Harley-Davidson Racing Department. On the left is Dick O'Brien, chief of Harley-Davidson racing since 1957; on the right is Carroll Resweber. *(AMF/Harley-Davidson, author.)*

The first BSA National Championship since 1972 was captured in the 1978 Ascot TT by Alex Jorgensen, and as of this writing, no subsequent BSA titles have been won. Although Harley-Davidsons out-scored its flat track rivals by a cumulative 33 to 9 during 1977 and 1978, Yamaha's road racing posture was even more dominant during the period. Yamahas won all six road races in 1977 and all five in 1978. Indeed, by the season's end, Yamahas had won twenty-one consecutive road race Nationals over a five-year span.

Disgruntlement with Yamaha's Daytona monopoly was revealed in Dan Hunt's June, 1977 *Cycle World* article entitled, 'They Held the Wrong Race on Sunday'. Hunt's title was a reference to the four-stroke formula racing in which BMWs, Moto Guzzis, Ducatis, and the ubiquitous Japanese fours had competed two days prior to the Daytona National. Class C had now turned 180 degrees off its original course, as water-cooled four cylinder two-strokes were as far away from the concept of standard motorcycles as can be imagined. Meanwhile, new definitions had to be invented to provide an equivalent of the old Class C setup. Time and inevitable engineering progress had made possible the racing metamorphosis, and the new power structure had permitted it. 139

1979; 1980: A privateer is champion

Steve Eklund campaigned a mixture of Yamahas and Harley-Davidsons all the way to the No. 1 plate in 1979. He was the first privateer to be the Grand National Champion since Dick Mann had done it in 1963. For 1980, the new 'Numero Uno' was factory rider Randy Goss whose consistency overcame a total of one win during the season.

Kenny Roberts entered the February 1980 Houston, Texas Astrodome Nationals, and won the TT event on a Yamaha to draw even with Bart Markel for most career wins. In August, Roberts' grand prix schedule allowed him time to win the Leguna Seca 200-mile National road race at Monterey, California, again Yamaha mounted. His total of 29 AMA National titles was beyond reach of any rider but Jay Springsteen, whose total of 25 titles did not increase until the latter won the Houston Astrodome National Championship in February 1982. Both riders then drew level with 29 titles each.

A signal event was the August 24 Indianapolis, Indiana mile-track National. Ricky Graham won the twenty-lap title race at an average of 100.947 mph, **the first Class C flat track National won at over 100 mph.** Of the 26 Championship races, Harley-Davidson riders won 15, for a 57.7 percent rate. Yamaha's championship winnings included not only their customary road race laurels, in this case five pavement titles, but three TTs and a short track as well.

A significant road racing rule change affected the outcome in one National Championship race. During 1980, 1025 cc four-strokes were pitted against 750 cc two-strokes breathing through carburetor restrictor plates and 500 cc two-strokes without carburetor restrictors.

Suzuki broke Yamaha's road race monopoly when Wes Cooley won the Elkhart Lake, Wisconsin 72-mile road race, the first Yamaha defeat in AMA Championship road racing since 1976. Moreover, Cooley's Yoshimura R&D machine was the first four-stroke road race win since Cal Rayborn's 1972 Indianapolis title.

Speculation persisted that Class C Grand National racing would convert from the 750 cc formula to 500 cc racing in the near future. Meanwhile, Harley-Davidson's latest production run of XR racers had been limited, as Dick O'Brien related that Milwaukee continually considered the possibility of a major rules change.

The author has emphasized the evolution of Class C in the Harley-Davidson section as this marque alone has survived throughout the era, and also for the benefit of readers making a cover-to-cover tour of the book. The Class C message of course applies also to Indian.

A recurring suggestion over the years had been to the effect that separate road racing and dirt track points chases should be conducted by the AMA, with a No. 1 plate being awarded for each category. In a sense, with the exception of some privateers such as Gary Scott and Steve Eklund, two separate seasonal battles had been conducted for some time due to the special competence of Yamaha and Harley-Davidson within their separate spheres. The traditional

American preference for flat track racing and the deterrent effect of Yamaha's road racing monopoly on rival manufacturers had combined to reduce spectator interest in the pavement events.

The outlook at the end of 1980

Barring some kind of handicapping formula analogous to the old mixed-bag rule, it appeared unlikely that significant technical variety would return to either American flat track racing or road racing. Some movement in this direction had occurred with a road racing mixture of 500 cc two-strokes and 750 cc four-strokes, as well as the use of carburetor restrictor plates on the 750 cc two-strokes, but these handicapping techniques had so far had little effect on the outcome. Accordingly, the AMA decided that the carburetor restrictor plate technique would be applied throughout Class C effective with the 1982 season. Beginning in 1982, all 750 cc racers were to run with carburetor restrictors, but 500 cc machines were to run unrestricted.

Thus, the AMA renewed its commitment to the handicapping principle which had been a cornerstone of the original Class C concept and the modus operandi of American motorcycle racing from 1934 through 1968. The abandonment of the old mixed-bag rule in 1969 had permitted a sort of Darwinian evolution of the species during the next decade. The inevitable but unpredictably rapid emergence of a dominant marque in each of the two highly different modes, the dirt and the pavement, had produced the European scenario so long dreaded. On the other hand, motorcycle racing in the USA had enjoyed a brief period without acrimonious debate over controversial handicapping formulae. At the end of 1980, it appeared that all the pros and cons of mixed-bag racing would once again return in the near future.

Harley-Davidson appeared mainly interested in holding on to the No. 1 plate and, as road racing had become a relatively small-time AMA affair, Milwaukee had little motivation to develop competitive pavement racers. Moreover, any competitive road racer under existing or foreseeable rules would bear no resemblance to Harley-Davidson's backbone, the big V-twin.

1981

In the February issue of the AMA official magazine, *American Motorcyclist,* the association announced an indefinite continuation of existing 750 cc dirt track racing rules. Despite the case against the Harley-Davidson dirt track monopoly, many Harley XR riders didn't like the idea of giving a handicap to the Japanese brands. The Harley riders stated that the orientals had the money and know-how to build competitive flat trackers and shouldn't be rewarded for their lack of interest. Ironically, the establishment of democracy in the new-generation AMA had largely been the by-product of an earlier rider's revolt against the old mixed-bag rules which had favored Harley-Davidson. But now, with the power in their hands, the riders looked at their own short-   141 run interests and lined up with the brand they were favoring – Harley-Davidson.

Also, in early 1981 it appeared likely that Yamaha would be ready for the 1981 season with their own 750 cc V-twin racer. In the off-season they had announced two touring model V-twins, a chain-driven 920 cc and a shaft-driven 750 cc. For their home market, Yamaha had announced a chain-driven 750 cc model, just the ticket for American flat tracking. They were thus able to meet the old 'stock' machine requirement by having built the minimum required number of motorcycles, the historical yo-yo minimum now being set at twenty-five. Moreover, rumors were rampant that Honda had their own Harley-Davidson XR which they were busily studying, with an eye towards building their own in-line V-twin racer.

In May, rumor became reality when rookie rider Jim Felice qualified for the San Jose mile on a Yamaha 750 V-twin. The motorcycle was backed up by a trio of famous number-one riders: Kenny Roberts, Mert Lawwill, and Dick Mann. Moreover, the noted C.R. Axtell had done the flow work and reshaping of the cylinder heads. Lawwill, in charge of engine work, announced that 25 of the Yamaha V-twins would be built for sale to interested privateers. Mann was responsible for frame design and fabrication.

The Honda rumor was likewise turned into fact. Honda had developed several 750 V-twin flat-trackers, at a unit cost of $13,500, each equivalent to the cost of three superbikes. Meanwhile, despite the outcry of the Harley-Davidson riders, and despite the rush of Yamaha and Honda to the 750 V-twin concept, the AMA seemed certain to require carburetor restrictors on 750 cc bikes effective with the 1982 season.

The V-twin Harley-Davidsons had been the number one sellers in the USA prior to the Japanese takeover of the market. Later, the Harleys had borne the brunt of condescension and ridicule by fans of the new mainstream Japanese big four brands. But by 1981, Milwaukee had the last laugh on the dirt tracks if not in the show rooms, for the V-twin was at last recognized as having technical merit. Harley-Davidson's V-twin policy had not been pure nostalgia after all, and two Japanese giants had flattered Milwaukee by following suit. Strangely, the forthcoming new rules might make it unnecessary for the Japanese firms to build V-twin racers. Paradox was paramount!

Moreover, the balance of the 1981 season provided even more irony. As Mike Kidd campaigned the Roberts-Lawwill-Mann Yamaha 750 early in the season, it became obvious that more development was needed before the Japanese V-twin would be highly competitive with the Milwaukee variety. The seasonal points race tightened and the Yamaha V team increasingly felt the pressure of competition and the frustration of moving slower than the Harleys. While not backing Mike Kidd effort officially, the Japanese concern was obviously stretching cooperation to the point of near sponsorship. Consequently, race fans were startled when Kidd switched over to a Lawwill-tuned Harley-Davidson to finish the season, this move apparently with the tacit approval of Yamaha. Kidd, 'the Yamaha racer', went on to annex the No. 1 plate on a Harley by finishing in front of Gary Scott in the season ending and

142

customarily climactic Ascot half-miler.

The proverbial 'cherry on the sundae' was the AMA's final fling at fickleness. Rider pressure at last prevailed and the AMA reversed itself for the third time during the season! At press time, the word was: a straight-out 750 cc rule for 1982, with no mixed bag of motor sizes and handicapping carburetor restrictors. Whether this would be a short-run plan, or whether long-run fundamental changes were yet forthcoming, was obviously a matter of conjecture.

Regardless of future rules changes or foreign challenges, one could expect that Milwaukee would continue to make whatever kinds of racing motorcycles would be required to challenge for the number one plate.

Henderson

Although the Henderson was never intended to be a racing motorcycle, the classic in-line four merits attention for its prominence as a long-distance record-setter. Born in 1912, the Henderson made its first mark within a year, as in October of 1913 Carl Stevens Clancy became the **first motorcyclist to circle the globe.**

Record runs began in earnest during 1916, when Roy Artley set four consecutive San Francisco-to-Los Angeles marks. In 1917, Artley set a 24-hour sidecar record of 706 miles, beating the old mark by 122 miles. He then clipped almost nine hours off Cannonball Baker's (Indian) Three-Flag record time for the Canada-to-Mexico journey, doing the trick in 72 hours and 25 minutes. Alan Bedell made the first Henderson transcontinental record in 1917, his time of 7 days, 16 1/4 hours bested Cannonball Baker's Indian feat by 3 days and 19 hours.

There followed a five-year drought in major record-setting activity, which was broken on May 31, 1922 by Wells Bennett, heretofore known for his Excelsior successes in all forms of competition. (The Henderson, by now, was an Excelsior product, the founders William and Thomas Henderson having sold out to Ignaz Schwinn in 1917.) Riding the rough creaky boards of the rapidly deteriorating Tacoma, Washington speedway, Bennett established a 24-hour record which would last for fifteen years. He motored 1,562.54 miles, an average of 65.1 mph, and beat Baker's Indian distance set at Cincinnati in 1915 by over 28 miles.

The nearest thing to a transcontinental race occurred in September of 1922, when Bennett departed from Los Angeles on a Henderson 28 hours after Baker left on an Ace. Hampered by his unfamiliarity with transcontinental routes, the Henderson rider gave up in Pennsylvania when it became obvious he would not better Baker's latest effort. As the 'Hen' had owned the cross-continent record for five years before bowing to the Ace, Bennett was not long in reattempting the feat. The following month, Bennett beat Baker's Ace time   143

Maldwyn on a Henderson four cylinder, ready for a try at the world's 24 hour record. Cincinnati two-mile board speedway, 1917. See clipping on Page 45 - Big Book.

Maldwyn Jones prior to his unsuccessful 24-hour record attempt at Cincinatti in 1917.

(Maldwyn Jones.)

by over 7 hours, and established a new motorcycle record of 6 days, 16 hours, and 13 minutes.

By this time, record-setting on public roads was drawing criticism from the general public, and in fact the M&ATA had refused to officially recognize such records as of 1919. It was therefore typical of the era when Wells Bennett was arrested in Los Angeles based on knowledge that he was in the process of a record run, and not for violation of the speed limit which he had carefully observed in the metropolitan areas.

A flurry of Three-Flag activity in 1923 culminated in Bennett's second Three-Flag title of the summer. On August 29, Wells Bennett set the last of the classic era's Three-Flag marks at 42 hours and 24 minutes, thus displacing by 37 minutes Paul Remaley's Indian Scout honor.

As the bulk of Henderson records were set by Bennett in 1922 and 1923, details of this Henderson vintage are provided as follows:

Motor   – Four cylinder sidevalve; bore, 2 11/16 inches stroke, 3 1/2 inches; displacement, 79.4 cubic inches (1301 cc).

Pistons   – Die cast split skirt alloy (optional, cast iron).

Crankshaft – One piece forged steel.

Bearings   – Plain bearings throughout engine.

Wells Bennett posed for this shot, in conjunction with his 24-hour record at the Tacoma Speedway in May 1922.   *(Bob Smith.)*

Lubrication– Wet sump, positive force feed through drilled crankshaft.
Valves   – Side by side.
Clutch   – Multi-disk wet plate integral with flywheel.
Brake   – Rear brake only, external contracting band.
Tires   – 20 inches (wheel diameter) by 3 1/2 inches.

After Bennett's exploits of the early twenties, Henderson's competitive laurels were few. In 1924, near San Bernardino, California, Fred Ludlow made an attempt on the American speed record of 129.61 mph made by Ace's Red Wolverton. Although good publicity was generated by the photos of the streamlined Henderson, the result was a disappointing 127.1 mph. Company advertisements of this effort were tricky, as they correctly but misleadingly stated that Ludlow's speed was the fastest sanctioned 1/4 mile ever turned. This statement was possible because the 129+ Ace record was over a measured   145

1/10 mile. Incidentally, timing of Ludlow's run was by four stop watches.

In 1928, at the Muroc Dry Lake in California's Mojave desert, C.A. Cameron set a 'stock' 100 mile record average of 94.5 mph. Cameron's ride was apparently the last Henderson record-setting experience.

In 1929, Henderson design reverted to the ioe layout originally used from 1912 through 1919. This was a tribute to the late Will Henderson, who stuck with the ioe idea when he left Excelsior and formed Ace. Although the resultant 'K' series Hendersons of 1929, 1930, and (early) 1931 were the fastest Hendersons ever, company headline-seeking was restricted to the hillclimbing exploits of Super X riders. Thus, unlike its 1929-1930 championship Super X brothers, when production ceased in early 1931 the illustrious Henderson four quietly passed from the competitive scene, its greatest glory some seven years distant.

Bennett after his record-setting transcontinental ride of November, 1922.

(Motorcycle and Bicycle Illustrated.)

Indian

The IOE era. 1901-1911
in the beginning....

During the dawn of motorcycling, the fortunes of Indian racing were inseparably linked to those of Jacob DeRosier. In 1902 Jake DeRosier entered the Indian factory shortly after production began, and remained a Hendee Company employee for several months. During this period he gave up motor-pacing work for bicycle racers and began demonstrating the new Indian motorcycle for its own merits. Shortly, he became a well-known figure at the earliest motorcycle race meets and hillclimbs.

In the **first public competition entered by Indian** on July 4 and 5, 1902, three Indians were entered in the Boston to New York endurance run, **the first such event ever held in the United States,** and each finished with a perfect score. DeRosier is believed to have been one of the three victorious riders. Their 1902 Indians were typical of the first four years of production. Each bike's single 15.85 cubic inch cylinder sloped rearward like the back half of a V-twin, and acted as its frame's down tube. Valve gear was intake over exhaust (ioe or pocket valve); the intake valve operated automatically by vacuum. These splash lubricated engines were rated at 1.75 horsepower, sufficient to propel the 110 pound lightweights from 5 to 40 miles per hour.

Motorcycle competition in these earliest days centered around efforts to prove the hill-climbing prowess, reliability, and economy of pioneer machines. Speed was self-evident in comparison to the horse and bicycle. Consequently, the second American enduro of July 3-5, 1903, was a real feather in the war bonnet of the winner, Indian President George M. Hendee. The route was over a course from New York City to Springfield, Massachusetts, and thence back to New York. On September 5, 1903, Indian rider George N. Holden won the nation's **first long distance track race** at the Brighton Beach dirt track of New York City. Holden covered 150 miles 75 yards in the allotted four hours. The happy nonchalance of low-speed motorcycle competition was near its end.

During the next two years, Indian competition continued in the same mode, with numerous events being held in the New England area. An exception to the northeastern emphasis occurred on January 29, 1904, at Ormond beach, Florida, when an Indian turned the mile in 1 minute, 9 1/5 seconds. In 1905 DeRosier entered the Federation of American Motorcyclists (FAM) National Enduro, using one of the first Indians equipped with a spring fork. These forks, comparable to those on the early English Triumphs and American Clevelands, actually provided more fore and aft wheel movement than vertical motion. The 1905 Indians also featured twistgrip throttle and ignition controls, an idea copied from the Curtiss motorcycle, but instead of Bowden wires, the control was accomplished through a system of rods and universal joints.

147

In 1906 a 42 degree V-twin was experimented with and entered by DeRosier in several races. This new twin-cylinder motor fitted in the conventional bicycle-type (or diamond) frame, and was adjudged sufficiently successful to market to the public effective with the 1907 model year. The 42 degree included-angle of the cylinders was to remain an Indian twin characteristic throughout the Redskin's life during the next 46 years.

On September 12, 1906, Louis J. Mueller of Cleveland, Ohio, and George Holden of Springfield, Massachusetts, set a long distance record which was to stand for several years. With each rider using his own new two-cylinder Indian, the pair completed their New York to San Francisco journey in the record time

Oscar Hedstrom poses with his first hand-built Indian in 1901. Indian singles remained quite similar until the advent of loop frames in 1909. Most endurance runs and speed demonstrations during the 1901-1906 era were made on machines similar to this original prototype.

148   *(Bob Smith.)*

of 31 days, 12 hours, 15 minutes, covering 3,476 miles. A most prominent motorcycle racer was Indian star Stanley T. Kellogg. On July 4, 1906, Kellogg won the fifth annual endurance run of the Federation of American Motorcyclists (FAM), and Indian co-founder Oscar Hedstrom finished second.

During 1907, T.K. Hastings won England's Thousand-Mile Trial, later to evolve into today's International Six Days Trial. This was the **first entry of an American machine by an American in an English contest.**

1908, 1909, 1910: competition intensifies

By 1908 the emphasis in motorcycle competition had shifted from endurance runs to speed contests. Speed events had been around from the beginning, but had originally been regarded as a sidelight during the annual FAM meets. In the east, Stanley T. Kellogg won numerous dirt track races during the summer and autumn of 1908. Los Angeles, California emerged as a motorcycle racing center during 1908, with record-setting activity at two dirt tracks; Agricultural Park and the original Ascot Park.

Indian design progress up to 1908 had focused on their stock bicycle-like machines. Racing had been conducted on either modified stock bikes or on experimental jobs destined for subsequent production as stock touring machines. An example of a preproduction test vehicle was the motorcycle loaned to DeRosier for a race on the Clifton, New Jersey velodrome (bicycle track) in July 1908. This machine was strikingly un-Indian in appearance, featuring a conventional 'loop' frame instead of the traditional 'diamond' bicycle-type frame. The resultant lower center of gravity greatly improved handling, and DeRosier was able to set a quarter-mile record of 13 1/5 seconds for an average speed of 68.2 miles per hour. Jake also won the three-mile event on the same day in 3 minutes, 3 seconds. As a result of his performance at Clifton, DeRosier was added to the official Indian racing team as a salaried rider.

A new twist in Indian policy was apparent in their 1908 catalogs, which included the Wigwam's (factory's) **first production model designed solely for racing.** This diamond-framed production racer gave ample evidence of Indian's total commitment to racing. The machine was available in both twin and single cylinder versions. The twin was a 61 cubic inch (1000 cc) model rather than the standard 38 inch twin, and the single was accordingly a 30 1/2 inch model. Valve gear was inlet-over-exhaust, but Indian had at last changed from automatic to mechanical inlet valves.

Two long-distance successes further highlighted Indian's 1908 racing season. B.A. 'The Terrible Swede' Swenson won the 978-mile New York to Chicago race in 33 hours and 26 minutes. Meanwhile, in England, T.K. Hastings again won the Thousand Mile Trial on his Indian twin.

On March 14, 1909, promoter Jack Prince opened the Coliseum motordrome in Los Angeles, his first track expressly designed for motorcycle racing, a short (1/3-1/4 mile) wooden oval, with corners banked at an angle of 25 degrees. Prince also put up sufficient financial inducement to lure DeRosier   149

The first production Indian racer was this 1908 diamond-framed model. For each cylinder, there was a single push-pull rod which actuated both the overhead intake and side exhaust valves.   *(Stephen Wright, author.)*

away from his familiar New England surroundings for a series of match races with Paul Derkum, Reading-Standard rider and local hot shot. DeRosier won every race, Derkum moved on to easier competition at other tracks, and the motordrome era was at hand.

It is almost impossible to underrate the impact of the wooden motordromes on American motorcycle history. From a technical viewpoint this kind of racing emphasized speed and neglected handling and braking, trends which lasted until the 1950s because of subsequent 'road race' course design. More importantly, during the motorcycle's critical period of competition with the automobile, the two wheelers emerged as the symbol of danger and recklessness.

By 1909, board track interest had mushroomed, the new tracks seemingly being built almost every month. Accordingly, the Hendee Company had joined forces with Jack Prince and built a 1/3-mile circular motordrome in Springfield, Massachusetts. Shortly after the track opened, Freddy Huyck displaced DeRosier as the record-holder for the mile, Huyck doing the trick in 43 1/5 seconds in July. In October Charles Spencer and Charles Gustafson Jr., each on his own Indian, used the new bowl to set new amateur distance records for three through twenty-four hours, and time records for distances of 200 through 1000 miles. They covered 1000 miles in 22 hours, 20 minutes, 59 seconds, and, for the 24 hours, logged 1,093 miles, 1,151 yards.

Buoyed by his several successful tracks, Jack Prince opened a second
150   motordrome in the Los Angeles area in early 1910, the site being the seashore

The cylinders of early Indians were secured by three long studs. The single left-side stud for each barrel are seen in this view. *(Stephen Wright, author.)*

community of Playa del Rey. As the new Playa del Rey track was a one-miler instead of a 1/3-miler, it was a much faster course and DeRosier set the 100-mile record at 1 hour, 26 minutes, 14 seconds. This new record came despite DeRosier's misfortune of running out of gas on the 99th lap, which cost him some 5 minutes of pushing.

1911: – The peak of prestige

At the Los Angeles Coliseum Motordrome on February 7, 1911, De Rosier rode perhaps his most brilliant ride ever in the United States. In attempting to lower his own 100-mile mark, Jake established new records for distances from two to ninety-two miles before running out of fuel. During this nonstop performance on his famous number 21 pocket valve (ioe), he averaged 43 2/5 seconds per mile and covered 83 miles in the hour. By comparison, DeRosier's time for 90 miles was 1 hour, 6 minutes, 33 2/5 seconds; while the best British time to date was 1 hour, 50 minutes, 59 4/5 seconds. Likewise, over all the shorter intermediate distances, it was the same story. For instance, the 10-mile rates were: DeRosier, 7 minutes, 1 4/5 seconds; Britain's best, 10 minutes 26 2/5 seconds. Continental 'official' records were only marginally better than British efforts and way off the Yankee pace.

Also in February 1911, the British correspondent of *Motorcycle Illustrated* commented about the great interest aroused in Britain over the announcement that, following his upcoming Isle of Man TT entry, DeRosier intended to compete man-on-man against Charlie Collier (Matchless), at Brooklands or

151

some other suitable venue. The correspondent was moved to remark: *'Only sheer patriotism permits us to prophesy a British victory...,'* and then somewhat suspiciously added, *'...the atmospheric conditions in America are alleged by our own technical experts to be more favorable for high speeds than ours, and nobody here will be surprised if DeRosier fails to repeat some of his home records whether he licks Collier or not'.* American records were indeed suspect.

On April 4, 1911, a youthful Don Johns, using DeRosier's number 21 Indian, set amateur records for two through twenty miles at the Playa del Rey board track near Los Angeles. His twenty-mile time was 14 minutes, 23 3/5 seconds, for an average speed of 83.37 miles per hour; this compared to the best British amateur twenty-mile ride of 56.39 miles per hour. However, in light of Johns' subsequent employment by Indian and his use of DeRosier's personal mount, Johns' classification as an amateur was somewhat artificial.

Meanwhile, Indians continued to win most races throughout the United States, whether on the boards or the horse tracks. The 'iron redskins' also held almost all speed and distance records. On June 26, 1911, Volney Davis departed San Francisco on his Indian twin, in an attempt to set a new transcontinental record. The stage was now set for what was surely the most dramatically successful month ever enjoyed by the Indian motorcycle.

On July 3, when Volney Davis arose at 4 am in Salt Lake City, it was 11 am in Douglas on the Isle of Man. Jake DeRosier, black theatrical tights and all, was running true to form and in first place in the TT. Jake had finished his first lap in 46 minutes, at just about the time that Davis was trying to find an open restaurant.

Having fallen six times during TT practice, DeRosier had already re-marked, 'This ain't gonna be no picnic.' He was, therefore, not in the best shape at the race's outset, and after crashing severely in the third lap, the dazed DeRosier finished the race in twelth place. But it mattered not to Indian adherents, for the Indian team finished one, two, three. Oliver C. Godfrey was the winner. After Charlie Collier (Matchless) was disqualified for taking on fuel at an unauthorized point, C.B. Franklin was awarded second place and A.J. Moorehouse, third. Their machines were breathed-on production ioe models, with the cylinders sleeved down to be within the 585 cc displacement limitation.

On July 4, at Indianapolis, Indiana, forty thousand people were on hand for the American Independence Day celebration. Among the festivities was 'The President's Race', which consisted of a five-lap duel between Johnnie Sink on a Flying Merkel and E.G.Baker on an Indian. Following his defeat of Sink, Baker was escorted to the President's box, where he was congratulated by the President of the United States, William Howard Taft. Little did either man know that someday Baker would be nicknamed 'Cannonball' and that his fame would be as enduring as Taft's.

At the famous Brooklands concrete oval in England, Jake DeRosier whose American records had been viewed skeptically, equalled his best American mile effort by turning the mile on July 8 in 41 1/5 seconds. One week later, in a series of three match races, DeRosier won two races to Charlie Collier's one.

Collier's Matchless seemed the equal of DeRosier's Indian, but the American was too trackwise and managed to outsmart Collier in the only race not marred by equipment failure.

On July 16, Volney Davis completed his transcontinental crossing at New York City in the record time of 20 days, 9 hours, and 11 minutes. Along the way he had time to sleep 4 to 6 hours every night, time to eat well, time to do an engine overhaul, time to do some mild partying, and time to stop in Cleveland for a respectful social call on the co-holder of the previous record. In a sense, and intending no belittlement of his extraordinary effort, Volney Davis was the last man able to set a transcontinental record in the style of a gentleman.

As for Indian's 1911 Isle of Man sweep, accounts vary. At least one current historian has termed the surprisingly good peformance of the Scotts, including Frank Phillipp's fastest lap, as the most significant development in the first TT over the long mountain course. Others have said that the American twins' all-chain drive and countershaft gear boxes, fortuitously matched against the newly laid-out steep mountain course, hastened the demise of the British belt-driven brigade.

The impact may have been even more far-reaching. Consider the words of none other than the famous British motorcycle journalist 'Ixion', who wrote for *Motorcycle Illustrated* under his real name, B.H. Davies: *'The trade was proposing to abandon the race next year, as it is very costly, and racing is a less remunerative advertisement with us then with you. But I do not see how it can decently be abandoned after such a smashing foreign victory.*

Before the end of that momentous Indian year of 1911, George Hendee fired Jake DeRosier, who then became an Excelsior factory rider. DeRosier would never quite rise again to the same prestige he enjoyed with Indian. As for Indian, at the close of 1911 their machines and riders held **every** one of the FAM's 121 recognized pro and amateur speed and distance records. Unknowingly, the manufacturer, like the rider, had seen its most glorious single season.

The 8-valve era, 1912-1915

During 1910, Oscar Hedstrom began designing the four and eight valve singles and twins, which formed the backbone of Indian record attempts until the mid-twenties, although curiously never part of Indian's several Isle of Man teams. These machines began to appear on the tracks in late 1911 and early 1912, and were expected to reaffirm Indian supremacy over the recently significant Excelsior. The 8-valve timing gear was similar to the standard (pocket valve) engines; however, the crankcase was much larger than standard.

Additionally, the cylinder heads were detachable and carried four vertically disposed valves operated by pushrods and forked rockers. The 8-valve twins were soon to prove out as the fastest motorcycles in the world.

Indian's most prestigious 1912 performance was at Brooklands, where C.B. Franklin passed through what was regarded as a performance barrier. He rode one of eight 8-valve Indians in Britain for 300 miles in less than 300 minutes   153

(4 hours, 42 minutes), establishing official world records for distances covered in 2, 4, 5 and 6 hours. In the Isle of Man, there was no factory backing, and the best Indian placed eighth.

Meanwhile, American board track design had evolved into its final shape for the short motordromes. Whereas the original track had been moderately banked at 25 degrees in the corners, the banking was repeatedly increased on subsequent tracks until 60 degrees became the norm. This had the immediate effect of producing higher speeds, and a less obvious but sinister impact of track safety, as riders were now becoming intimately familiar with the phenomenon of 'G' forces. To lose traction in the steeply banked turns was exceedingly dangerous to both rider and spectator, as centrifugal force could send rider and machine high into the air.

Above: **Jake DeRosier** shortly before his departure for the Isle of Man in 1911. Curiously, upon his return DeRosier was not immediately provided with one of Oscar Hedstrom's new 8-valve machines. Consequently, the DeRosier/Indian partnership was dissolved and Jake headed for Chicago, where he was hired to race Excelsiors. *(Bob Smith.)*

Right top: A 1913 ioe engine, representing the ultimate development of the original Hedstrom design. As there was little oil sling to the front cylinder, an auxiliary supply line was provided. *(Dewey Bonkrod, Sam Hotton.)*

Right bottom: The 8-valve twins which Hedstrom introduced in mid-1911 had much larger than standard crankcases. They were therefore later termed 'big base' 8-valves to distinguish them from the 8-valve machines designed after 1914 by either Charles Gustafson Sr. or Charles B. Franklin. The rider is Charles 'Fearless' Balke, and the location is the one-mile Playa del Rey board track near Los Angeles. *(Stephen Wright.)*

Standing behind this big-base 8-valve is Fred Luther. The high profile of these big-base bikes led some to call them camels. On such a big-base, Britain's Bert LeVack missed by 24 hours the honor of being the first motorcyclist to exceed 100 mph in Britain. That these 1911-born 8-valves were well ahead of the British and European mainstream is clear, for in 1921 LeVack set a British speed record of 107.5 mph on his ten year old 'outdated' camel. Unfortunately for Indian, LeVack's record came the day after a Harley-Davidson was the first 100+ mph motorcycle in Britain. *(Stephen Wright.)*

1912: An accident changes history

Early in 1912, a young Indian rider named Eddie Hasha began to make his mark on an 8-valve Indian at the Los Angeles Coliseum Motordrome, defeating all the established stars such as DeRosier. Hasha repeatedly set professional class records, while Indian's Don Johns cleaned up in the amateur races and record books. Hasha then headed east to conquer new worlds.

On September 8, 1912, at Newark, New Jersey, Eddie Hasha's Indian began to miss during the third lap of the day's last race, number 13, and Ray Seymour shot past. Hasha reached down with his left hand to adjust something, the motorcycle at once picking up speed and closing the gap with Seymour. In the next instant, Hasha and his Indian shot up the bank coming out of the number four turn in front of the grandstand. By the time the machine came to rest, Hasha, a rider named Albright, and six spectators were dead or dying. The grim reality of Newark and the resultant publicity and local

Charles B. Franklin at Brooklands in 1912, after becoming the first rider to travel 300 miles in 300 minutes. From 1914 through the late twenties Franklin designed some of the fastest motorcycles in the world. Surprisingly, his sidevalve bikes were generally swifter than any competing overheads. *(Ted Hodgdon.)* 157

threats marked the beginning of a slow decline for the 1/4-mile midget motordromes, or 'murderdromes' in the language of the press. It was one of the few cases in the history of the *New York Times* that motorcycling was front page news. The Newark accident was perhaps the single most damaging blow ever to affect American motorcycling.

1913: No more DeRosier, no more Hedstrom

On February 5, 1913, Jake DeRosier returned from California to Springfield, Massachusetts, following the second operation on his leg injured the previous March. DeRosier, a member of the Excelsior team since being fired by Indian in mid-1911, had gone down in a Los Angeles match race against Charles 'Fearless' Balke on March 12, 1912. Three weeks after returning to Springfield on February 25, 1913, DeRosier died as a result of the third operation on his leg. On March 1, 1913, almost a year after his accident, DeRosier was buried. President Hendee ordered the Indian factory flag half-masted and all work suspended for 5 minutes while DeRosier's funeral procession passed by the giant Indian works.

Motorcycle Illustrated said *'During his career Jake DeRosier won over 900 races. He was a unique figure, developed by a rapidly rising sport, and possessed to a full degree the peculiarities of the racing motorcyclist, in addition to a magnetic personality. There was but one Jake DeRosier, there never will be another, for the conditions under which he achieved fame never will return. He was without question the most famous racing motorcyclist the sport has known in any clime'.*

On the same day that DeRosier was buried, Oscar Hedstrom's retirement became effective. As the engineering brain behind all Indian's success, his departure was a serious blow to future Indian racing. During the 1913 racing season Charles 'Fearless' Balke became the standout Indian star, winning important road races, board track, and dirt events.

1914: The Cannonball epic begins

On May 14, 1914, E.G. Baker established the first of his several transcontinental records. Using an interesting strategy, he timed his San Diego, California departure so as to ride most of the distance between weather fronts. Seemingly as a blunder, he left San Diego during steady rain. However, within an hour he was greeted by sunshine, and did not encounter rain again until two thirds of the way across the continent. His record time of 11 days, 12 hours, and 10 minutes meant good-bye forever to the more civilized efforts of predecessors like Volney Davis. Henceforth, with ever improving roads and motorcycles and with a growing population of service stations, increasing importance would be placed by the transcontinentalists on the ability to persevere with minimal sleep and rest. It should not be understood, however, that 'Cannonball' Baker had an easy time of it. Like Volney Davis, he also endured axle deep sand in the southwestern desert and axle deep mud in the midwest. Baker's machine was equipped with the swinging-arm leaf spring

158

The legendary Erwin G. 'Cannonball' Baker stands beside rider Fearless Balke at Rockford, Illinois in 1913. Balke's wet right leg is the result of oil mist from open-ported cylinders.

(Stephen Wright.) 159

frame, termed the 'cradle spring' frame, and much was made of this by the Wigwam's Publicity Department.

On May 16 and 17, 1914, 'Fearless' Balke won several events at Chicago's Hawthorne dirt track, using an eight-valve twin. Three weeks after his Hawthorne triumphs, Balke's luck ran out. As a testimony of the careless racing supervision of the times, Balke was killed on June 8 when he ran into a track roller hidden in the hanging dust clouds.

In 1914, Independence Day was again sufficient reason for a major motorcycle race. At Dodge City, Kansas, in the heart of the great plains country, a 300-mile 'road race' was staged on a two-mile flat dirt oval. Indian fulfilled its traditional role by taking first in the hands of Glenn 'Slivers' Boyd, so named because of an earlier board track fall and long slide over the splinters. Indian fielded both ioe (pocket valve) machines and 8-valves, a fact not reported in either *Motorcycle Illustrated* or *Motorcycling*, and typifying the American motorcycle press' noninterest in things technical. In a change of policy, Harley-Davidson had dared to challenge Indian's supremacy and Excelsior's customary second honors, but all the Harleys suffered mechanical problems.

The other big event of 1914 was the Savannah, Georgia 300-mile road race of November 26. The course was more of a genuine road race layout than Dodge City, as the Savannah 300 was accomplished by turning twenty-seven laps over an 11 1/2-mile circuit. Indian was again triumphant, Lee Taylor being the rider.

1915: 'Crevvy' and the first sidevalves

Indian's 1915 racing and record setting efforts were noteworthy on two accounts. These were the emergence of yet another star rider, and the introduction of a motorcycle power plant which was to change the future of American motorcycling.

More fundamental to an understanding of Indian racing trends was the resignation of co-founder George Hendee as the company's general manager. While Hendee remained as president, reports of his increasing interest in his newly constructed country estate were the evidence of a managerial chasm within the Hendee Manufacturing Company. Coupled with the 1913 departure of Hendee's original partner and engineering genius Oscar Hedstrom, this degradation of managerial expertise was to play no small part in the coming challenge to Indian's traditional role as racing champion.

This is a small base 8-valve. Credit for design of these engines has been attributed to both Charles Gustafson Sr. and Charles B. Franklin by different writers. At the various race meets and record attempts both Gustafson and Franklin were usually in attendance, so it is probable that they were more or less equals at the time of the small-base's debut in 1916. Note that the lines of the fuel tank differ considerably from those fitted to the earlier big-base 8-valves, and that the small-base model is smaller overall than the big-base. The small-base crankcase was the same as that used for the standard production ioe models. Both the big and small-base 8-valve twins and 4-valve singles used plain crankshaft bearings, a bronze bushing at each end suspending the crankshaft.

160   *(Stephen Wright, Sam Hotton.)*

Throughout the summer of 1915 Ray Creviston was the dominant flat tracker in the sport, recording wins over Excelsior's newest hope Bob Perry, as well as 'X' riders Carl Goudy and Glenn Stokes, and Cyclone's brilliant Don Johns. But Crevvy's longest win of the summer was 50 miles. On the heels of Harley-Davidson's Venice 300 win the previous November, the Milwaukee brand had now added the Dodge City 300, the Le Grand 200, and the Saratoga 100-mile road races to its 1915 trophy case. Meanwhile, Excelsior's Bob Perry had won the only other long event, a 100-mile flat track tour at Madison, Wisconsin. Therefore, when Erle Armstrong rode his Indian to victory on August 16 in the Tacoma, Washington 300-mile board track event, there was at last a measure of restored redskin prestige.

In the autumn months, track racing honors were divided between Indian and Excelsior, with the Chicago 'X' getting slightly the better end of it, and Harley-Davidson out of the limelight. Another Indian star was rising, as Jim Davis won his first major event, using an 8-valve and taking the Columbus, Ohio 25-mile flat track feature.

In the long distance record setting field for 1915, E.G. Baker began the 'Three Flag' tradition by riding his Indian from Vancouver, British Columbia to Tijuana, Mexico in less than 3 1/2 days. Advertisements in the motorcycle press mysteriously referred to Baker's machine as having a new type of motor which would be standard in the forthcoming 1916 models. However, the accompanying photos showed an earlier picture of Baker and a typical ioe Indian twin. In fact, Baker had used one of the first of the soon-to-be famous Powerplus motors, the L-head or sidevalve design which was to remain an Indian hallmark henceforth. Moreover the successes of this new Wigwam strain would eventually divert the American motorcycle industry from the mainsteam of worldwide motorcycle development. The 8-valves, designed primarily for board tracking, were still a force to be reckoned with, particularly in short record-setting attempts. But although the 8-valves would be around for some years yet, a new era of Indian racing was at hand.

1916: The sidevalve era

It will be recalled that Indian's pioneering designer, the great Oscar Hedstrom, had left the Wigwam in 1913. The behind-the-scenes difficulties of Indian's early-teens management have been well chronicled in Harry V. Sucher's *Iron Redskin*, and do not merit repeating here. It is sufficient to note that the departure of Hedstrom cleared the way for the transition into a more economically producible sidevalve design originally engineered by Reading-

Right top: **This is a rare photo, for Bob Perry is known to have raced an Indian only on this one occasion at Denver, Colorado. Perry was synonymous with Excelsior, but he borrowed this 4-valve Indian after his own 'X' broke down. The machine is a 'half-twin', a genre popular for many years in the USA's racing.** *(Stephen Wright.)*

Right bottom: **After Cannonball Baker's several Three-Flag and transcontinental Indian records, much favorable publicity was generated for the cradle spring frame. The spring frame was introduced in 1913.** *(Dewey Bonkrod, Sam Hotton.)*

Standard's Charles Gustafson, Sr. now the Wigwam's Chief Engineer.

While the original managerial motivation of the Powerplus was its economical producibility, Gustafson was able to demonstrate that his new L-head engine was in fact more powerful than the Hedstrom ioe layout. Additionally, the new Powerplus was a quieter and cleaner design, as the valve mechanism was now entirely enclosed. Of slightly smaller bore and longer stroke than either the ioe or 8-valve models, its measurements were 3 1/4 inch (bore) by 3 31/32 inch (stroke), for a displacement of 60.88 cubic inches. The crankpin was beefed up and the connecting rods were mounted on a four-row set of rollers. Wristpins and bearings were of larger diameter. The right hand (timing side) bearing was of roller design, while the left hand (drive) side was a plain bronze bearing.

Following Hedstrom's ioe practice and industry standards, the new motor operated all four valves from a single camshaft via bell cranked cam followers acting on valve lifters. The continued use of the 42 degree included cylinder angle resulted in short intake plumbing. As in the later Hedstrom engines, an oil supply line was provided near the base of the front cylinder, as flywheel action provided less oil sling into the front cylinder than into the rear. Likewise, the magneto drive arrangement was similar, although the driving gears appeared more robust. The same attribute applied to the motor as a whole, the entire layout presenting a less dainty though perhaps less artistic image as compared to the Hedstrom F-head motors.

While the immediate public response to this new 1916 'un-Indian' powerplant was one of suspicion, Erwin G. Baker continued to demonstrate the stamina and power of both machine and man. On January 29, 1916, Baker set another notable record, this time in Australia. The Powerplus carried him to a new 1000 mile record, in the time of 21 hours and 3 minutes. By comparison, the previous professional record for 21 hours was slightly over 690 miles by England's Harry Collier (Matchless) in 1909, and the best amateur distance was 945 miles by America's Charles Spencer (Indian), also in 1909.

In 1916, Ray Creviston remained the most successful flat tracker. Indian again suffered an important defeat at the July 4th Dodge City 300. At Dodge City, Springfield's top man was Speck Warner, whose fourth place finish was over half an hour behind Harley's winner, Irving Janke.

The following month, Australia's Jack Booth set three records which the Hendee company advertised as 'world's road records' these being 1, 5 and 10-mile distances covered near Melbourne, Australia on July 25. However, on the whole 1916 was not a good year for Indian racing.

The Motordromes fall from favor

The press coverage of 1916's motorcycle events was notable for the almost complete absence of board track happenings. The general public's initial curiosity had apparently been satisfied, while the dangers of the dromes had cooled the ardor of even devout motorcycle fans. Harley-Davidson had never

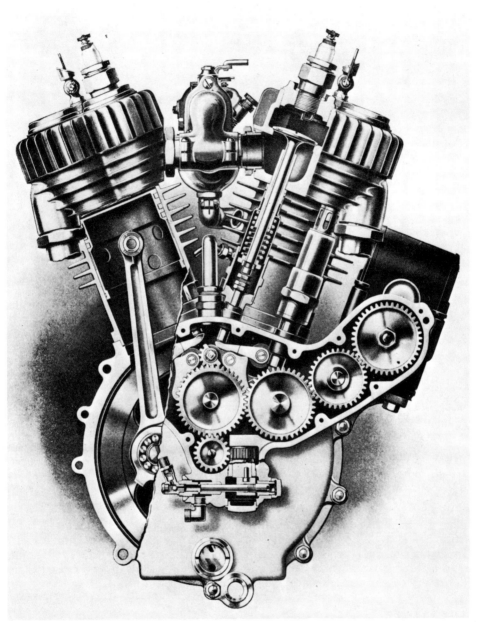

In 1915, the sidevalve Powerplus engine of Charles Gustafson Sr. superseded the Hedstrom ioe design. Whereas the ioe models had used plain bearings on both ends of the crankshaft, the Powerplus had roller bearings on the right (timing) side and a plain bearing on the left (drive) side. *(The Antique Motorcycle.)* 165

A typical Powerplus racer is seen at the Marion, Indiana 200-mile road race in 1919. The rider is New Zealand's legendary Percy Coleman. Although Coleman had lost the sight of one eye in a workshop accident, he set many Australasian records using Excelsior, Harley-Davidson, and Indian machines. His particular strength was in New Zealand's unique grass track format. Hampered by being relegated to secondary equipment not desired by Indian's American team riders, he nevertheless mightily impressed the USA's fans during his 1919 tour. *(Emmett Moore.)*

played the motordrome game anyway and had now proved that greater prestige was to be won in the long road races. Consequently, both Indian's and Excelsior's managements de-emphasized motordrome racing after 1913. Some of the short dromes, like Detroit's and Cleveland's, had quietly closed their doors after fatal accidents and others would soon follow.

1917, 1918: A slowdown

With the entry of the United States into the World War I, Indian became preoccupied with military production and problems; and in concert with Excelsior and Harley-Davidson, Indian gave no consideration to active racing support during the years 1917 and 1918. There was, however, a good deal of record-setting activity during this period. The Cincinnati, Ohio board speedway was the site of four record attempts in the summer of 1917. In June, Cannonball Baker displaced Harley-Davidson rider Alan T. Bedell as the 24-hour solo titlist at 1,386 1/4 miles. Some three weeks later Maldwyn Jones's Henderson effort was unsuccessful. Baker and Teddy Carroll then copped the 24-hour sidecar mark at 1,275 3/4 miles in August. Also in August, Baker won back the 24-hour solo record held for three weeks by Harley's Leslie 'Red' Parkhurst, Baker logging 1,534 3/4 miles.

1919

After the war, the Wigwam's top rider was Alabamian Eugene E. 'Gene' Walker. During 1919, Gene Walker won four of the nine dirt track National Championships, taking the one, five, ten and twenty-five mile titles. Although motorcycle racing continued on the big board tracks of one mile or larger circumference, the original 'motordromes' of 1/4 to 1/3 mile were no longer sanctioned.

1920

'Alabam' Walker continued his successful flat track battles in 1920. Moreover, between April 12 and April 15, Gene made a series of successful assaults on some American records established by Red Parkhurst on a Harley-Davidson. Using an 8-valve 61 cubic inch Indian tuned by Charles B. Franklin, Walker was timed on the Daytona Beach, Florida sand at 114.17 mph, but this was wind-assisted. Following international convention, he made the required two-way runs and averaged 103.56 mph. For a change, this American speed record also received recognition by the FICM, and thus Eugene E. Walker's name and his Indian's speed were duly recognized. Walker thus displaced Britain's Herbert LeVack, whose previous official record of 94.79 mph on an Indian had already been unofficially but routinely surpassed by Walker in lap after lap at the big Sheepshead race meet. Walker's 61 inch Indian not only topped Parkhurst's official 61 inch records, but also surpassed Parkhurst's unofficial 68 inch speeds.

The genius of Franklin

By now Charles B. Franklin, Ireland's gift to American motorcycling, was establishing himself as an outstanding engineering talent. His brilliantly conceived 37 cubic inch (600 cc) sidevalve Scout had become a most popular member of the Indian tribe, and its seemingly impossible power output had been rewarded by the little twin's wide adoption as a police model – and this in the land of really big motorcycles.

On September 19, 1920, near Cleveland, Ohio, Albert 'Shrimp' Burns set a 10 mile dirt track mark of 7 minutes, 53 seconds on one of Franklin's new   167 sidevalve racers. While logging this 76 mph average, Burns defeated Jim Davis on an 8-valve Harley-Davidson. How could a sidevalve defeat an 8-valved, hemispherical ohv motor? One wonders even today at this turn of events. But it was to happen again and again under Franklin's wizardry.

Although Indians won 14 of 17 National Championships in 1920, their cumulative championship mileage was only 200 miles. Harley-Davidson, on the other hand, racked up 513 miles of titles in only three events, as Milwaukee won the Dodge City 300 and the Marion 200. An oddity was the 50-mile National Championship at Ascot in which Shrimp Burns had repeatedly shown his Indian's speed margin over the factory Harleys. Although Burns was declared the winner the race was declared null and void after a protest by the Harley-Davidson forces. The issue was over the age-old problem of lap scoring.

The year of 1920 was also notable for the increasing prominence of Indian hillclimber Orie Steele. Steele won three of the five events at the Wharton, New Jersey meet, and was to remain the pre-eminent Indian hillclimber for some

Indian used a variety of frame designs. This one is similar to the 'Marion' type shown in the previous figure, but has a different upper tube and tank. Frames such as this one-off special and the Marion were termed keystone frames by the Wigwam. The rider is Albert 'Shrimp' Burns, one of the most daring of his day. The photo was taken atop the Indian factory.

(Emmett Moore.)

ten years. Albert 'Shrimp' Burns and Bert LeVack entered their names in the record books. Burns set a 100 mile mark of 1 hour, 22 minutes, 11.08 seconds during the Marion, Indiana 200-mile road race. LeVack rode a 1912 8-valve to new international records for times of 1 hour through 6 hours, and traveled over a measured Brooklands mile at 95.4 mph, which was the fastest speed yet credited to a motorcycle in Great Britain.

1921: Harley-Davidson dominance

At England's Brooklands concrete track D.H. Davidson, on a Harley-Davison, and Bert LeVack, on an Indian, vied for the honor of being the first motorcyclist to travel over 100 mph in Britain. The honor fell to Davidson on April 28. The next day, LeVack upped the British mark to 107.5 mph on his 'outdated' Indian, nicknamed the Camel for the characteristic high profile of the big-base design. In June, Freddy Dixon and Bert LeVack finished 2nd and 3rd in the isle of Man TT, and Indian won the Team Prize. Both Dixon's and LeVack's times were over ten minutes better than the previous year's winner. Their machines were 'half twins', each being a big twin sidevalve with the front cylinder removed.

The following month, at Brooklands, LeVack rode a 61 inch sidevalve twin to victory in the Brooklands Gold Cup 500-mile race. Dixon, on a Harley-Davidson, finished 2nd, and Harveyson on an Indian was 3rd. These were the only 'classy' 1000 cc machines in the field, as a 500 cc Norton finished ahead of all other 1000s. Owing to the roughness of the Brooklands oval, LeVack's winning time of 7 hours, 5 minutes, 59 3/5 seconds was some 6 minutes off the 1917 500-mile American record set by Cannonball Baker on the Cincinnati board track.

At Toledo, Ohio, Albert 'Shrimp' Burns was killed after bumping into Harley's Ray Weishaar. A top-flight factory rider for both Harley and Indian, Burns had won a number of championships. A recent notable victory was the Beverley Hills, California 15 miler in April, which Burns won with a sidevalve twin, averaging 102.55 mph and beating a field of 8-valve Harley-Davidsons. In the words of Maldwyn Jones, *'Burns was a very wild rider and took a lot of chances. He took one too many.'* Also at the Toledo meet, Indian's best sidecar pilot, Floyd Dreyer, set 61 inch sidecar dirt track records for the mile (51.60 seconds) and for 25 miles (21 minutes, 47 seconds). These records stood for many years.

The overall American racing message of 1921 was the dominance of Harley-Davidson. Milwaukee won *every* National Championship event. Having proven their point at considerable expense, Harley-Davidson withdrew factory racing support from their riders at the season's end. Excelsior also de-emphasised racing, having found the results very discouraging. The 'X' had not won a big-time race since 1916. Effective with the 1922 season they would sponsor only two riders, primarily in midwestern half-miles. Indian kept their racing organization intact, and consequently would have things their own way in 1922.

169

1922

As Indian's 1922 victories were somewhat hollow, they will not be chronicled in detail. Some individual efforts were noteworthy, however, such as Jim Davis's Beverley Hills board track record of April 14. Davis made the **all-time fastest 1 mile lap on the boards** at 110.67 mph (although this would be surpassed on a 1 1/4 mile course in 1926). Davis then used his sidevalve twin to set new records for 1 through 100 miles.

Because of numerous racing fatalities, the Motorcycle and Allied Trades Association (M&TA) decided to experiment with smaller motors during the 1922 season. Thirty and one half cubic inch (500 cc) racing had been sanctioned for several years, but now, the thirty-fifties were granted National Championship stature along with the sixty-ones. The machines used were 'half-twins,' built by removing one cylinder of a 61 inch V-twin.

Orie Steele continued his winning ways in hillclimbs. Steele was the 1922 National Hillclimb Champion by virtue of his winning the 37 inch, 61 inch and 80 inch events of the National Championship climb at Egypt, New York. A new face in hillclimbing was Joe Petrali, who won the Vallejo, California free-for-all event.

1923 through 1926: Transition

In 1919, the M&ATA had refused to grant sanctions to intercity record attempts. Indian followed this up in 1923 by announcing it would no longer support or publicize such unofficial record runs, for as a major supplier to the nation's police departments, the Wigwam could no longer endorse the required illegal speeds. The closing moments of this old Indian tradition were filled with the exploits of Paul Remaley, who twice broke the Canada-to-Mexico 'Three Flag' solo record. Remaley used the surprisingly peppy 37 inch sidevalve Scout designed by C.B. Franklin.

1923

Indian won six of the eight nationals in 1923. For a change, the Harleys were not all conquering in the long events, as Curly Fredericks took the 200-mile 61 inch crown at Wichita, Kansas.

1924

The move to smaller motors was continued in 1924, for all national championships were confined to the 30.50 inch class. Harleys again dominated, winning six of the eight title bouts. Paul Anderson, who'd transferred from Excelsior, set a one-mile 30.50 inch dirt track record pace of 79.33 mph over a 20 mile distance.

The bad news stories of 1924 were the deaths of Harley-Davidson's Ray Weishaar and Indian's Gene Walker. Walker, probably the most talented flat tracker of his time, was noted for riding carefully, never taking chances. Nevertheless, he was killed while alone on the Stroudsburg, Pennsylvania track, practicing. A winner of nineteen national championships during his six-year career, his loss was keenly felt.

1925

The on-again, off-again attitude of M&ATA towards big motors was evidenced in 1925. The 61 inch jobs were reinstated to national championship status, but Harley-Davidsons took them all. However, Indian won four of the five titles for 30.50 inch machines. Of the Indian riders, Johnny Seymour was most consistent, winning the 5, 15, and 25 mile events on half-mile tracks.

At Sellick's Beach, South Australia, Paul Anderson was reported to have made a 125 mph run, which if true and properly sanctioned, would have made him the world's fastest motorcyclist. Later in 1925, Anderson had a two-way

Johnny Seymour on a circa 1924 4-valve 30.50 cubic inch (500 cc) racer. Note the cast aluminum exhaust manifold. This machine appears to be the same one on which Seymour set an American 30.50 record of 115 mph at Daytona in early 1926. *(Emmett Moore.)* 171

record attempt at Arpajon, France. Anderson's two runs of 159.08 mph and 112.34 mph gave him an average of 135.71 mph, lifting him to a lofty height not surpassed until J.S. Wright reached 137.32 in 1930 on an OEC-Temple. However, although Anderson's speeds were recognized by the Motorcycle Club of France, they were not recognized by the FICM due to questions about the accuracy of the electric timers.

1926

In January of 1926, at Daytona Beach, Johnny Seymour set American records of 132 mph on a 61 inch 8-valve and 112.63 mph on a 30.50 inch 4-valve. Once again, these records were not given international recognition, but it is interesting to note that LeVack's current Brough Superior JAP official mark was well down, at 119 mph. On the other hand, Seymour made his run in one direction only, and the winds were not specified. So the reader can make anything of it he wishes.

The next stage of motor reduction was the advent of the 21.35 inch (350 cc) Harley and Indian ohv singles. Actually, Harley-Davidson had unveiled their 'Peashooters' at Milwaukee in August of 1925, but Indian lagged behind in this field. Nevertheless, Jim Davis rode his Indian to victory in the first 21.35 inch national championship, held at Altoona, Pennsylvania. Davis' time, on July 10, was 3 minutes, 22.4 seconds for the 5 miler, a rate of 88.9 mph. For comparison, Curly Fredericks won the 10 mile 30.50 inch at a speed of 92.5 mph, so it is difficult to see what safety progress was being made by shrinking the engines.

Curly Fredericks set a record on August 21, 1926, which was destined never to be broken. Riding on the 1 1/4 mile Rockingham, New Hampshire, board speedway, Fredericks registered the **fastest lap ever turned on the boards at 120.3 mph.** His mount was a 61 inch sidevalve equipped with dual Zenith carburetors. On the whole, Indian had the better of it, winning eight of the twelve solo National Championships in 1926.

Owing to the popularity of Excelsior's Super X 45 inch ioe, introduced for the 1925 season, the M&ATA began sanctioning championship events for 45s during 1926. Moreover, there was still a solitary 61 inch National on the 1926 agenda, so the American sport was still indecisive as to its future.

The total 1926 lineup of National Championships by motor size was: 61

Right top: M.L. 'Curly' Fredericks aboard a 2-valve racer derived from the stock Prince model, a 21.35 cubic inch (350 cc) sidevalve. Both 30.50 cubic inch (500 cc) and 21.35 cubic inch 2-valves were built, and the engines were virtually indistinguishable. *(Emmett Moore.)*

Right bottom: The twin carburetors of this motorcycle's engine mark it as an 'Altoona' motor, the name being derived from some successes at the big Pennsylvania board track. An Altoona model was used by Curly Fredericks to make the all-time fastest board track lap, 120.3 mph, but the site was the Rockingham, New Hampshire track. The frame of this particular example is not the type used on the board track version, but is the keystone type used for the hillclimbers. *(Sam Pierce.)*

inch, one; 45 inch, two; 30.50 inch, five; and 21.35 inch, five. In one of those curious twists of fate, the first 45 inch National didn't go to a Super X. Jim Davis won the 20-miler at Salem, New Hampshire (Rockingham) on a 30.50 inch Indian ohv single.

In 1926 and 1927, Indian produced a total of twenty-six 45 cubic inch overhead valve engines. Most of the engines were fitted to hillclimbing machines, two were mounted in flat track racers and at least one was configured for road/TT racing. Two of the accompanying photographs show one of the flat-trackers, which is outfitted with the last of the twenty-six engines. All of the special motorcycles were modified extensively by their owners, so that there can be no meaningful definition of a factory-original configuration.

The two camshafts ran in self-aligning ball bearings, and the crankshaft

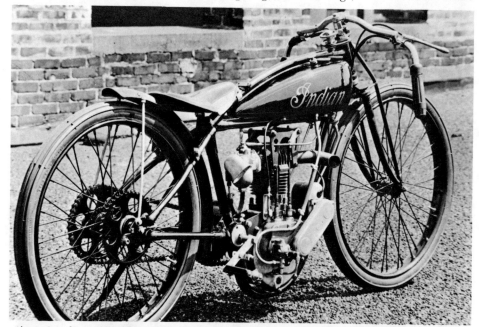

Above: **Another Prince derivative, this one a 30.50 cubic inch 2-valve engine in a frame usually used for the 21.35 cubic inch (350 cc) racer. The photo was taken on the roof of the Indian factory.**
(*Emmett Moore.*)

Right top: **The frame on this 1928 2-valve road race is similar to that of the machine in the previous figure, but in this case provision has been made for a transmission. This model won a number of victories in Germany during 1928. This machine and the previous two all feature the Schebler barrel carburettor. The photo was taken in a courtyard of the Indian factory.**
(*Emmett Moore.*)

Right bottom: **This hillclimber is the first of twenty-six overhead valve specials built by Indian in 1925-1926. All were 45 cubic inch (750 cc) machines. The serial number is A45-1.**
(*Chuck Vernon, author.*)

was also ball bearing mounted. The connecting rod big end was equipped with roller bearings, while the little end was the conventional plain bearing. One of the two oil pumps fed the lower end, and the other supplied oil to the rear of the front cylinder. The first few engines had cast iron cylinder heads but later engines were equipped with aluminum heads.

Performance of the twenty-six 45 overheads was formidable, as they used a 15:1 compression ratio and burned alcohol. In 1928, at the Muroc Dry Lake racer Jim Davis edged Fred Ludlow by two feet in the 25-mile feature event. Both Davis and Ludlow had been timed at over 126 mph on their 45 overheads.

This flat tracker, one of only two built, is the last of the 45 ohv specials built for the 1926 season. The frame is different from that of the hillclimbers. There was considerable experimentation with frames, the twenty-six engines being moved in and out of several configurations. The brake was added to permit riding at antique bike meets, as the Class A flat trackers were brakeless. The serial number is A45-26. *(Chuck Vernon, author.)*

At least one road racing version of the 1926 overhead 45s was built, as seen in this official factory photograph. *(Archives of the Indian Motorcycle Company, Sam Hotton.)*

The further forward of the two oil pumps supplies lubrication for the front cylinder walls.

(Chuck Vernon, author.) 177

Bob Armstrong, son of longtime Indian figure Erle 'Pop' Armstrong. Using this 80 cubic inch (1300 cc) motorcycle, Bob was the top amateur hillclimber of 1929. Except for the curved upper tube, this machine's frame appears identical to the 1926 45 ohv hillclimber frame.

(Emmett Moore.)

1927, 1928 and 1929

During 1927, the Wigwam won five of the nine nationals. Indian riders won every National Championship in both 1928 and 1929, a back-to-back feat unprecedented and unrepeated.

Indian's special 45 cubic inch overheads were put to good use on August 4, 1928 at Rockingham. Bill Minnick, Jim Davis and Curly Fredericks won several races with the 45s, including National Championships in both 45 and 61 cubic inch classes. These 45 overheads thus displaced the Wigwam's historic 8-valve and sidevalve 61 inchers as the stable's fastest horses.

Indian's faith in the 45 class had been endorsed earlier. In April of 1929, the Wigwam announced it would no longer support other than the 45 inch class in hillclimb competition. On the west coast, Californian P.A. Bigsby and his employer, Al Crocker, produced a number of kits for converting the

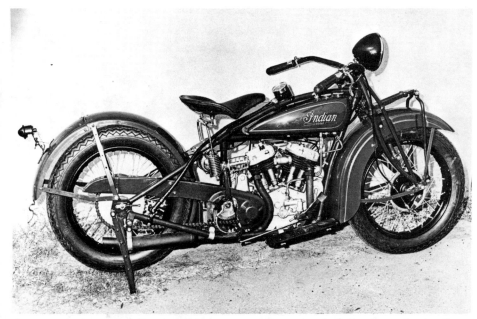

The 101 series Scout, the most popular amateur sports motorcycle during its production from 1928 through 1931. Note the T-shaped intake manifold.   *(Harry Sucher, George Hays.)*

sidevalve Scout into a hemispheric ohv machine. Swede Mattson rode an ohv Scout to victory in the 45 inch expert event of the Fresno, California hillclimb in April of 1929. Mattson continued to campaign the overhead Scout with success in the California climbs.

In 1929, Jim Davis won the only 45 inch National. Davis also took four of the six 21.35 inch titles, the other two falling to Curly Fredericks.

1930 through 1933: The dark ages

During this period both Indian and Harley-Davidson showed increased interest in hillclimbing. The Super X victories of Joe Petrali and Gene Rhyne had produced much good publicity for Excelsior/Henderson, and Springfield was naturally in a mood to reap some of the same rewards. When the Super X and Henderson marques folded in March of 1931, Indian managed to hire Gene Rhyne, the 1930 National Hillclimb Champion for the 1931 season. As well as Rhyne and the perennial Steele, the Wigwam's stable of slant artists including a young man named Howard Mitzell. Mitzell was at the beginning of a forty-year career which would eventually make him the grand old man of hillclimbing.

Flat track racing was a dying sport, as the harsh economic times and the dissimilarity of racers and stock motorcycles combined to kill spectator appeal. 179

The Al Crocker machine shop in Los Angeles built overhead valve conversion kits for the 101. These ohv 101 Scouts were either 30.50 cubic inches or 37 cubic inches. The 30.50 cubic inch version was used for Class A short-track racing while the 37 ohv was eligible for hillclimbing events. *(Chuck Vernon, author.)*

Nevertheless the twenty-ones were now circling the tracks much faster than the thirty-fifties of a decade ago.

In October of 1932, Charles B. Franklin died at the age of 46 while on a medical leave of absence from the Wigwam. As he had been the man behind the most successful of the 8-valves, the surprisingly powerful Indian sidevalves, and a few later ohv specials, one can but wonder at what might have been Indian's competition future had Franklin lived a normal life span.

By 1933, racing had been reduced to a local amateurish exercise. Many races were 'outlaw' events, that is, unsanctioned. It was also about this time that the European style of speedway racing became popular, and as the most successful of the speedway bikes were JAPs or Rudges, Indian's racing interest was at an all-time low. Moreover, such racing interest as there might have been was killed by economics. The giant Wigwam was now operating at only five percent of its production capacity.

Another immortal design

At the end of 1931, Indian discontinued the famous model 101 Scout because of severe financial constraints. During the following season, they offered a 45 inch Scout which was admittedly a Scout engine in a Chief frame, and consequently essentially unacceptacle as a sporting motorcycle. To fill the gap left by the 101's departure, and to make use of existing surplus stocks, the Wigwam decided it was sufficiently healthy to bring out a new series for the 1933 season.

This new series consisted originally of a 30.50 inch V-twin, which was announced in the early summer of 1932 and joined by a 45 inch version in the autumn. The smaller version was initially termed the Scout Pony, and survived until World War II under two more labels, the Junior Scout and the Thirty-Fifty. The 45 inch job was given a rather uncharacteristic name, Motoplane. Both machines were based on the defunct 21.35 inch (350 cc) Prince single

This is a Class A short tracker (speedway) bike built around a 101 Scout ohv unit. Although the tank has the Indian logo, the frame, cylinder, and valve gear were produced by Al Crocker. These motorcycles were campaigned in both the USA and Mexico during 1932. In 1933, Crocker had his own ohv single cylinder engine ready for use in this same frame. Thereafter, the tank carried the Crocker logo. The rider is Earl Farrand.   *(Stephen Wright.)*   181

offered from 1925 through 1928. The 45 inch Motoplane proved unreliable, as the lightweight Prince frame, clutch, and transmission were overstressed by the 750 cc engine.

However, the Motoplane was the impetus for a completely new model launched in early 1934, the Sport Scout. The Sport Scout combined the best attributes of the Prince-Pony-Motoplane layout with the semi-unit construction advantages of the 101. Another carry-over was the dry sump oiling introduced on the Scout Pony and Motoplane. The front forks were of the English style girder pattern, as were the Motoplane's, but the Sport Scout's all new forks were considerably more robust. The wheelbase was 56 1/2 inches compared to the 101's 57 1/8 inches. Tires were 18 inches by 4.00 inches, and total weight was 385 pounds (dry), about 25 pounds more than the 101.

The engine dimensions were the traditional 2 7/8 bore and 3 1/2 inch stroke. Intake and exhaust valves were 1 5/8 inches, a surprising fact since the 101 had 1 7/8 inch valves. The pistons were T-slotted and cam ground (i.e., elliptic) in order to provide for unequal growth under heat caused by the eccentric sidevalve configuration. The cylinder heads were aluminum.

The engine was linked to the transmission by a three-row primary chain running in cast aluminum oil bath. The clutch was a multi-disk steel and Raybestos unit of the wet type. The transmission was a three-speed sliding gear unit identical internally to the 74 inch Chief. Ignition was battery and coil or optional magneto.

1934 through 1941: The Sport Scout revitalizes racing

As the new Class C racing rules were intended at the outset to bring in the amateurs and keep out the factories, the Sport Scout was not an overnight success. In fact, Harley-Davidson had the better of it throughout 1934, as the Sport Scout had not been distributed in sufficient numbers to make a dent in the racing results.

1935

In February, Rody Rodenburg rode a Sport Scout to victory in the Jacksonville, Florida 200-mile National Championship Class C road race, the forerunner of the Daytona 200. An unusual record was accomplished by Steve and Roger Whiting in May. The brothers alternated in the saddle of their solo Indian Chief and set a new transcontinental record of 4 days, 20 hours, 36 minutes. This time bested by about 6 hours Steve's go-it-alone effort of 1934. Another Chief Class C record was accomplished in May on the Muroc Dry Lake of California, when a Chief rolled 100 miles in 1 hour, 17 minutes, 48 seconds.

At Langhorne, Pennsylvania 'Woodsie' Castonguay won the 100-mile Class C national in September on a Sport Scout. Other Indians took all the next seven spots except fourth.

1936

On January 19, 1936, Ed Kretz won the 200-mile Class C National Championship at Savannah, Georgia at an average speed of 70.03 mph. Fred Ludlow reached an almost unbelievable speed of 128.57 mph on a Sport Scout during a speed meet in April at the Muroc Dry Lake. However, closer study makes the figure believable for two reasons. First, this was not a Class C mark, so presumably both the motor and the fuel were very non-standard. Second, two-way runs were still not required. On the Muroc Dry Lake, the wind can literally, continuously, and steadily blow at a 30 mph rate for hours at a time. With some one-hundred square miles of dry lake in which to mark off a course, it was a simple process to insure one had the maximum wind assistance. Nevertheless, Ludlow and crew had shrewdly accomplished their work, for among the defeated were 61 inch, 74 inch, and 80 inch motorcycles. In fact, second spot went to a 74 inch Chief which also set a class record.

Lester Hillbish won the Langhorne, Pennsylvania 100-mile National at a record 81.06 mph, and six of the first ten finishers were on Indians. In preparing for the race, Howard Mitzell made an interesting discovery. He eliminated the characteristic heart shape of the internal side of the cylinder head and between the valves. The improved breathing more than compensated for the lower compression ratio. This approach was to be the cornerstone of subsequent sidevalve racing development for the next thirty years.

An interesting episode was the Sports Scout transcontinental run which entered the mythical record books to the credit of Rody Rodenburg of Indianapolis. In June of 1936, Rodenburg was acknowledged as the new coast-to-coast champion with a time of 71 hours, 20 minutes, despite getting off course and covering some 300 miles more than necessary. Rodenburg's time was the generally acknowledged solo transcontinental mark until 1959. However, the late Rollie Free, Indian dealer at Indianapolis during this period, told the author that Rodenburg had cheated. According to Free, Rodenburg and an accomplice towed the motorcycle, taking turns sleeping and driving.

Another transcontinental record was captured in September by L.C. Smith, who took the sidecar honors, riding alone at 86 hours, 55 minutes, breaking the 1935 record of Earl and Dot Robinson. At Syracuse, Fred Toscani won the 25-mile Class A National on a 21.35 ohv single, one of the last Indian wins in this dying branch of the sport.

1937, 1938

From 1937 through 1941, the man of the hour was Ed Kretz. Kretz won the inaugural Daytona 200 on the beach in January of 1937, and led each of the next four pre-war 200-milers before dropping out. He won two consecutive 100-mile Nationals on the Langhorne, Pennsylvania one-mile dirt oval in 1937 and 1938, and again won in 1940. In 1938, Kretz copped the original Laconia

183

National, a 200-miler which was termed a TT. This event was so physically demanding that Ed earned the nickname 'Iron Man' which stuck with him the rest of his career.

Several other Sport Scout riders helped Indian dominate the 1937 and 1938 seasons. Among them was Lester Hillbish, winner of the 1936 Langhorne 100 and four status events during 1937. After Kretz and Hillbish took most of the 1937 honors, the 1938 winningest pair was Kretz and Woodsie Castonguay. By May of 1938, Indian held every Class C record for half-mile tracks.

On March 17, 1938, Rollie Free hung up two new Class C records, hitting 109.65 mph on a fully equipped 74 inch Chief and 111.55 mph on a Sports Scout. The latter was also a stock machine as required by Class C, but had its front fender and headlight removed. Free did not bother to modify the cam profiles. Instead, he concentrated his efforts on careful assembly.

Production assembly techniques left much to be desired, particularly with respect to cylinder mounting. Free's assembly procedure included a multi-step cylinder base nut torquing technique which minimized eccentricity caused by hurried assembly. While on first thought this may seem inconsequential,

The 101 Scout was superseded by the Sport Scout. Here, Rollie Free is congratulated by E.C. Smith at Daytona Beach in March 1938. Free has just set a Class C record of 111.55 mph. Smith was the de facto boss of American motorcycle competition for over 20 years. *(Emmett Moore.)*

consider the following: Free had some time previously placed an extended micrometer in the cylinder bore of a removed Sports Scout barrel, so that the micrometer would barely stay horizontally suspended snugly in the bore. He then placed his hands on opposite sides of the cylinder and squeezed the iron casting. As a result, the micrometer fell from its tenuous perch. He therefore reasoned that the torquing of the cylinder base nuts was a critical procedure, as well as the more commonly appreciated importance of proper cylinder head torquing.

Another Free trick was valve grinding. His technique included removal of most of the small 'flat' annular surface immediately below the valve contact area with the seat, the purpose of this annular surface being to form a conical seal against the valve seat. Hence, Free's valve heads had a curved profile in a cross-sectional view except for the very thin annular ring which mated with the valve seats. Still another distinction was Free's exhaust plumbing. He carefully mated the exhaust headers to the cylinder ports, assuring that a smooth

Six months after Free's Daytona record, Freddie Ludlow raised the 45 cubic inch and 74 cubic inch marks at Bonneville, Utah. Ludlow turned 115.126 mph on this Sport Scout 45, and 120.747 mph on a Chief 74. Noticeable changes from standard 101 specification include the magneto drive, now taken from the rear of the primary chain, and the Y-shaped intake manifold with correspondingly reoriented cylinder intakes. *(Sam Pierce.)* 185

interface was achieved, which in turn eliminated turbulence of the exhaust gases.

But the most importance of Free's techniques was the tear down and assembly procedure. He used to describe this process as a matter of taking the engine apart, wiping off all the parts with clean rags, and putting everything back together. On one occasion, an out-of-state disciple had no success with this approach and wrote Free a letter asking for a set of his rags.

1939

Sport Scout riders were less successful in 1939, as Harley-Davidson had devoted increased attention to their WL series 45 inch twin. Still, there were some notable wins. Bob Hallowell won the Chattanooga, Tennessee 200-mile National TT on a Sport Scout, competing against 61 inch ohv and 74 inch sidevalve machines. Stanley Wittinski won the Springfield, Illinois 25-mile National on the one-mile oval, Indian's third consecutive victory in this prestigious race. Springfield was so highly regarded that the AMA would eventually reward the Illinois mile's winner with the number one plate.

1940

Melvin Rhoades won the Springfield, Illinois mile in 1940, the Wigwam's fourth consecutive 25-mile title. Kretz accomplished his third Langhorne 100 victory, and Ted Edwards won two National Championship TT events on a 74 inch Chief. Much was made of Edwards' praise of the new plunger rear suspension of the Chief.

The Sport Scout's impact was evidenced by Harley-Davidson's two most recent racing models. In 1940 there was the model WLDR, and in 1941 there was the WR, an out-and-out Class C racer without the pretence of highway equipment to be immediately removed.

1941

Although Norton's Billy Mathews won the 1941 Daytona 200, the race was an important if covert Indian bench mark. Several newly designed Sport Scouts appeared quietly on the scene in the hands of favored riders. To the casual observer, these were typical Sport Scouts, but in fact, they were considerably different. For openers, they had larger crankcases in order to lessen crankcase ventilation problems. This fact in itself made these 'big base' Scouts illegal under AMA Class C rules, since this constituted a basic new design and necessitated the building of a minimum of fifty such units. The additional details of these 'big base' Sport Scouts are provided under discussion of the 1948 models, when Indian 'went public' with their machines and built the required fifty units. In the 1941 Daytona, these big base Scouts all retired, and their influence would not be felt until after the upcoming war.

As the 1930s were hard times, a popular and economical performance booster was to install Sport Scout cylinders and heads on a 101 crankcase. Indian always made their new designs compatible with previous ones. The rider is Art Hafer, who set an 8-mile record for one-mile tracks in 1940. The record stood for over a decade. Hafer is best remembered, however, for his abilities as a builder tuner. A Hafer-tuned Sport Scout, ridden by Ernie Beckman, won the last National Championship for Indian in late 1953. *(Art Hafer.)* 187

The most famous of all Sport Scouts was this machine, campaigned for several years by Indian's top rider, Ed Kretz.
(Ed Kretz Sr., Sam Hotton.)

Overall, 1941 was a year somewhat favoring Harley-Davidson. In the Chattanooga 100-mile National TT, Bob Hallowell's win was protested and the race declared 'no contest' due to scoring problems. Thus, after some forty plus years of American racing, the old scoring bugaboo was still around. At Hatfield, Pennsylvania, Frenchie Castonguay set a new Class C 8-mile record for half-mile tracks. Class C racing was on the verge of being as fast as the old 30.50 inch ohv Class A game. By the USA's entry into World War II in December of 1941, Indian still held most Class C records, although they had slipped somewhat. The breakout of Class C records was: Indian, 9; Harley-Davidson, 4; and Norton 1. The Class A game was dead at the end of 1938.

1946

The next organized full season of racing occurred in 1946. However, it should be noted that there was a reduced number of National Championships. For example, there was no Daytona 200, as it could not be organized in time. Sport Scout riders captured the year's two most prestigious wins. Ed Kretz won the Laconia 100 and Johnny Spiegelhoff won the Langhorne 100.

1947

Jack Horn and Bill Huguley gave Indian a good start for the 1947 season on February 22 by finishing first and second in the Amateur Class Daytona 100-miler. The following day, Johnny Spiegelhoff rode one of the under-the-

Kretz updated his bike with the vertically-mounted magneto driven from the oil pump. The earlier rear-mounted magnetos provided somewhat erratic spark timing once appreciable wear was experienced. The oil pump is the aluminum gear type introduced in 1948, its plumbing compatible with the under-the-seat oil tank mounting used for road racing. In the bike's present flat-track trim, the oil supply is carried in the forward part of the right tank.

(Ed Kretz Sr., author.)

table big base Sports Scouts to victory in the Expert Class 200-mile classic, taking over the lead from Ed Kretz after 48 miles and never relinquishing it. Kretz made several pit stops for various problems before retiring. Finishing second was another Sport Scout rider, Ted Edwards.

On May 31, Max Bubeck accomplished an extraordinary feat. Riding an Indian Four, modified with Vard telescopic forks, Bubeck won the famous Greenhorn Enduro. The grueling Greenhorn was a two-day 500-mile affair which included the dusty Mojave Desert and finished Saturday night atop the 6,800 foot peak of Greenhorn Mountain before the Sunday riding. The second and third place finishers were on Harley-Davidson 61 ohvs, which also seems incredible from the vantage point of today's world of specialized enduro bikes. 189

At the time, however, the big Harleys were considered a staple of enduros. But to win such an event on a huge Indian Four was fully appreciated even in 1947 as a tribute to remarkable riding and preparation.

Bubeck had his own approach to setting up the four, which included an oil cooler fashioned from a refrigerator condenser, and the use of Chevrolet valve springs. A key reliability modification was the drilling of the crankshaft for uniform oil distribution. In the stock Indian Fours, oil was pumped through the number one (forward) bearing to the number one rod's big end. The number three (center) bearing provided oil access to the number two and three big ends in the stock setup, but there were no drilled passages to 'join' the number one to the number two rod, and to connect the number three rod to the number four rod. Moreover, the stock configuration had the number four rod lubrication supply shared with the transmission. Bubeck drilled the crank, between the first and second bearings, and between the third and fourth bearings. He thus solved the infamous overheating problems, popularly but erroneously attributed to lack of air flow over the rear cylinders.

Another trick was emery cloth buffing of the pistons until about one thousandth inch of metal has been removed. The total package was an unusually reliable and speedy four cylinder Indian. The bike went 104 mph after 4000 miles of road and enduro use, and was later clocked at 108.43 mph, using a twenty tooth transmission sprocket instead of the normal eighteen tooth sprocket.

Indian's racing position was now noticeably slipping, for although they had captured the Daytona 200 on one of their six prewar big base Sport Scouts, the run-of-the-mill Indian 45 was no longer as powerful as its latest Harley-Davidson counterparts. As there were but a handful of the special Sport Scouts, the odds in any particular big event were definitely in Harley-Davidson's favor. There was also the matter of the Sports Scouts' nonproduction status, complicating the twin tasks of bringing new racing blood on board and keeping traditional Indian riders in the fold. Naturally, there was a growing spare parts problem.

The impact on Indian's racing position can be gauged by observing the results in the 1947 Laconia 100. Of the nineteen finishers, eleven rode Harley-

Left top: **Although this circa 1948 shot was posed for a spark plug advertisement, Ed Kretz did, in fact, do almost all his own wrench turning. The Indian company provided him with pit men at some of the more prestigious events such as Laconia and Daytona. Indian also paid Kretz's expenses until things fell apart in 1949, at which time he transferred his racing allegiance to Triumph. The stories about Indian providing Kretz engines in batches of four to six, however, are incorrect. Kretz says he always had just enough parts to carry on, and was never provided with extra engines.** *(Ed Kretz Sr.)*

Left bottom: **Ed Kretz today. The bike seems small compared to both its ancestors and later spring framed machines. Although the frame carries a 1939 serial number, the motorcycle is fitted with a circa 1948 big base engine. The oil pump is the more squarish aluminum one used on the Chief road models, rather than the type used on the Ludlow machine. The other principal change from earlier practice is the vertically-mounted magneto, which provided more positive timing control than the old rear-mounted unit.** *(Ed Kretz Sr., Sam Hotton.)* 191

Left to right: **Dick Gross, Walt Brown, Bobby Hill, and Brownie Betar. Hill has just won the 1952 Syracuse, New York 10-Mile National Championship on the one-mile track.** *(Bobby Hill.)*

192

Max Bubeck after winning one of the most prestigious cross-country events, the 1947 Greenhorn Enduro
(Max Bubeck.)

Davidsons compared to seven on Indians. More importantly, Ted Edwards' second-place ride was the only Indian in the top ten, the balance being Harley-Davidsons. June 22 had definitely been a bad day for Indian.

Origin of the Model 648

Accordingly, on the very next day, Indian's General Policy Committee decided to build-up the AMA minimum of fifty big base Sports Scouts. Production of fifty model 648 big base Sport Scouts required 500 different parts, of which 490 were standard parts. Of these 490 standard parts, 420 were in stock and Indian was already committed to produce another 65 standard parts to fulfill existing back-orders. Consequently, as far as standard parts were concerned, the decision to build the model 648 required a negligible additional cost outlay. The total direct cost of 490 standard parts was estimated at approximately $340 per motorcycle. The special parts situation was different. The estimated cost of obtaining these 10 special parts from outside the factory was $365 per motorcycle. There was also the matter of factory overheads, so the end result was that the machines had to be sold at a loss. In fact, the no-profit cost to the factory was about the same as the retail price of a BSA Gold Star in the USA.

Sales Manager Al West was to see to it that Indian got a 'fair' dollar return on the project. His guidance in this area was to obtain a minimum of $600 for each model 648, for a maximum company loss of about $400 per motorcycle so that Indian's maximum cost for the project would be $20,000.

As an indicator of where Indian's top managerial emphasis was, the $20,000 cost to Project 45-45 compared pathetically with Indian's current investment in the vertical twin Scout and single cylinder Arrow programs. These new 'gentlemen's' touring motorcycles ultimately consumed about $6.6 million dollars of investment capital over a three-year period, according to company President Ralph B. Rogers.

Despite having a 98 percent commonality of parts with the defunct prewar Sports Scouts, the new 'big base Scouts' had significant internal and external differences. The 648 was, in essence, an updated version of the several experimental prewar racers.

The 648's internal differences from the touring Sport Scout were as follows:

The flywheels were different, being of cast steel, narrower and using the counterweight pattern as on the Army shaft drive models. The crankshaft assembly was also different, featuring oil holes graduated in size, and the timing side (pinion) shaft was tapered on the end to mate with a tapered-holed pinion gear. The front camshaft was modified to drive a new aluminum oil pump. The pistons were more domed than in the standard Indian Bonneville Sports Scouts, and required modification to the combustion chambers.

Externally, the big base motors were very different. The crankcase had a large sump cast in the rear. There was no sump valve on the bottom right side of the motor. The new aluminum oil pump was the same one as used on the 1948 Chief except that the intake and return fittings were on the side in order to link up with the new oil tank, mounted under the saddle. The pump had a breather at the top rear and also required a special cam case cover. The new vertically mounted Edison-Splitdorf magneto required the cutting away of some cylinder cooling fin surfaces.

1948

The big base project paid off handsomely on March 14, 1948. Floyd Emde, heretofore a prominent Harley racer, won the 200 mile beach classic at the record pace of 84.01 mph. For 1948, the Daytona course had been lengthened from its former 3.2 miles distance to 4.1 miles, resulting in the lengthening of each of the two straights to almost two miles. Consequently, a new race record was virtually assured.

The starting line-up of the 1948 Daytona 200 was symbolic of the changing balance of power in American motorcycle racing. In the pre-war era, Indian had usually entered almost as many motorcycles as Harley-Davidson in the premiere events, and sometimes there would be more bikes from the Wigwam than from Milwaukee. The 1939 200 could be considered typical of the immediate pre-war period. In that race, the breakout of the forty-seven finishers was: Harley-Davidson, 40 percent; Indian, 36 percent; others, 15 percent. In 1948, the competing marques shared thusly: Harley-Davidson, 51 percent; Indian, 25 percent; others, 25 percent. Except for a single BMW in each of the referenced races, "other" meant British motorcycles. Harley-Davidson was holding its share of competition racers, but Indian was losing ground to Norton, BSA, and Triumph.

The growth of Norton support previewed later victories. In the 1939 Daytona 200, there had been only one Norton finisher, amounting to about two percent of the field and thirteen percent of the foreign bikes. In 1948, Norton motorcycles accounted for ten percent of the field and forty percent of the foreign machines.

Indian speed was convincingly demonstrated at the June 27, Rosamond Dry Lake, California speed trials. The builder-rider team of Frank Chase and Max Bubeck won top honors with their special 'Chout', a combination of a Chief engine and 101 Scout frame. The Chout was equipped with telescopic forks built by the Vard accessory firm. Skinny tires were used, an 18 by 4.00 rear and a 19 by 3.20 front. Twin Schebler carburetors fed methanol to the

Left to right: **Frank Chase, Max Bubeck, and 'Pop' Shunk stand behind the Chase/Bubeck 'Chout'. Having achieved over 135 mph in 1948, this was the fastest unstreamlined Indian ever built.** *(Max Bubeck.)* 195

motor which had special cams designed by 'Pop' Shunk. This was a four lobe cam setup instead of the normal two lobe, and the lobes were 1/4 inch wide instead of 1/2 inch wide. To reduce drag, only the high gear ratio was installed, there being no gears internal to the transmission case. The bike's 2.6:1 gearing gave 4600 rpm at 135 mph. The engine produced 65 hp at 4400 rpm at the rear wheel, as measured on Frank Christian's dynamometer. The toughest competition for the Chout was Bus Schaller's overhead valve Harley-Davidson; but the Chout emerged victorious at 135.58 mph. Bubeck's ride thus became an interesting entry into Indian's rich folklore, for **his speed was the highest ever to be officially recognized for an unstreamlined Indian.**

One week later, Ed Kretz won the 100-mile National TT at Riverside, California on July 4. Of the thirty entries, ten were on Indians, nine were on Harleys, and eleven were on British makes, evidence of Indian's more competitive West Coast position and the 'missionary' work of long time West Coast distributor Hap Alzina.

At Langhorne, Pennsylvania, on September 5, Kretz again came out on top making him only the four-time winner of the demanding 100 mile flat track event. The entry list at Langhorne was more representative of Indian's declining national strength. Of the 36 starters, only eight rode Indians. The rest of the field included: 20 Harley-Davidsons, 6 Nortons, 1 Matchless, and 1 BSA.

1949

Nineteen forty-nine was practically a 'non-year' for Indian. At Daytona, their share of the top twenty places consisted of Ted Edwards in seventh place, Walter Troxel in fourteenth place, and Earl Givens in twentieth place. Kretz, as usual, was a factor early in the race, running second on his big base Sport Scout for a number of laps. His fastest lap was turned in 2 minutes, 47.87 seconds, while winner Dick Klamfoth's best circuit on his overhead cam Norton was quicker by 0.52 second. The design work on the model 648 big base Scouts had not been followed up by continuous development in contrast with Harley-Davidson's constant caressing of their WR 45s.

When Indian entered twelve of the new vertical 498cc twin Warriors at Laconia on June 10, 1949, all saddled by factory-sponsored riders, it was an impressive show of confidence to the spectators and the press. But there was nothing in Indian's illustrious racing heritage that could be passed on to the Warrior. The Warrior was an enlarged 249, which had been designed outside of the Wigwam and brought into the tribe by Rogers. While the vertical twin received the full attention of the Indian's handful of dedicated race-wise technicians, their efforts might just as well have been ceremonial. In the sidevalve world, Indian's race-wise men were near-immortals; but in the overhead valve world, they were on very equal terms with their competitors.

In racing the 249 Scout, Indian had needlessly spotted their overhead valve rivals approximately thirteen percent of extra displacement. Although the Warrior update eliminated this fundamental flaw there was a most improbable happening – absolutely unreliable magnetos. Edison-Splitdorf had built Indian's magnetos for a generation. Tens of thousands had demonstrated reasonable reliability, the most recent example of which was the magneto used on the 648 Sport Scout. Yet, incredibly, all twelve factory Warrior entries suffered magneto failure at Laconia.

Not long after Laconia, Hap Alzina purchased the right to distribute BSAs in the eleven western states. Indian was already finding it difficult to hold on to its dealers because of reliability problems with the 249 Scout and 149 Arrow. As Alzina had been Indian's most successful distributor, his surprise move was a serious psychological setback for Springfield and no doubt influenced more dealers and racers to abandon Indian's ship. The growing number of Indian deserters left behind loyalists who could not face reality or those who had not yet found a better deal. Ed Kretz was in neither category. The man whose racing career has been synonymous with Indian would switch his racing support to Triumph in 1950.

Details of the vertical twins

The 1949 440 cc overhead valve Scout was never catalogued as a production racer. However, its race-ready statistics must have been virtually identical to its successor, the 1950-1952 Warrior model, except that the latter's displacement was increased from 435.6 cc to 498 cc by enlarging the cylinder bores. Key data on the vertical twin Indian is summarized below.

The bore on the 1949 Scout was 2.375 inches and the stroke was 3 inches, giving a displacement of 435.6 cc or 26.6 cubic inches. On the 1950-1952 Warriors, the bore was enlarged to 2.54 inches and the displacement was 498 cc or 30.5 cubic inches. The Scout's 19/32 inch diameter overhead valves had a ninety-degree included-angle, acted through bronze guides, and were actuated by aluminum push rods. The inclined push rods and the extreme 'outboard' mounting of the rocker arms increased the direct exposure of the cylinder head's middle surface to cooling air, and provided a distinctive and esthetic appearance. Conversely, the configuration inhibited future development, as there was insufficient room between the inlet push rods to provide optimum twin-carburetor induction.

The compression ratio was 7 1/2 : 1, the maximum allowable under AMA rules at that time. There were no particularly unusual features of the design apart from the previously mentioned inclined push rods, with the possible exception of the cylinder fins. The cooling fins were very thin and closely spaced for that era due to the centrifugal casting technique in which the aluminum cylinders were cast around iron liners. The connecting rods had removeable lower sections to accommodate replacement of the plain big-end bearings. The little ends were also of the plain bearing type. The mainshaft had ball bearings on the drive side and roller bearings on the timing side. Primary drive was by a double row 3/8 inch pitch chain running in a cast aluminum oil bath housing.

197

The clutch was a four plate cork-faced unit linking the engine to a four-speed constant mesh transmission. Lubrication was dry sump, with an aluminum gear-type pump. The wheelbase was 53 1/2 inches. Total weight of the stock version, fully serviced, was a relatively light 300 pounds. In race trim, the bike weighed less than 250 pounds.

Output of the 1950-1952 Warriors was specified as 29 horsepower, so by inference the 1949 stock Scouts probably produced about 25.5 horsepower. The 1949 Scout was down in size and horsepower by almost 13 percent compared to British motorcycles, but its light weight was sufficient to equalize acceleration. *Cycle* magazine road-tested a 498 cc Warrior TT in January 1951 and obtained a top speed of 91 mph, using the standard off-road gearing, indicating a probable maximum of about 95 mph for a standard-tuned Warrior TT with pavement gearing.

The maximum speed of the 498 cc Warriors at the 1949 Laconia was approximately 100 mph according to Ed Kretz. It is interesting to note, however, that Laconia's one-mile circuit of hills and hairpins put less emphasis on speed than on acceleration and handling. Kretz says that the vertical twin Warrior accelerated on a pair with his V-twin Scout. Top speed was a different story, for Kretz's big base Sport Scout, was capable of 115 mph at Daytona. It should be noted that no Indian vertical twin ever won an AMA flat track or road race National Championship. This statement is mitigated by the fact that no top-flight riders stuck with them after the 1949 Laconia disaster.

The racing debacle of the 1949 Laconia was but another facet of Indian's larger problem of survival. Incidentally, the motorcycle press was very kind to Indian, as accounts of the 1949 Laconia were quite vague. Nevertheless, a sympathetic press couldn't hide the decline. Indian's production in 1950 would fall to about half its 1949 output. In their first issue, *Cycle* commented in April 1950, '... *With the reduction in competition within the industry, motorcycle development stagnated. Finally, just two motorcycle manufacturers were still doing business – Harley-Davidson and Indian. Then, in mid-1949, Indian ceased major production. The field had indeed dwindled to one of near monopoly.*' The editorial continued with praise of the competitive situation among motorcycle manufacturers outside the United States, and the resultant engineering progress that benefited the riders. Clearly, an American motorcycling revolution was in progress, led by British motorcycles. After 1949, the entry of Indians in a National Championship race became increasingly regarded as an oddity. But there was still a measure of glory to be won on Indian motorcycles, as will be seen.

1950

The Indian dealer network was now engaged in the sale of AJS, Matchless, Norton, Royal Enfield, and Vincent motorcycles, as well as the reduced supply of Indians being built in Springfield. Indian, now under the control of the British Brockhouse firm, was enjoying a good market for their Union Jack imports, aided by the 1949 devaluation of the pound sterling which had lowered stateside prices almost twenty-five percent. As a concept basically similar to the British bikes, the Indian Warrior was now priced above most of its peers. For example, the 1950 suggested list price for a Deluxe spring frame Warrior was $870, compared to a Norton twin at $770 (12 percent cheaper) and the prestige road model Norton, the 500 cc International overhead cam single, at $875. The cooking version of the 500 cc single cylinder models of AJS, Matchless, Norton, and Royal Enfield were arguably better motorcycles than the Warrior. These machines were available from the same salesrooms as the Warrior, while undercutting its price by some twenty-five percent.

Consequently, since these British machines were the essence of survival for the company, and among them were models more speedworthy than the Warrior, it made little sense to provide company support for Warrior development and racing at the level of the national circuit. Instead, those pounds sterling and dollars were funneled into the support of the Indian-distributed imports, primarily Norton and to a lesser extent, AJS/Matchless.

The accelerating motorcycle revolution was clearly illustrated in the 1950 Greenhorn Enduro. Just a few years before, this long-time classic had been a Harley and Indian affair. Now, in 1950, the lineup was: 7 Indians, 38 Harley-Davidsons, and 101 British motorcycles! Del Kuhn won this 500-mile cross-country event on an AJS single.

Three weeks later, Ed Kretz entered the Laconia 100 on a Triumph. Indian's top rider came in fourteenth, while Harley-Davidson not only won but took six of the top ten positions. But the year had its Indian moments. Max Bubeck won a stoutly contested California enduro, the Cactus Derby, riding a Warrior TT. Bill Tuman won the 5-mile and 8-mile Nationals on a big base Sport Scout.

1951–1953: The twilight years

1951

In the early part of 1951, things continued in accordance with the new definition of normalcy. In February, the Daytona 100 field included but ten Indians, compared to 44 Harley-Davidsons, and 58 British motorcycles. Dick Klamfoth won America's biggest race for the second time on his Norton overhead cam single.

By June, there were still no Indian National titles. On June 17, at Freemansburg, Pennsylvania, the grand old man of hillclimbing had his day. Fifty-four year old Howard Mitzell won the main event on an Indian 61. In a reminder of the glory days of full factory support, one of the spectators was another Indian hillmaster, Orie Steele, whose career had lasted from 1919 to 1935. Among the competition at Freemansburg was Gordon Mitzell, Howard's son.

At this juncture, Harley-Davidson's premier engine builder/tuner was Tom Sifton. Sifton was held in awe, as evidenced by the titles of articles appearing now and then in *Cycle* magazine. In November 1950, there was 'Tom Sifton, Sovereign of Harley-Davidson Speed,' and in September 1951, there

199

was 'Sifton Harleys Sweep Bay Meadows.' In recalling those days, Sifton told the author that three Indian builders had more speed in their Sport Scouts than the Sifton Harley-Davidsons during late 1951 and all of 1952 and 1953.

Dick Gross, Art Hafer, and Bill Tuman had indeed built three superlative Indian Sport Scout racers, ridden, respectively, by Bobby Hill, Ernie Beckman, and Bill Tuman. It is significant that these riders favored the overhead cam Norton singles for road racing, where good brakes, modern suspension front and rear, and a four-speed transmission paid dividends. But in flat track racing, the over-riding need was high power output over a wide rpm range. In flat tracking, suspension requirements were minimal, while shifting gears was illegal, and brakes were forbidden. Bucking the trend towards British motorcycles, and with minimal to zero factory support, Hill, Beckman, and Tuman knew that a well-prepared Sport Scout was a more competitive flat tracker than their cammy Nortons.

Of the three 'twilight' Sports Scouts, Hill's was the most radical, the most powerful, and the least reliable. The most extreme of all Gross' modifications was the use of ball bearings on both ends of the mainshaft as well as the connecting rod big ends. The ball-bearing setup required the machining away of considerable connecting rod metal, a drawback in terms of reliability.

Hill's remembrance, as related to the author, differs somewhat from Sifton's suppositions. There was no formal information exchange program between Hill, Beckman, and Tuman, however Tuman did eventually ride on Gross-prepared bikes. Moreover, Bobby Hill credits Tuman with being a 'very good mechanic', so it seems likely that there was at least some cross-feed going on.

Bobby Hill had three Sport Scouts in his stable. One of these was fitted with a four-cam valve mechanism, or rather with four cam lobes instead of two lobes. Each lobe was half as wide across the face as the standard Indian lobe, there being two lobes per cam. The 'four-cammer' was Hill's primary mile-track motorcycle.

Although he had a few problems, Hill says he actually only blew up on one occasion, that being the 1953 Springfield mile. The reason for that failure was oil starvation. Gross had determined that less oil in the crankcase would provide extra speed, but at Springfield the oil circulation had been overly restricted.

Dick Gross had almost turned the inside of Bobby Hill's mile-tracker into a Harley-Davison, for its four cam lobes, Harley rods, and ball bearings were all hallmarks of the Milwaukee brand! The Gross brand of trickery further illustrates the nearly impossible problem of regulating 'stock' motorcycle competition. Although the AMA-stated ideology argues against such ingenuity, the use of non-standard internal parts was practiced by virtually all serious competitors. Gross was simply craftier than most.

Bobby Hill, describing Dick Gross, said: *'He was a smart machinist. He could make anything to do anything. In fact, Dick worked for Giddings and Lewis, and he was one-of-a-kind. He would maybe work all year and only do the job once. You know, he was a special person. And that's the way it was on motors. He could make anything. He was*

200

very knowledgeable, like for heat treating and this and that. He wasn't just a machinist; he knew what he wanted to make, and he could make it himself.'

The twilight Scout built by Art Hafer, for Ernie Beckman, was ball-bearing outfitted for awhile, but Hafer returned to rollers. In the Hafer engine, the pistons were forged solid-skirt Lynite made by the Zollinger Company of Fort Wayne, Indiana. The pistons were somewhat lightened for balancing purposes. Later, Hafer used German-made Hepolite pistons. Hafer left off the third compression ring and ran his motors with two compression rings and one oil ring.

Valves in the Hafer motor were the standard 1 5/8 inch diameter Sport Scout valves. To actuate the valves, Hafer devised his own cam action which incorporated Sport Scout cam followers (lifters) instead of the Bonneville Sport Scout followers. The intake valve was timed to leave its seat at 30 degrees before top dead center, and the exhaust valve closed 30 degrees after top dead center, giving a valve overlap of 60 degrees. Hafer fed his intake port through an inlet duct which was 1/8 inch larger than stock. His biggest problem was the reliability of connecting rod bearings.

Although the TT Warrior engine was attractive, the pushrod configuration precluded an effective twin carburetor setup. More importantly, the machine was not competitively priced with comparable British bikes. *(Chuck Rouse, author.)* 201

Hill's two 1951 titles, at Springfield, Illinois and Milwaukee, Wisconsin, were both accomplished in record time. Following the custom, Hill was granted the No. 1 plate for winning the Springfield 25-miler.

1952

At the 1952 Bay Meadows, California mile, Bill Tuman and Bobby Hill convincingly demonstrated their horsepower gains since the previous year's Harley-Davidson runaway. Hill was the fastest qualifier at 43.60 seconds. Tuman won the 20-mile National Championship in 14 minutes, 49.41 seconds, a 20-mile record. Bobby Hill again won the Springfield mile, thus holding on to the number one plate. Over the past four years, Hill had racked up two firsts and two seconds in this most prestigious mile-track event. He then finished out Indians' 1952 winnings on the Syracuse, New York one-mile track in September, winning the 10-mile Championship. It had been a good year, considering that there were only three serious Sport Scout campaigners against a dozen or more stars on Harley-Davidsons and British motorcycles.

1953

Nineteen fifty-three was not quite as successful, Hill experiencing several mechanical failures. Bill Tuman won the Springfield mile and kept the No. 1 plate in the possession of the Indian organization, although like Hill, Tuman would bolt the number one tag to his overhead cam Norton single for road races. Bobby Hill won the 10 and 15 mile titles on mile tracks, the latter being his eighth mile track Championship.

At Williams Grove, Pennsylvania on October 11, 1953, history was made. Ernie Beckman set the day's fastest qualifying time of 29.97 seconds, and then went on to win his third consecutive 8-mile National Championship. **This was the last AMA National Championship race won on an Indian motorcycle.**

Post-1953

In the 1954 season, Tuman abandoned the Indian marketing organization and began road racing on Triumphs. Likewise, Hill road raced BSAs and won the Daytona 200 on a Star Twin. As the Indian organization was no longer manufacturing Indian motorcycles, and as they had offered little or no help anyway to Tuman, Hill, and Beckman, the 1954 season provides an interesting tribute to the Indian Sport Scout. Tuman, Hill, and Beckman continued to campaign these unsponsored V-twins during the 1954 circuit, garnering a couple of third-place finishes and one second-place finish in National Championship events. The second-spot placing was in the Springfield, Illinois 25-mile National, won by Harley-Davidson's Joe Leonard.

The Scouts were no longer competitive with Leonard's Tom Sifton-built motorcycle, for reasons explained in the Harley-Davidson section. Spare parts for the Sports Scouts, particularly the unobtainable female rods, had already been a problem which Hill's builder Dick Gross had solved by using Harley female rods. But there were limits to such ingenuity, and besides, the trio of twilight Scout riders could grab at least some measure of sponsorship by flying the Union Jack. Moreover, Sifton's Harley-Davidson secrets spilled over into the Harley mainstream in 1955, and the twilight Scouts were finished. Hill did manage a second place in the Springfield 25-miler in 1955, losing to Everett Brashear, but that was the Sport Scouts' last brush with glory. The Indian banner was flown for a few more years by lesser riders in decreasing numbers. The marque had the distinction of competing in all the old beach races of the Daytona 200 series, right up to the last one in 1960.

The grand old man of hillclimbing, Howard Mitzell, and his son, Gordon, continued successfully to run Indians in hillclimbing for a number of years. Howard won the 74 inch Class A event of the 1953 Laconia meet and the 1954 Class A National Championship. On the West Coast, Frank Chase remained an Indian loyalist and won the 1955 Greenhorn Enduro on a special built from an 80 cubic inch Chief engine and a military shaft-drive frame. Max Bubeck was second on his Warrior TT.

Up to a decade after Indian's 1953 production stoppage, National Championship races were occasionally won at paces no faster than in 1953, so it is interesting to ponder what additional Redskin victories might have been possible with factory support. As it was, since no genuine assembly line Sport Scout production had occurred since 1941, the model had no need for further championships to add to its luster.

Diminishing returns

The 1962 sixteenth annual Greenhorn Enduro fell to Max Bubeck and his Warrior TT. The tough 445-mile desert run defeated most riders, as only 23 of the 170 entries finished.

In the sixties, a unique gentleman from New Zealand earned the last loud applause for the immortal Indian. From 1962 through 1967, Bert Munro was the standout attraction at the Bonneville, Utah speed weeks. His motorcycle was a streamliner built around what had started life as his brand new 1920 596 cc sidevalve Scout. In its original guise, the Scout had been timed at a top speed of 54 mph in 1926. Some forty years later, Bert remarked, *'I've got it going faster every year since.'*

In 1962, Munro established a class record of 162.149 mph with his 51 cubic inch (850 cc) overhead valve Scout. In 1963, he suffered a broken connecting rod while traveling an estimated 195 mph. A year later, he had a run of 184.00 mph, the fastest of any motorcycle during speed week. However, Bert was unable to log record time due to wheel bearing failure, poor salt conditions, and strong winds.

Bert was unsuccessful in 1965, but in 1966, with the Scout engine enlarged to 56 cubic inches (920 cc), the New Zealander upped the S.A. 1000 cc class record to 168.066 mph. For what proved his last ride, Munro punched the   203

Scout out to 58 cubic inches (950 cc) for the 1967 speed week. His two-way average of 183.586 mph was another class record. To qualify, Bert made a one-way run of 190.070 mph over the Utah salt, **the fastest speed ever recorded on an Indian.**

As remarkable as Munro's speeds were, they take on a more special meaning when one considers the circumstances. The pistons were cast using holes in the New Zealand beach sand! In place of the standard single-cam valve gear, Bert substituted his own four-cam design to actuate the overhead valves. Power was transmitted through a Munro-built seventeen-plate, 1000-pound pressure, clutch and a triple chain drive. Replacement parts were used over and over again, and were hand made with hack-saw, file, lathe, and grinder. The list of consumables included: flywheels, pistons, cylinder barrels, cams and cam followers, bushings, the lubrication system and connecting rods. The latter, in their ultimate form were literally hand-carved from a Caterpillar tractor axle, and were tempered and hardened to 143 tons of tensile strength. Truly, the perseverance, skill, and loyalty of this man from half a world away, were the very essence of the vitality that had long sustained Indian against improbable odds.

Bert Munro's last run amounted to the end of Indian's illustrious competition history. The long rivalry between Indian and Harley-Davidson was the most enduring and fiercely competed battle in the history of sport. The glory of Indian is today reflected in the strong enthusiasm of Indian fans, especially those dwindling few whose riding experience predates the collapse of the once mighty Indian tribe. As was said of DeRosier, there can never be another motorcycle like the Indian, for the conditions under which Indian achieved fame never will return. The Indian was unquestionably the most beloved American motorcycle of its time.

Merkel

The Merkel motorcycle, better known as The Flying Merkel, evolved from the Light marque established in 1901 by the Light Motor Co. of Pottstown, Pennsylvania. These early Lights were essentially carbon copies of period Indians. After engineer Joe Merkel joined up with Light in 1909, the firm was redesignated as the Merkel-Light Motor Co. Joe Merkel at once began to improve the product, devising a spring frame consisting of pivoting rear frame

Left top: **After the last Indian TT Warrior was built in 1951, it was rolled aside and photographed. This is the last of the breed.** *(Emmett Moore.)*

Left bottom: **Bert Munro and the fastest Indian ever built, his highly modified 1920 Scout. Besides being punched out from 600 cc to 1000 cc, Bert had fashioned the engine's pushrod-operated overhead valve gear. An unusually resourceful and dedicated enthusiast, Munro cast his pistons in the beach sand of his native New Zealand!** *(Cycle World.)* 205

Maldwyn Jones and his Merkel-Jefferson. The frame was later used to house a 4-valve Harley-Davidson single.
(Maldwyn Jones.)

structure and analygous to the scheme employed by England's Vincent, and more recently, Japan's Yamahas. Joe Merkel also designed a compact spring fork which looked for all the world like an unsprung trussed fork. The fork's action was telescopic in principle working through dual coil springs. While offering but limited travel, the precise steering of the lightweight Merkel fork resulted in these being sought-after components for modified racing and record setting motorcycles over a generation after the Flying Merkel's demise.

In April of 1910, Merkel rider Fred Whittler defeated Indian's Jake DeRosier in several races over the Los Angeles Coliseum boards. And on April 18, Whittler set new professional records for 17 through 50 miles, his 50 mile time being 40 minutes, 13 seconds (74.6 mph) versus the old professional record of 48 minutes, 21 seconds (62 mph). (Curiously, however, Freddie Huyck's amateur times, on an Indian, for 17 through 22 miles were still the best for those distances.)

In late 1910, Graves set new records for distances of 2 through 20 miles at the Los Angeles Motordrome, again taking the glory from Indian's star, Jake DeRosier, and also beating the earlier Merkel records of Whittler. The latter entered the record books again by establishing a Los Angeles track record (not a 'world' record) of 74.8 mph. Whittler's ride on November 6, 1910 was

Early Merkel engines like this circa 1911 unit had automatic (suction operated) intake valves. Similar machines were raced during the brief period of full factory involvement in racing, from 1909 through 1911. *(Ken Lewis, author.)*

essentially the end of Merkel's serious committment to racing and record setting, as the company was now preoccupied with moving from Pennsylvania to Ohio.

In April of 1911, Merkel riders won several events of lesser stature, and one rider, A.G. Chapple, was itching for another chance to do in the famous DeRosier. Amid much press publicity, DeRosier bowed out of his scheduled match race with Chapple in May, claiming a need to depart early for Isle of Man TT practice.

In May of 1911, *Motorcycle Illustrated* announced that the Miami Cycle and Mfg. Co. of Middletown, Ohio, had bought out Merkel-Light and was transferring operations to Middletown. Soon after Merkel production began in Ohio, a young amateur rider named Maldwyn Jones met up with Joe Merkel in front of the plant. Maldwyn asked for a job as a motorcycle racer, citing his two years' experience at various county fairs and his enthusiasm for Merkel motorcycles. Joe Merkel declined to hire Jones as a racer, stating that his firm wasn't doing any more racing, but he did offer Maldwyn a job in the Repair Department, road testing repaired machines. The Merkel firm's newly acquired disinterest in racing is well revealed in the following account furnished by Maldwyn Jones to the author.

'When I went to work for Merkel, I worked in the Repair Department, road testing repaired engines. I somehow got hold of an ancient Merkel racing machine, a model 'U' with ported cylinder and flat belt drive, and an open chain drive to the magneto. It had only been used in short races, because oil from the ports made the belt slip. I made a guard to keep the belt dry, and at Hamilton, Ohio on July 4, 1912, won some races, with Cannonball Baker as my main competition. After that, I had a corner of the basement as my unofficial racing department, and was able to get things from the racing 'junk' room. The factory officially had no interest in racing, but the Sales Department took care of my shipping expenses. I tested for the Repair Department, but always managed to find time to work on my racing stuff, none of which was new. I am sure Joe Merkel knew what I was doing, but he never came around to offer any advice. I saw him frequently in other parts of the factory and talked to him, mostly about the new models.

The Dayton, Ohio motorcycle club was holding a 100 mile race, on the Fairgrounds half-mile dirt track, early in 1913, and I got a bike ready for it, but when I got ready to ship it, always by rail express in those days, I was told that I had to get Joe Merkel's consent. And he just said no, that with that old equipment I was using, I could not possibly finish a 100-mile race. He said that was his policy not to go into a race unless you had a good chance to win. Maybe he was right from an advertising angle, but it was a big letdown for me after I had done so much work.

I quit Merkel the next day, and two or three weeks later at Dayton, in some short races, I rode a Thor built by a friend who was the Thor dealer in Dayton. He had a fine machine shop and was an excellent craftsman. The engine....had as much care in building as the proverbial 'Swiss watch'. And how that bike would accelerate! In those days, the races were always standing starts, and in the first race against a lot of factory competition, even other Thors, I think I was halfway around the first turn before the other riders knew the race was on. I won three races and fell in the fourth, the last of the day. Joe Merkel was there, with other officials of Miami Cycle (Merkel), and was betting that I would not finish as good as third. He left right after the first race, as he couldn't take the kidding from the other men.

The next week, the President of Miami Cycle, Kelly Jacoby, sent for me and asked me to come back to work in the final assembly. I went back, doing inspection and some road testing. after that, I no longer worked on my racing stuff down in the basement. I graduated to the top floor and could have most anything made that I wanted. It was some time before Joe Merkel would speak to me'.

Following his return to the Merkel firm, Maldwyn managed to devise an interesting racing hybrid, a 30.50 cubic inch (500 cc) single primarily for half-mile track competition. Again, quoting from Maldwyn:

"About that side valve Merkel engine that I converted to a 2-valve overhead job.... As I remember, I had considered a choice of one of three makes of cylinder heads – Pope, Waverly, and Jefferson, all pretty much alike.... I finally bought the head from a Jefferson dealer in northern Ohio, who did some racing in that area – naturally on a Jefferson. This man, 'Peg' Triesch, a pretty fair rider, was usually one of the 'also rans' without whom the racing game would have died for lack of entries. Peg got his nickname because of the loss of part of one leg, but he didn't let that keep him from racing....

I could not use the Jefferson cylinder, as it would not fit the Merkel crankcase, so I sawed the top off the Merkel cylinder and machined it to fit the gasket seat of the Jefferson head. The long bolts (or studs) needed to hold the head and cylinder down to the crankcase had to be bent slightly outward, as the bolt circle on the crankcase and that in the head were not the same. I had to make a rocker arm support, rocker arms, push rods and other small parts. I got blank cams (the gear teeth were finished) and worked out the contours with a hacksaw and file, and then had the cams hardened. My idea at that time was to have the highest valve lift at the point of greatest piston speed and let the valve down to the seat as gently as possible, more like an eccentric action. Incidentally, those big ball bearing cams were a source of vibration in the engine, and in my racing engine I balanced the cam somewhat by drilling holes in the side of the heavier part. Lacking suitable aluminum pistons at the time, Merkel used a steel 'hourglass' piston, and in my racing engine, for the sake of lightness, I used just a 'skeleton' of the standard piston – and only one ring.

When I first tried out the engine on my 'home' track at Lebanon, I found that it needed very much more spark advance than it did as a pocket valve, and I later found that to be true of the Indian four valve – why, I don't know. With some further refining, such as lighter rockers and push rods, it was generally as fast, and often faster than my competition.

Some time later, Lee Taylor was hired to run the Final Assembly Department, a job he had held at the Yale motorcycle factory. I had a friend in the Frame Department (foreman) who was a racing enthusiast, and who would build anything I wanted in the way of frames or handlebars, without the formality of an order, and I was progressing in building my own engines. Still later, after Taylor's arrival, Pineau came into the picture, doing road testing, as I remember. Pineau, with some help from the Advertising Department, made a near copy of my ohv engine, but it was never quite as fast as mine, due I believe to my cam action. He used standard cams.

Taylor also had his own idea of a racing machine built in the factory, still without sanction. So there was no real Merkel racing team and no Experimental Department, as far as racing was concerned. Taylor did not build an ohv engine, and that was a mistake, as he was never the competition he would have been with a little more power. Lee was a very good rider.

What I have been writing about up to now was the racing on half-mile dirt tracks, a weekly affair during the summer. Incidentally, I don't think Joe Merkel ever saw the ohv 30.50 engine that I built, though there was plenty of opportunity for him to see it, if he wished.

Frank Valiant, who was Head of Advertising, did tend to the shipping of our machines. A couple of road races, such as Savannah, and two or three like Dodge City, the Merkel factory did support, as the machines were supposedly stock twins, but when Pineau and I went to Savannah in 1913, we had no one with us from the factory, in the way of help, and very few extra parts. In contrast, Indian had a big crew of riders and mechanics, and a lot of checkers to keep track of what was going on'.

In the 1913 Savannah, Georgia 300-mile road race, Maldwyn Jones and the Merkel motorcycle were the victims of poor officiating.

'I really won the 1913 race, but due to faulty scoring, I rode an extra lap, 11 1/4 *miles, and was given second. I had no trouble during the race, but Perry was in the pits for 20 minutes and never passed me at any time. The Savannah Club finally gave me credit for the win, but the official record shows that Perry won, as I did not protest within the prescribed half-hour. Cannonball Baker told me later that the Indian crew knew that I had won, but didn't feel like 'mixing in.' I wish they had.'*

When asked if he considered the 1913 Savannah 300 his best career effort, Maldwyn surprisingly commented,

'About my best effort in racing, I don't think it was Savannah – that was a kind of joy ride, as it was in a beautiful setting of palm trees and Live Oaks, hung with Spanish Moss. I had no idea of my position in that race till it was over, as our 'pit crew' was just two (locally hired) men, who knew nothing about giving signals to Pineau and me. It was an easy ride for me, and I believe I could have gone on for another 300.'

1914 was a better year for Merkel racing, as the home-brewed ohv singles of Jones and Cleo Pineau generally had the horsepower edge over competitors in the popular midwest half-mile dirt track events. As a highly unofficial team,

When Jones and fellow Merkel factory employee Cleo Pineau raced at Savannah in 1913, they received no factory support other than the loan of the machines and time off from their jobs. Pineau's right hand rests on the housing for the coil spring of the rear suspension, which is analogous to the Vincent setup of the thirties, forties, and fifties. (Modern riders might term it a monoshock suspension, after Yamaha's reintroduction of the system.) *(Maldwyn Jones.)*

Jones, Pineau, and fellow Merkel employee Lee Taylor did not venture far from home. While the greater glory has always been reserved to the longer 'classic' events, it should not be construed that these midwestern events were unimportant. Racing over the ever-present horsetracks had been sanctioned by the FAM at least as far back as 1909, and some of these local events drew bigger crowds than today's National circuit. Then, as now, horsetrack racing was the predominant mode in American racing, rivaled only for about three years by the motordromes, and even that rivalry was confined to the larger cities.

In the 1914 Savannah 300, Maldwyn Jones was again unlucky.

'In thinking of the Merkel as a reliable machine.... I went back to Savannah the following year (1914) for the 300-mile race, with the same bike, all stock, except handlebars, and at 200 miles was in second place, 20 seconds behind the leader, when our pit crew (again hired locally) let me run out of gas, a long way from the pits. More than five hundred miles of racing with this motorcycle and a lot of practice, without any trouble of any kind with the machine.'

Continuing his comments on Merkel reliability,

'The Merkel was a good reliable bike, and I have no idea how much of the design came

Jones could still smile after being robbed of the Savannah 300-mile title on Christmas day of 1913. In this view, the rubber boots atop the front forks can be seen, and their short lengths give evidence of the limited telescopic travel. The vertical cylindrical oil tank is apparent, behind the engine. The lap-counting problem which cost Jones official victory remained an American weakness for another generation. *(Maldwyn Jones.)* 211

from racing experience before they moved to Middletown. The engine was all ball bearing – German, Hess-Bright, even the cams and the gear train to the magneto. I never saw any bearing trouble, unless the engine had completely run out of oil. Merkel had the first spring frame, the best, as the up-and-down movement of the rear wheel did not change the tension of the drive chain as happens in most spring frame bikes of today. Merkel's spring front fork was a good one too – used on most all of the later Harley-Davidson racing motorcycles.'

That was about the end of the line for Merkel, which had introduced a disastrously unsuccessful (and even dangerous) spring-powered self starter on its 1914 touring line. The resultant service and legal difficulties were costly. Moreover, Miami was now unable to obtain the German-made ball bearings featured on the crankshaft, cam and magneto drives, and connecting rod big ends. These facts, and the general decline in America's motorcycle interest, forced Merkel to the wall at the end of 1915. Joe Merkel had left the firm in June of 1913, and it seemed that his commonsensical engineering talents and his once-enthusiastic support of racing were sorely missed during a critical period.

Nevertheless, during its seven years of racing (1909-1915), the big orange Merkel 61 cubic inch (1000 cc) V-twins and their companion 30.50 cubic inch singles had provided formidable competition to the big three. The special 'Merkel-Jefferson' developed by Maldwyn Jones, and copied by Cleo Pineau, stands out as an early example of the individual Yankee's special knack for workshop engineering. Happily, that trait would be proved again and again in thousands of races long after the Merkel's end.

Mitchell

On August 22, 1902 at Chicago, Illinois, a Mitchell motorcycle set the **first American 24-hour record.** Riding on the cement Garfield Park track, A.A. Hansen covered 634 1/4 miles.

The 1902 Mitchell was a diamond (bicycle type) framed single, with a bore and stroke of three inches, yielding 21.2 cubic inches (347 cc). The motor was set high in the frame above the pedal cranks in order to maintain the standard bicycle width between the right and left pedals. The power was transmitted directly from the engine to the rear wheel via an endless rawhide belt. Due to the position of the motor, the belt had to be raised over the crank bracket, so an idler pulley was clamped to the seat mast tube. This also provided a means of belt adjustment.

The carburetor was merely a mixing valve consisting of a vertically acting check valve with a taper seat about 3/16 inch in width. The only adjustment was through a needle valve checking the flow of gasoline to the valve seat. Gasoline was admitted through a needle point opening in the intake port.

Speed control was by spark only. Lubrication was by the total-loss system. The Mitchell was manufactured by the Wisconsin Wheel Works of Racine, Wisconsin from 1901 through 1910.

Orient

On July 31, 1900, six months prior to the Indian motorcycle's debut, the Orient machine made its first public appearance at a Boston, Massachusetts race meet. Albert Champion rode 5 miles in 7 minutes, 16 1/4 seconds at the Charles River Park Track in **the first motorcycle speed performance conducted in the United States***.

Mr. Champion's Orient and its several earliest companions are believed

Guy M. Green won the 1906 5-Mile National Championship of the NAM at Providence, Rhode Island using this Orient. These machines used a French made coil, spark plug, and battery as well as the French Aster engine. *(Motorcycle Illustrated.)* 213

actually to have been French machines to which the race promoter, Charles H. Metz, affixed his own Orient label. Later, these bikes were termed Orient-Asters because of their French built Aster engines, so the exact point at which Orient machines became at least half-American cannot be confirmed. The Orient was manufactured by the Waltham Manufacturing Company of Waltham, Massachusetts. Their Chief Engineer was the previously mentioned Charles H. Metz who was later to produce motorcycles under the Metz and Marsh-Metz trademarks.

On May 30, 1902, **the first road race in the United States** was conducted between Irvington, New Jersey and Milburn, New Jersey, a distance of ten miles. Five of the six riders finished, and W.T. Green was the winner on an Orient at an average speed of 31 mph. On November 19, 1902, Ralph Hamlin, riding an Orient-Aster, defeated C.W. Risden in a 3-mile dirt track race at Agricultural Park in Los Angeles, California, averaging 46.65 mph.

The newly formed National Association of Motorcyclists (NAM) held their first National meet from September 1-3, 1906 at Providence, Rhode Island. Guy M. Green won the 5-mile National Championship on a 4 hp Orient single. However, it should be noted that the NAM did not include the top riders of the USA who belonged to the older Federation of American Motorcyclists, the FAM. Of the riders participating in the NAM Providence meet, only Ralph DePalma would gain fame, and that as an automobile racer.

The second annual NAM meet was held at Horse Neck Beach, Massachusetts on August 31, 1907. Orient machines won all three feature events; the 1-mile open, 3-mile scratch, and 24-mile handicap.

*This is a tricky subject. The reference source from which the above was taken states also that the USA'S 'first motorcycle race' was won on April 28, 1900 in Louisville, Kentucky by a French-made Aster. And if you consider motorized three-wheelers in the mainstream, then the first American motorcycle race was won on an Ariel trike in late 1899, as detailed in Peter Hartley's *The Ariel Story* (Argus Books Ltd., Watford, Herts., 1980).

Pope

Like the Cyclone, the Pope was another example of a 'world-beater' design on paper, but one which was not backed up by a strong managerial base. Upon their introduction in 1911, Popes were nothing more than typical ioe singles with rigid frames and leaf spring front forks. But for the 1913 season Pope brought out push rod overhead valve singles and twins.

To this point, Indian was the only major American manufacturer to have built ohv engines, and these were limited to the special racing 4-valve singles and 8-valve twins. Accordingly, amateur riders of these new stock Pope overheads suddenly found themselves competitive with some professionals on the well-known Indians and Excelsiors. Throughout the summer of 1913

214

The Pope's advanced specifications could not overcome poor management.

(The Antique Motorcycle.)

Popes won more than their share of locally contested events.

Buoyed by these successes, Pope's management fielded a factory team for the big Venice, California 300-mile race in March of 1914. However, the outing was disappointing, as all machines entered suffered mechanical failure. Likewise, on July 4, the Pope team members all retired early in the Dodge City 300-Mile National Championship. Their beautiful-appearing overhead valve gear proved fragile, as the machines experienced broken rocker arms and valve failure. After the 1914 Dodge City, Popes were never heard from again in the major races. However, their brief flurry of amateur victories in 1913 had at least been partially responsible for increased racing emphasis by Excelsior, Harley-Davidson, and Indian.

On paper, the Pope management position was also imposing. Whereas Excelsior, Harley-Davidson, and Indian had found it challenging to achieve financial support, the Pope Motorcycle Division was the happy beneficiary of the huge Pope automotive empire. Pope automobiles were industry leaders, and were manufactured in both Hartford, Connecticut and Toledo, Ohio. In 1915, the company President, Albert L. Pope was elected President of the prestigious National Association of Manufacturers.

However, beneath Pope's imposing assets and large cash intake was also a record of increasing liabilities and heavy spending. The Pope motorcycles were a sideline of the automobiles, and the two-wheeler's fortunes rose and fell in tandem with the firm's overall financial health. Indeed, during their brightest year of 1913, receivers had been appointed because of the Motorcycle Division's difficulties. In 1915, one of the Pope automobile factories was sold to the Pratt and Whitney aircraft engine firm, in an effort to increase Pope efficiency. However, despite continuing improvements in its product, the Pope   215 motorcycle folded during 1918. Meanwhile, on the racing scene, the early potential of the Pope was not exploited by the company's management, probably because of financial pressures. As the 1913-1916 period was one of rapidly improving racing performance for the big three brands, the undeveloped stock Popes were never serious threats at the championship level.

The Pope illustrated also reveals the marque's interesting rear suspension, which was of the plunger type almost universally adopted during the forties and fifties. Another nicety was the shaft-driven Bosch magneto, the drive being mounted in SKF double annular ball bearings.

Key specifications included:

Bore – 3 21/64 inches	Stroke – 3 1/2 inches
Bearings – plain	Wheelbase – 56 1/2 inches
Tires – 28x2 3/4	Displacement – 60.89 cubic inches

Reading-Standard

The most lasting contribution of the Reading-Standard was its pioneering of the sidevalve engine design in the United States. From 1903 through 1906, Reading-Standard machines, commonly referred to as R-S, had been patterned after the earliest Indian ioe motorcycles. However, for the 1907 season, Reading-Standard introduced **the first sidevalve motorcycles built in the United States,** under the design of Charles Gustafson Sr. Gustafson was later to be a key figure in Indian design development, and would be responsible for Indian's switch from ioe to sidevalve engines in 1916.

Reading-Standard flirted with serious competition support during the 1907-1910 period. Two of its sponsored riders, Ray Seymour and Frank Hart, later went on to much success on Indian Motorcycles after leaving the R-S firm in 1910. (On Indians, Seymour won a number of professional class events, and Hart was ultimately the nation's amateur Champion.) Among R-S successes during this period were J.H. Shafer's winning of the 1907 Los Angeles-San Francisco 1000 mile Endurance Run and Paul Derkum's 1908 3-mile dirt track record at Bakersfield, California, in which he averaged 57 mph.

But even more successful was Ray Seymour's 1909 R-S season. In June, he set the following records at the Los Angeles Coliseum motordrome: 73 mph over 4 miles; and 72.8 mph over distances of 7, 8, and 9 miles. In July, he lowered the one mile record to 47 seconds, a rate of 76.6 mph.

During 1910, Reading-Standard management opted to withdraw from

Right top: **The first Reading-Standards were identical to Indians. This 1908 model still follows Indian practice closely, but is equipped with the American industry's first sidevalve powerplant.**
(Jim Lucas.)

Right bottom: **Ray Seymour rode this 61 cubic inch Reading-Standard twin at the Los Angeles Coliseum board-track during 1910. The Coliseum may be seen in the background. The engine is unusual in that the front cylinder valve gear is on the left side while the rear cylinder valve mechanism is on the right side.**
(Motorcycle Illustrated.)

competition and concentrate on its touring line. By 1914, the firm was in financial trouble, a state from which it would never emerge. Still, the R-S line survived the critical slump caused by World War I.

In the early twenties, Reading-Standard emphasized endurance runs in its advertising campaigns, and it scored several successes in the eastern part of the United States. Reggie Pink also did well with R-S bikes in hillclimbing competition.

In 1920, the racing bug bit the R-S management, and it constructed both 30.50 and 21.35 cubic inch overhead valve singles for flat track racing. Neither bike was successful.

Likewise, Reading-Standard had no luck with its 1921 overhead cam 61 cubic inch twin which was campaigned by Ray Creviston, the standout Indian flat tracker immediately prior to World War I. The cammer was actually nothing more than a Cyclone with a slightly modified upper frame, a different fuel tank, and different forks. The engine castings had, in fact, been purchased from the failing Cyclone firm which had been promising production resumption in 1921 advertisements.

With little to distinguish the R-S from its competition, and with a poor dealer representation, the Reading-Standard firm folded in 1922. Surplus stock and (perhaps) tooling was purchased by the Cleveland motorcycle company, which marketed the R-S in 1923 as an addition to its one-model line of two-stroke lightweights. Prices of the Cleveland R-S machines were artificially low, and apparently Cleveland was merely grabbing a short-term sales opportunity made possible by buying below cost from the bankrupt Reading-Standard company. In any event, Cleveland probably had its own big motorcycle concept already in mind, the Cleveland four which appeared in 1926. Thus, at the end of 1923, the Reading-Standard faded into oblivion.

Thomas Auto-Bi

The oft-stated claim that Indian (born in 1901) was the first American motorcycle is apparently in error. Disregarding some crude exhibitionary machines, **the honor of being the first Yankee machine probably belongs to the Thomas Auto-Bi.** In the April 17, 1913 issue of *Motorcycling*, W.C. Chadeayne penned an article entitled 'The Ancestry of the Motorcycle,' in which Chadeayne claimed the honor for the Thomas Auto-Bi. Chadeayne further stated that the Thomas company established the *'first factory to be devoted exclusively to the manufacture of motorcycles in America.'* In the same article, captioned illustrations indicated the arrival of the Hafelfinger, Holly, Marsh, and Orient machines in 1900.

Besides being about seventy years closer to the topic than we are today, Chadeayne should have been quite familiar with the Thomas Auto-Bi. On October 31, 1905, he had arrived in San Francisco, setting a new transcontinental motorcycle record of 47 days, 23 hours, and 50 minutes on a

Thomas Auto-Bi.

Another success was E.F. Edmond's first place in the 1902 economy run in New York City, which was the **first motorcycle economy run in the United States.** Edmond covered 50 miles on 4 5/16 pints, an average of 92.7 mpg. In the 1903 New York City enduro, Lincoln Holland tied Indian founder George M. Hendee, but Hendee was given a disputed victory based on a tie-breaking secret check.

The Thomas Auto-Bi and its successor, the Greyhound, were never significant competition machines after Chadeayne's 1905 transcontinental record. At the time of the transcontinental record, the Thomas Auto-Bi was a typical belt-driven, single-speed, single-cylinder machine of the era. The engine was mounted high and forward, resting on the front down tube of the diamond frame.

Thor

Although the Thor was one of the more prominent of early motorcycles, it was not very successful in competition. The Thor's initial fame was due to the arrangement between the infant Hendee Manufacturing Company, marketers of the Indian, and the Aurora (Illinois) Automatic Machinery Company. The Indian firm did not initially have facilities to manufacture Oscar Hedstrom's single cylinder ioe engine, so this work was subcontracted to Aurora, which in turn was authorized to distribute Thor engines built in excess of Indian requirements.

Accordingly, Aurora built its own Thor motorcycles and also wholesaled Thor engines to a number of fledgling firms. This resulted in several makes of machine basically identical to the 1901-1904 Indians and a confusing similarity

This 1911 Thor twin typifies their early Aurora designs.   *(The Antique Motorcycle.)*   219

of names. These Indian copies included the: Thor, Thor-Bred, and Thorough-bred marques. Meanwhile, Oscar Hedstrom was sometimes embarrassed by being termed the inventor of the Thor engine.

The Thor's only major racing success occurred on Sept. 9, 1908. On the Los Angeles Agricultural Park dirt track, Howard Shafer broke every 'world' record from 23 through 48 miles and established new records for 49-56 miles. These records were made in the course of a one hour race, at the end of which Shafer had motored a record 56 miles and 600 yards. The flamboyant Paul Derkum also raced Thor machines occasionally during this era at Los Angeles, but Thors were outpaced in the top-flight programs by Indians and Excelsiors.

At the semi-professional and amateur level, Thor's relatively heavy early sales resulted in the make being well represented, especially in the midwest. Endurance runs were more prestigious than race meets during the first half-dozen years of this century, and enduros were still important in 1910 when the Thor team won the FAM enduro in Philadelphia, Pennsylvania. In 1913, the season's fastest five miles on dirt was 4 minutes and 7 seconds (72.8 mph) by a rider named Camplejohn at Jacksonville, Florida. Likewise, Ray Creviston made the year's best time for 50 miles on dirt at Columbus, Ohio, in 45

Maldwyn Jones and tuner Harry Gross at a 1913 Hamilton, Ohio, race meet. Temporarily at odds with Joe Merkel, Maldwyn's fine showing at this meet got him rehired by the Merkel firm. Maldwyn said Gross' craftsmanship rivaled that of the proverbial Swiss watchmaker. The bike was exceptionally fast but prone to speed wobbles. *(Maldwyn Jones.)*

minutes, 41 3/5 seconds (65.6 mph).

The Thor's closest brush with a National Championship was the 1914 Dodge City 300-mile road race, in which Bill Brier finished second to Indian's 'Slivers' Boyd. Subsequently, Thor racing manager Bill Ottaway transferred to Harley-Davidson and was tremendously successful with the Milwaukee firm. With the fading of memories and documentation, the passage of time has tended to enhance the Thor image, as it has been presumed that the renowned Ottaway must have made Thor a serious threat to Harley-Davidson and Indian. However, this was not the case.

The 1911 Model O Thor twin pictured is characteristic of the firm's early two cylinder production. Principal specifications included the following:

Motor: Roller bearing with roller bearing connecting rods and mechanical valves; capacity, 59.72 cubic inches.
Wheelbase: 55 1/2 inches
Wheels: 28x2 1/2
Ignition: Bosch magneto

Yale

On May 16, 1903, George Wyman mounted his Duck motorcycle and headed east from San Francisco. Fifty-three days later, on July 6, Wyman rode into New York City, having completed the **first transcontinental motorcycle ride.** Wyman was sponsored in this historic project by *Bicycling World & Motorcycle Review*, the first motorcycle trade paper in America. His Duck machine was a crude belt-driven single cylinder model with an outside flywheel. The Duck had a saturated wick carburetor built into a big rectangular tank hung from the top frame tube.

Wyman's 1903 transcontinental run drew national attention to the previously obscure Duck. Consequently, later in the year the Duck people were persuaded to sell the Duck manufacturing rights to the Kirk Manufacturing Company of Toledo, Ohio, then making Yale and Kirk bicycles. Thereafter, the Duck became the Yale; however, there are also accounts of a Duck-California and, more commonly, a Yale-California motorcycle. Apparently, the California concern enjoyed a period of overlap with their Ohio successors during which Ducks, Duck-Californias, and Yale-Californias were marketed. The evolution of the names is probably in the order depicted, with the machines being marketed from the two locales during 1904 as the Yale and Yale-California. The Yale-California label was continued as late as 1907.

Yale competition efforts centered around endurance runs. On July 9, 10, 11, 1909, a Yale team of three riders won the Chicago Motorcycle Club Endurance Contest at an average speed of 20 mph over the 600-mile course.

The Yale continued to have some success in locally-sponsored enduros up until the outbreak of World War I, but the marque never seriously contested the premier race meets. Motorcycle production was accomplished in batches   221 and, for alternate work, the factory began taking on munitions items. The opportunity for quicker profits in war-related work, and the disappointing response to Yale's ambitious national advertising program in all the leading magazines, convinced the Consolidated Manufacturing Company it was time to kill off the Yale motorcycle.

The Toledo, Ohio concern announced the end of motorcycle production in December of 1915. Thus, another pioneer American motorcycle slipped away, but not without leaving a permanent imprint. The Yale was the first motorcycle to cross the North American continent, and that's a pretty big first.

On a machine such as this, George Wyman made the first American transcontinental run. Moreover, Wyman finished three weeks ahead of the first transcontinental automobile trip.

(Howard Heilman.)

ABBREVIATED BIBLIOGRAPHY

The Antique Motorcycle
Archives of the Harley-Davidson Motorcycle Company
Archives of the Indian Motorcycle Company
Barth, Dick, 'The Story of the 648 Scout,' Pow-Wow, Summer/Fall 1978, pp.39-41
Bayley, Dr. Joseph, The Vintage Years at Brooklands, Goose and Son, Norwich, 1968.
Bowman, Hank Wieand, Motorcycles in Competition, Fawcett Publications, Greenwich, 1952.
Carrick, Peter, Motor Cycle Racing, Paul Hamlyn, London, 1969.
The Cincinnati Public Library
Clymer, Floyd, A Treasury of the Motorcycles of the World, McGraw-Hill, New York, 1965.
Cycle
Cycle Guide
Cycle News
Cycle World
Davis, Jim, telephone interview by Jerry Hatfield, April 1981; Hatfield at Edwards AFB, CA.; Davis at Buckeye Lake, Ohio
Hartley, Peter, Bikes at Brooklands; The Pioneer Years, Goose and Sons Limited, Norwich, England, 1973.
Hendry, Maurice, Harley-Davidson, Ballantine Books Inc., New York, 1972.
Hill, Bobby, interview by Jerry Hatfield, April 1981, Grove City, Ohio
Hodgdon, T.A., Motorcycling's Golden Age of the Fours, Bagnell Publishing Co., Lake Arrowhead, CA, 1973.
Hough, Richard and L.J.K. Setright, A History of the World's Motorcycles, Harper and Row, New York, 1966.
Indian Motorcycle Club of America
Interviews: Sam Arena, Rollie Free, Hap Jones, Maldwyn Jones, Ed Kretz, Dick O'Brien, Carroll Resweber, Gene Rhyne, Tom Sifton.
Ixion, Motorcycle Cavalcade, Iliffe and Sons, Ltd, London, 1950.
Klamfoth, Dick, interview by Jerry Hatfield, April 1981, Columbus, Ohio
Letters and Phone Calls: Ernie Beckman, Jimmy Chann, Dick Gross, Art Hafer, Bobby Hill, Maldwyn Jones, Red Wolverton.
The Los Angeles Public Library
The Los Angeles Times
Modern Mechanics and Inventions
Motorcycle Illustrated
Motorcycle Sport
Motorcycling and Bicycling
Motorcyclist
The late Bert Munro, speed ace, Program of the 7th National Veteran and Vintage Motorcycle Rally, Otago (New Zealand), February 27, 28, March 1, 1981, pp. 31, 32.

The New York Times
Page, Victor W., *Early Motorcycles, Construction, Operation, Service,* Post Motor Books, Arcadia, California, 1971.
Scalzo, Joe, *The Bart Markel Story,* Bond/Parkhurst Books, Newport Beach, California, 1972.
Schilling, Phil, *The Motorcycle World,* Hamlyn, London, 1974.
The Scientific American
Sheldon, James, *Veteran & Vintage Motorcycles,* England, 1961.
Tragatsch, Erwin, *The Complete Illustrated Encyclopedia of the World's Motorcycles,* Rinehart and Winston, 1977.
Tragatsch, Erwin, *The World's Motorcycles,* Motor Racing Books, Inglewood, California, 1964.
Wallace, P.J., *Brooklands,* Ballantine Books Inc., New York, 1971.
Wright, Stephen, *American Racer,* Megden Publishing Co., Huntingdon Beach, CA, 1979.